To Claudette,
A committed professor.
Keep up the good work!

Merline Pitre
2-27-86

Through Many Dangers, Toils and Snares:

The Black
Leadership
Of Texas
1868–1900

Merline Pitre

EAKIN PRESS
Austin, Texas

Library of Congress Cataloging-in-Publication Data

Pitre, Merline, 1943–
   Through many dangers, toils, and snares.

   Bibliography: p.
   Includes index.
   1. Afro-American leadership — Texas.   2. Afro-Americans — Texas — Politics and government.   3. Afro-American politicians — Texas — Biography.   4. Texas — Politics and government — 1865–1950.   5. Texas — Race relations.   I. Title.
   E185.93.T4P57   1985   976.4'00496073'0922   85-15927
   ISBN 0-89015-524-0

FIRST EDITION

Copyright © 1985
By Merline Pitre

Published in the United States of America
By Eakin Press, P.O. Box 23066, Austin, Texas 78735

ALL RIGHTS RESERVED. No part of this book may be reproduced in any form without written permission from the publisher, except for brief passages included in a review appearing in a newspaper or magazine.

ISBN 0-89015-524-0

For My Parents
Florence and Robert Pitre

Benjamin Franklin Williams, cattle rancher and member of state legislature after Civil War, 1885.

— University of Texas Institute of Texan Cultures at San Antonio

This is a proud day. There is nothing like it in the history of the past . . . We are entitled to the candidate; we do all the voting and are entitled to the offices. Shall we turn the mill forever and somebody else eat the meal?

— MATTHEW GAINES
Brenham Banner
August 18, 1871

Richard Allen — was prominent in Houston after the Civil War. Portrait painted in 1865. From J. Mason Brewer's Negro Legislators of Texas, *Dallas, 1935.*

— University of Texas Institute of Texan Cultures at San Antonio

Contents

Foreword	vii
Preface	ix
Part One — The Toils: The Making of Biographical and Political Profiles	1
Introduction	3
1 The Constitutional Convention of 1868–1869	7
2 The Reconstruction Legislature	21
3 Blacks at The Crossroad 1872–1875	37
4 The Post-Reconstruction Legislatures	53
Part Two — The Snares: White Over Black in Party Conventions	83
5 A Thorn in the Side	84
6 Miscalculation or Manipulation	99
7 Fusion or Fission	116
Part Three — The Dangers: Methods of Removal	129
8 Rejection, Reduction, Retrenchment	130
Part Four — The Personalities: Neither All Good Nor All Bad Men	153
A Preview	155
9 Matthew Gaines: The Militant	157
10 George T. Ruby: The Party Loyalist	166
11 Richard Allen: The Opportunist	174
12 Robert L. Smith: The Accommodationist	179
13 Norris W. Cuney: The Climber of Sorts	188
Postscript	199
Appendix A. Roster of Black Legislators of Texas	205
Appendix B. Roster of Black Legislators' Committee Assignments	209
Appendix C. Black Legislators Who were Delegates to Republican National Convention	214
Notes	215
Bibliography	245
Index	255

10	George T. Ruby: The Party Loyalist	166
11	Richard Allen: The Opportunist	174
12	Robert L. Smith: The Accommodationist	179
13	Norris W. Cuney: The Climber of Sorts	188

Postscript		199
Appendix A.	Roster of Black Legislators of Texas	205
Appendix B.	Roster of Black Legislators' Committee Assignments	209
Appendix C.	Black Legislators Who were Delegates to Republican National Convention	214
Notes		215
Bibliography		245
Index		255

Illustrations

Photograph	Members of the Thirteenth Legislature	38
Photograph	Composite Picture of Black Lawmakers	54
Photograph	Norris Wright Cuney	189
Maps		133–142

Foreword

The Southern Black Reconstructionists and their performance have been a topic of much historical debate. From the outset of their gaining the vote to their holding elective office, the whole experiment was questioned and criticized as well as praised. A wide range of reactions were voiced. For the most part, the earlier accounts shaped a negative image of their achievements which became a stable interpretation in most textbooks. Only within the last several decades have we gained more information, and fairer evaluations about their backgrounds, performance and what the Reconstruction experiment meant to Southerners as well as to America.

Within Texas, the blacks were a majority of the party voters but held a minority of the political power. Professor Merline Pitre's *Through Many Dangers, Toils and Snares* reevaluates the entire performance of the black political leadership on the state level. Not content to merely identify black leaders as good or bad, competent or incompetent, this judicious and scholarly study utilized numerous sources — primary, secondary, local, state and national — to give us an insightful and astute account. All possible sources have been included.

Moreover, Professor Pitre asked and answered the difficult questions about these almost invisible men of Reconstruction. She goes beyond their backgrounds to inquiry as to how they emerged in their relationship to their constituency, their role in the Republican party, as well as reasons for their demise.

On the whole, black elected officials offered, as W. E. B. DuBois observed in 1910, beneficial proposals and legislation. In many instances, they were ahead of their times and had an advanced program. Their approach to achieving their goals ranged from uncompromising to accommodationist, and all other areas of the spectrum. Some were charismatic committed leaders while others were loyal to the Party, and a few free lancers and opportunists.

For the most part, the methods and mechanism used to remove them from a share in the political power were brutal and violent. The strategies of elimination when not violent were often unethical. When political power was wrest from the black population, their precarious economic and social positions declined. Thus, retrenchment and Jim Crowism became the order of the day. But in failing to achieve all their goals, and there were failures, the insights and issues they raised are still not completely answered by modern society. Their efforts to overcome the dangers, toils, and snares, as Professor Pitre reminds us, should receive our applause.

CHARLES VINCENT
Professor of History
Southern University

Preface

The purpose of this study is twofold: to examine the role of the black political leadership cadre in Texas, 1868–1900, and to fill a void in the history of Afro-Texans. This work explores the complexities and contradictions that led to the emergence of black legislators in Texas; examines the nature and degree of these lawmakers' influence upon their constituents, as well as upon their white colleagues; analyzes whether or not blacks shared in the overthrow of Reconstruction; seeks to find out if the black leadership formulated or manifested a clear unifying ideology and attempts to respond to the suggestion of W. E. B. Du Bois, that "there is a need to establish what blacks wanted, did and achieved." This study follows the path of recent scholars who have paid close attention to Afro-Americans during the post-Civil War era. But it departs from that road by placing more emphasis on what blacks were doing for themselves as opposed to what was done to and for them. In other words, this study strives to put a focus upon the active and determined roles of these black politicians in reconstructing their lives, their communities, and their state.

Using a descriptive, analytical and interpretive approach, I have divided this book into four parts. Part One — The Toils: The Making of Biographical and Political Profiles. This chronicles the rise of these black politicians to power as well as their activities in the various constitutional conventions. Part Two — The Snares: White over Black in Party Conventions. This portrays the action or inaction of blacks in party conventions, where blacks were more often than not in the majority, but yet did not control those organizations. Part Three — The Dangers: Methods of Removal deals with forces in Texas that led to the demise of these black politicians. Part Four — The Personalities: Neither All Good Nor All Bad Men are character analyses of some of the black political leaders about whom I could procure ample data.

During its various stages of development, this book has benefited from suggestions and criticism of many friends. My indebtedness to my mentors, L. D. Reddick and Henry Cobb, is considerable. Since its inception, they have given this study encouragement and searching criticism. I am also grateful to Billy Joe Turner, Franklin Jones, Mary Wanza, and Dottie Atkins for their careful reading of the entire manuscript and their helpful comments and corrections. Moreover, I owe a debt for the typing of this manuscript to Lucille Boston.

The Independent Research Fellowship, awarded by the National Endowment for the Humanities, enabled me to conduct my research in various parts of this country, as well as Texas. A Faculty Research Grant from Texas Southern University permitted me to prepare the manuscript for publication. I am also appreciative for the cooperation and courtesies extended to me by the staffs of the Archives of the State Library in Austin, the National Archives in Washington, D.C., The Eugene Barker Texas Collection at The University of Texas, the Texas Collection at Baylor University, the Houston Public Library, Prairie View University Library, Bishop College Library, the Heartman Collection at Texas Southern University and Rice University Library. I am also grateful to the Housing Staff at Huston Tillotson College for providing me with a place to live while I did research in Austin.

Finally, the debt that I owe my family for this study can never be measured adequately. It must suffice to say that their encouragement helped to make this book possible.

MERLINE PITRE

Part One
The Toils:

The Making of Biographical and Political Profiles

Introduction

In 1895, Booker T. Washington wrote: "One of the surprising results of the Reconstruction period was that there should spring from among the members of a race that have been held so long in slavery, so large a number of shrewd, resolute, resourceful and even brillant men who became during this brief period of storm and stress, the political leaders of the newly enfranchised race." This statement is especially true of the black lawmakers of Texas. Although Texas did not elect any blacks to the United States Congress during the postwar era, forty-one men of color sat in the Texas Legislature and fifteen helped to draft two constitutions for the state. Still, very little has been written about these gentlemen. Despite the myriad monographs on Texas history, until 1970, there remained a hiatus in the history of the state concerning the black population. Most of the existing studies referred to blacks only secondarily, if at all. Perhaps because of blacks' minority status, the authors of these earlier works considered blacks relatively unimportant in contributing to the advancement of the state and its people. However, since 1970, revisionist historians such as Lawrence Rice, Alwyn Barr, and James Smallwood in their respective works, *The Negro in Texas, Black Texans,* and *Time Of Hope, Time Of Despair,* have helped to shed more positive light on the activities of blacks during the post Civil War era. But despite these and other works written about Texas history in general and black Texans in particular, we still do not know very much about these black legislators who served this state from 1868 to 1898. In other words, the origin, political development, attitudes, and aspirations of the black leadership cadre remain somewhat distorted by gross errors, silly caricatures and myths.

The problem of source material or the lack thereof has played a large role in preventing us from having a clear picture of who these men were, what they wanted, did, and achieved. Thus, individuals who relied solely on newspaper accounts in an effort to assess the activities of these blacks were almost certain to form negative images of blacks. For example, of these black legislators, one contemporary newspaper editor wrote: "They are perfect types of the ones that have warmed seats in the legislative hall." Referring to one black legislator in particular, this same editor went on to say: "If any other member speaks to him, no matter how seriously, he laughs immoderately and goes on wrapping House Journals and scribling addresses that no postmaster on earth could ever read." To be sure, this view evolves from a racist stereotype. And the danger of such a stereotype is not so much that it is untrue or even that it projects an image of a Sambo personality, but rather the danger is that such stereotypes have discouraged further investigation into the political activities of these black legislators. It is true that few, if any, of these lawmakers' personal papers have survived and many of the contemporary reports about them are extremely biased inasmuch as they were written by and for whites. But by utilizing available sources, which include not just newspaper accounts, but legislative and convention journals, census reports, voter registration lists, city directories, letters, almanacs, and other primary sources, one can come up with enough information to form a biographical and political profile of these black politicians.

Unfortunately, the only full-length book on black politicians of Texas, is J. Mason Brewer's *The Negro Legislators of Texas (1935)*. In this work, Brewer identified many of the black leaders according to their prewar status, nativity, and education. Yet, while Brewer's study is certainly an inspiration and beginning point, it is far less responsive to the questions regarding the black political leadership, especially with respect to social origins and political activities. For example, Brewer's work does not set out to answer the following questions: what were the backgrounds of these men; how did they rise to positions of leadership (that is, did they emerge from obscurity or were they recruited); were blacks unified or divided in their political perspectives; how did they relate to their black constituents; what was their role in the Republican party where they had a majority; and were there fundamental social, political and economic forces in Texas that weakened the will of these politicians and thus hastened their demise from politics?

That newspaper editors of the postwar years presented stereotypes of these black politicians without seeking answers to the above questions seems to suggest that these editors were waging war against these black legislators with their most potent and available weapon — bitter and truculent words. By using and accepting stereotypes without analyzing the above questions, many historians have confused facts with fiction and sympathy of ancestors' view with critical judgment. On the other hand, if one is to get a better understanding of the social and political history of Texas from 1868–1900, the historical judgments made about these black lawmakers cannot be left unquestioned. It must be pointed out that investigation into the lives and activities of these men does not mean that one will find all good or all bad men; that blacks were faultless; that they were a monolithic group or even that any of them were embraced *in toto* by white Republicans or Democrats. Rather, an analysis of their background will reveal that blacks came from a various social mix; that they had differences among themselves, and that they worked to safeguard the interest of blacks, as well as the welfare of the State of Texas when obstacles were not placed in their path.

An analysis of this period further reveals that the actions of black leaders were impacted upon by whites. Without a doubt, white conservative Texans were not ready to abandon in 1865, what they regarded as their rightful way of life. They had lost the military war, but they were not yet ready to lose a political battle in Texas to blacks. It is not surprising, then, that immediately after the Civil War, there was little inclination or will on the part of the Texas government to grant blacks equal rights. Thus, when General Gordon Granger arrived in Galveston on June 19, 1865, and placed the Emancipation Proclamation into effect, blacks received freedom, but not civil and legal rights. Two days prior to Granger's arrival, on June 17, 1865, President Andrew Johnson appointed Andrew Jackson Hamilton the Provisional Governor of Texas. Johnson instructed the former legislator to "prescribe such rules and regulations as may be necessary and proper for convening a convention . . . for the purpose of altering and amending the Constitution of Texas . . . to restore the said to its constitutional position with the Federal Government." It should be noted that the presidential requirement for readmission to the Union did not include granting blacks political rights. In fact, Johnson ordered Hamilton to use the state's election laws as they existed prior to February 1, 1861, laws which excluded blacks from voting for and serving as delegates to the proposed convention. Thus, the Constitution of 1866, drawn up entirely by native Texans, denied equality to blacks by prohibiting them from voting, holding office and serving on juries. In addition, the document established a system of segregated public education and guaranteed minimal civil rights to freedmen. In the fall of 1866, the Eleventh Legislature of Texas further restricted the freedom of blacks when it prohibited their service in the state militia, set up a separate insane asylum for freedmen and passed the first Jim Crow railroad law in the South. These lawmakers also passed labor bills which were designed to greatly curtail black economic freedom.

This denial of legal and political equality did not endure. March 2, 1867, the Congress of the United States intervened through a series of Reconstruction Acts and demanded that Texas grant full legal and political rights to blacks. As a result of those Reconstruction Acts, eleven unreconstructed southern states, including Texas, were placed under military rule and the military commander of each district was given full power to remove and appoint state officials. Congress also ordered these states to summon constitutional conventions and to write new constitutions that denied legal and political rights to no one on account of "race, color, or previous condition of servitude."

It was, in effect, the black inclusion and the nature of that inclusion in the framework of the Texas government that complicated the task of the would-be black leaders. The redefining of the freedmen's status within the context of the Texas government both expanded and limited the manner in which black legislators were able to pursue the goal of equality of opportunity. Their concern first and foremost was to further the blacks' struggle for power and participation in the existing political, social and economic institutions. The extent to which blacks would participate in and partake of the benefits of these institutions would depend in a large degree upon the black leadership. That black politicians did not achieve all they could have even within the Republican party where they had a majority has also to be laid at the steps of the black leaders. On the other hand, the black leadership was adversely affected by violence, the economic plight of blacks, and the large scale of white immigration into the state. So if blacks were to achieve anything in this atmosphere, it would have to come through blood, sweat, and tears; through many dangers, toils and snares.

[1]

The Constitutional Convention of 1868–1869

The blacks of Texas, like those in many other Southern states, did not take an active part in politics until the passage of the Reconstruction Acts of 1867. These acts, which declared all previous actions of the state null and void and called for the drafting of a new constitution, made it possible for blacks to become actors rather than merely objects in Texas politics. It soon became clear to the freedmen that these acts of Congress only opened the doors to voting and office holding; if they wanted to effectuate any change in the system, they themselves would have to take the initiative. So, in keeping with their idea of making political rights a reality, blacks went to the polls in Texas, February 10, 1868, and not only cast 35,952 votes in favor of a constitutional convention, but elected nine blacks to serve as constitutional delegates. To many white natives, events in the Lone Star State in that winter month clashed sharply with fond remembrances of the old regime and the people they thought they knew best. The sudden politicization of their ex-slaves was inexplicable. Unable to explain and to understand the activities of blacks, these whites conjured up powerful and tenacious images about blacks in general and black delegates in particular. Created by the Democratic and Conservative and white Republican press and nurtured by succeeding generations of historians and publicists, depictions of these black delegates as poor, ignorant ex-slaves ascending straight from the cornfield to the legislative halls were rife. These traditional images have been sustained to the present, largely by continued ignorance of who these delegates were and the roles that they played in the constitutional convention.

In order to better understand these men who helped draft the Constitution of 1869, it is necessary to take a look at their backgrounds. Probably, the black who stood out most in the convention — by virtue of his training and background — was George T. Ruby. A freeborn black, Ruby was a native of New York. After acquiring a sound liberal arts education in the State of Maine, Ruby journeyed to Haiti, where he worked as a correspondent for the *Pine and Palm*, a New England newspaper edited by James Redpath. Ruby's job was to collect information about Haiti, and send it back to the United States to be read by black Americans who were searching for an alternative to slavery and discrimination. After the Civil War, Ruby returned to the United States and settled in Louisiana, where he was employed in 1866 as a schoolteacher. In September of that year, Ruby left Louisiana and became an agent for the Texas Freedmen's Bureau in Galveston. One year later, he became President of the Loyal Union League of Texas. With a firm base in the urban setting, his acquaintance with leading Republicans of the state, and his support of blacks, Ruby at twenty-seven years of age was elected as a delegate to the 1867 Republican National Convention. Later, he became a senator and served in the Twelfth and Thirteenth Legislatures. After failing in his bid for reelection to the legislature in 1874, Ruby returned to Louisiana.[1]

Another black elected to the legislature was James McWashington. He represented Montgomery County where blacks outnumbered whites by only 250 in 1868. McWashington was born a slave in Alabama, but had lived in Texas sixteen years before his election to the convention. After serving as a delegate, he remained active in politics, attending many of the Republican party's conventions. Siding with Andrew Hamilton in 1869, McWashington ran on the Conservative ticket for a House seat, but met with defeat.[2]

From Harris County came Charles W. Bryant, a minister and a native of Kentucky. Born a slave, he became an agent for the Freedmen's Bureau of Texas before entering politics in 1868. No doubt this experience with the Bureau was very beneficial to Bryant, since it helped him to establish contact with many freedmen, which in turn aided him in establishing a political base. Because of his popularity with fellow blacks, when Bryant ran for delegate, he polled more votes than were cast for the calling of the constitutional convention. He received 1331, while the referendum for the convention received 1131. Though Bryant was a young man of thirty-eight years when elected to the convention, after his tenure in this body, he did not become involved in politics again.[3]

Benjamin Franklin Williams was one of the most active black delegates of the Reconstruction Convention. He was born a slave in Brunswick County, Virginia, in 1819. As a slave, he was taken to South Carolina, then to Tennessee in 1830, before being brought to Colorado County, Texas, in 1859. After Emancipation, Williams became a traveling Methodist minister. He was the officiating minister when the Wesley Methodist Chapel in Austin was established in 1868, a church, according to the *Galveston Daily News*, which forbade blacks from attending if they were not Republicans. Combining religion with politics, Williams became a militant spokesman for his race. As early as 1868, he was Vice-President of the Union Loyal League and as such kept the white Unionists abreast of what was happening in the Black Belt area. It was Williams's involvement in politics that won him a seat at the constitutional convention at the age of forty-eight. Apparently, Williams made a good impression on his fellow blacks while serving in the convention, because he was subsequently elected by Lavaca and Colorado counties to the Twelfth Legislature; by Waller, Fort Bend and Wharton to the Sixteenth; and by the counties of Waller and Fort Bend to the Nineteenth. Likewise, Williams's popularity was manifested among his colleagues in the Twelfth Legislature when they nominated him for Speaker of the House and he lost by only three votes. It was Williams, the land speculator, mechanic and engineer, along with other blacks, who was instrumental in the settlement and development of Kendleton, Texas.[4]

Two other delegates on note were Benjamin O. Watrous and Sheppard Mullins. Mullins was born a slave in Lawrence County, Alabama, in 1829, and continued in that status when he arrived in Texas in 1854. The skill of blacksmith which he acquired while in bondage served him well in freedom. After Emancipation, he began to labor in his own behalf and as such, acquired several lots in Waco and a block of land in McLennan County. Mullins was elected to serve in the second session of the convention when McLennan County chose him as their delegate after the death of the incumbent.[5] On the other hand, Mullins's colleague, Benjamin O. Watrous, was born a slave in Tennessee, where he was known as Ben Carter. Upon being set free, he took the name of his last owner, John Watrous. A wheelwright and property owner, Watrous was also a minister, and had lived in Texas twelve years when he was elected delegate from Washington County.[6]

A dearth of biographical information existed on the other delegates, Mitchell Kendall, Ralph Long, Stephen Curtis and Wiley Johnson. Kendall, a blacksmith from Georgia, represented Harris and Panola Counties. He was fifty years of age when elected to the convention, but he probably was the wealthiest of the black delegates. Despite his slave birth, while serving as a delegate, his assets were valued at two thousand four hundred dollars.[7] His colleague, Ralph Long was not as wealthy. Long, of Limestone County, was a Tennessean by birth and a farmer by occupation. Though he was considered by some of his contemporaries as a land speculator, this property was amassed after his tenure in the convention. At twenty-five years of age, Long became the youngest member of the convention. He had lived in Texas for only two of those twenty-five years before he became a delegate.[8] In contrast to Long's youth, the oldest black man to serve in the constitutional convention was Stephen Curtis, sixty years of age. He was a carpenter by trade and was born a slave in the Old Dominion state. He became involved in politics almost from the organization of the Republican party in Texas. Thus, he could be found at most, if not all, Republican gatherings held throughout the Reconstruction era.[9] Wiley Johnson, a man much younger than Curtis, represented Harris County in the convention and was a shoemaker by profession. His slave birth took place in the state of Arkansas.[10]

Of the stereotypes drawn about these men, namely, that they were a group of illiterate ex-slaves and penniless farmers, only the one of their antebellum status as slaves stands up to close scrutiny. As to occupations, there were two blacksmiths, three ministers, one carpenter, one teacher, and three farmers. Of the ten blacks who served in this convention, only three could not read or write. This does not mean that the other blacks were highly educated, but with the exception of Ruby, who was a teacher, all of the others had acquired a rudimentary education or better. As to the image of a penniless worker, at least three blacks had some form of property, real or personal, with one man's assets totaling $2400. Although the majority of these blacks did not own property and although the property held by a few of them was minimal as compared to that of whites, these blacks cannot be classified as penniless farmers who were not interested in the fiscal policies and economic development of the state. In truth, these men were not drawn from a middle class *per se* (because none existed in Texas at that time), but rather they came from a rank that was far below the ruling white class and a little above the black masses.

The process by which black delegates arrived at their political opinions generally involved a realistic appraisal of their vital self-interests. It is not surprising, then, that blacks joined the western bloc in the constitutional convention. At this point, it should also be noted that when the convention assembled in Austin on June 11, 1868, there were four major blocs — individuals with similar voting patterns. The first and largest block consisted of individuals who were loyal to Governor Elisha Pease and who probably best represented statewide Unionist opinions. This bloc supported the basic political and civil rights of blacks as defined in the Civil Rights Act of 1866, but was not willing to move beyond that point. The second bloc represented the interests associated with what was then the most populous part of the state — East Texas. These individuals were hostile to the interests of blacks, in large part, because the majority of blacks resided in that section of the state. Fearing the potential of black power in that area, they rejected the civil rights of blacks as defined by the federal government and looked for ways to avoid its implementation. The third bloc was sectional in that it consisted of individuals who resided in Western counties, which made up the Fourth Congressional District. This group held the broadest view on the rights of blacks among whites in the convention.

Moreover, westerners made more concessions in the area of officeholding and education to blacks than did any other group. It goes without saying, then, that they became blacks' strongest ally. Unlike the first three blocs, which typified political division that existed prior to the Civil War, the fourth group consisted of the black delegates, who operated in a manner designed to achieve the interests of blacks. Among other things, these blacks desired political and civil rights and worked for free public education.[11]

In keeping with their interests, blacks took an active part in the *ab initio* controversy, the first major issue to appear before the convention. The *ab initio* controversy began when Andrew J. Evans, of McLennan County, introduced a resolution which stated that since the United States government was constituted by the people and their representatives in Washington, rather than by the states, "the constitutional convention of Texas should not recognize or sanction the Ordinance of Secession of March 1861, or any bills, laws, ordinances, acts, resolutions, or rules that were passed, made or enacted since the passage of the Ordinance."[12] In other words, Evans's proposal called for the nullification of the civil government which existed in Texas during the period of 1861–1866. Since rejection or approval of *ab initio* would determine which direction the constitutional convention would take, the delegates took a long time discussing it and were mixed in their reactions toward *ab initio*. Some sided with Evans because they wanted the nullification of laws which granted lucrative railroad charters to a group of former Confederates; others wanted to invalidate land seizures made during the war; still others (blacks) joined Evans because the school fund was attached to *ab initio* and they believed that restoration of the school fund would hasten the organization of public schools. Conversely, many Democrats opposed *ab initio* on sheer principles.

Because of the diverse interests represented at the convention, it soon became apparent to the Republicans that Evans's bill would not pass unless it was altered. Thus, a number of substitute bills were introduced in order to keep the idea of *ab initio* alive. After several days of lengthy discussion, the convention adopted an amendment which stated that the Texas Constitution would make valid all legislative enactments and decisions since secession, insofar as they did not interfere with existing federal laws, aid rebellion or "operate to bring harm to any class of citizens." That blacks were not satisfied with this amendment became evident when six out of nine (Ruby, Williams, Long, Johnson, Bryant and Watrous) voted in a losing cause to defeat this measure. Not willing to accept defeat, Ralph Long offered a resolution similar to that of Evans's, one week later, declaring invalid all obligations incurred by the purchase of slaves or debt payments made with Confederate money and asking to set the statue of limitation ahead to include the war years. Needless to say, this motion was soundly defeated.[13]

After the *ab initio* issue was settled, blacks and other delegates turned their attention to other matters. Because blacks had supported West Texans on *ab initio,* the West Texans came to the aid of blacks in trying to get civil rights clauses inserted into the constitution. When B. F. Williams introduced a resolution to ensure that blacks would have equal access to public accommodations, his bill was referred to the committee on General Provisions, a committee which was controlled by a westerner, Morgan Hamilton. Hamilton knew that on its merits William's bill would not pass; therefore, he tried to attach it to Section Four of the proposed Bill of Rights of the constitution, which was being drafted and discussed. Section Four, if adopted as originally proposed, would have gone beyond equal protection before the law to equal treatment in the areas of the private sector. Without a doubt, Section Four provoked outrage among most white delegates, Democrats, Conservatives and Republicans, because they viewed this section as an attempt to accord blacks social equality. Thus, barring some form of compromise, this bill was doomed to failure. Because Edmund Davis, a westerner who controlled that bloc realized that this section would never pass as written, he offered a substitute bill which outlawed racial discrimination, but authorized the owners whose facilities were in question to prescribe rules and regulations necessary to secure "comfort, good order and decency." In a word, this bill committed the state to civil rights on paper, but not in practice; and at the same time the state took a *laissez-faire* attitude toward the owners. Still, the majority of the delegates refused to pass even this modified proposal. Rather, they substituted their own, which only recognized the "equality of all persons before the law."[14] But all was not lost for blacks; while they failed to get Williams's resolution incorporated into the constitution, they nevertheless secured a political ally in West Texas.

Contrary to Ferdinand Flake, editor of the *Flake's Daily Bulletin*, who asserted that black delegates did not add one constructive idea to the work of the convention, blacks did offer some resolutions, declarations, and bills which showed not only merit and thoughts, but also their concerns for the people they represented. Thus, early in the first session, and then again in the second session, George T. Ruby offered a declaration that "no one should prevent any qualified elector of the state from free exercise of the elective franchise by violence or bribery, or by threat of violence or by injury of his person or property or by depriving an elector of employment or threatening to deprive him of employment." Such a misdemeanor would carry a fine of five hundred dollars or six months in jail. Moreover, if someone were to hire another person to vote for someone else, the hirer would be charged with bribery.[15] It was Ruby's hope that this ordinance would be published and circulated to the voters. But this declaration had first to be passed by the convention. Consequently, when Ruby moved to suspend the rules to take up discussion on the declaration, his motion was defeated by a vote of 18 to 44. It is interesting to note that only the so-called black radicals, Long, Ruby, Williams, Watrous, and Bryant, voted for this motion. The other blacks, for some unknown reasons, did not feel it necessary to suspend the rules at this time. As a result, this declaration never reached the floor. Instead, it got lost in the legislative shuffle.

Concomitant with their efforts to achieve suffrage, blacks were also concerned with the right to hold office. Hence, Watrous presented a resolution to the convention urging that the right to hold office be extended to all men without regard to race, color, or creed. This act was referred to the Committee on Bills of Rights, reported back favorably and was incorporated in Article I, Section 2 of the Constitution.[16]

Blacks were not only concerned with the problems of blacks, but also with promoting the general welfare of the state. This idea became evident in resolutions which they presented to regulate the practice of medicine and law. For example B. F. Williams proposed that "no one should be allowed to practice medicine in the state without having first attained a diploma from some medical college or otherwise a certificate from some regular medical board." Williams's resolution called for a penalty of five hundred dollars or five years in jail, if one were found in violation of the law.[17] The favorable passage of this resolution was predicated on the fact that it was aimed not at physicians who had practiced medicine for years and were known to have been useful to students in the field, but rather to those just entering the medical field. Wiley Johnson drafted a similar successful resolution with reference to lawyers: "that no person shall be eligible for the office of judge of the Supreme Court, or Criminal Court without being admitted to the bar of counselor-of-law at the Supreme Court of the state." [18]

Discussion of reforming marriage laws was also crucial to black delegates. McWashington and Bryant championed the cause in this regard. McWashington, concerned with the fact that the marriages of many free people of color were never actually recorded in the courthouses in many towns and cities of Texas, introduced a resolution that "all marriages solemnized among free people of color during slavery should be declared legal and binding and that all the children born to that marriage should be declared legitimate." [19] After no action was taken on this resolution, Bryant of Harris County offered one of his own. His resolution called for making illegitimate black children, or children of slave parents, legitimate with all the legal rights of inheritance upon the marriage of their parents.[20] Unlike McWashington's resolution, Bryant's was adopted and was incorporated in Article XII, Section 27, of the Constitution. McWashington would not be easily silenced nor discouraged on marriage reform. A pioneer in his thinking and a man ahead of his time, McWashington proposed that a section be added to the constitution on women's rights. If it had been adopted as originally proposed, this section would have read as follows:

> The real and personal property of any female in this state acquired either before or after marriage, whether by gifts, grant, inheritance devise or otherwise, shall, so long as she may choose be and remain separate estate and property of such female and may be devised or bequeathed by her the same as if she were a *femme sole*. Laws shall be passed providing for registration of the wife's separate property and when so registered, and so long as it is not entrusted to the management of her husband, otherwise than as an agent, it shall not be liable for any of his debts, engagement or obligation.[21]

After being rehashed and reworded in the committee, this resolution was reported back favorably and subsequently became Article XII, Section 14, of the Constitution.

While some blacks showed remorse for former Confederates in their demands and actions, others did not. Early in the first session, when *ab initio* was still a very hot issue, in an effort to get back at railroad companies that had been chartered prior to 1861, Bryant introduced a resolution "that all laws granting public land to railroad companies are hereby repealed and all charters of the said railroads in Texas are declared null and void." [22] Following *ab initioists,* McWashington introduced an act to repeal an act to incorporate the Central Transit Railroad Company. The reason for this act was that "the notorious and unmitigated rebels, Duff Greens, G. W. Carter and Pryor Lea were incorporators." [23] On the other hand, Wiley Johnson of Harrison County appeared more sympathetic. He presented a declaration suggesting that "the delegates at the convention set apart 250,000 acres of land for the support of the widows, orphans and the aged who were not able to support themselves." [24] Observedly, aside from Bryant and McWashington, blacks did not introduce legislation designed to punish whites.

One of the most crucial matters debated by this constitutional convention was that of violence. In the minds of many black delegates, discussion of this issue ranked in importance with that of public schools and suffrage. Violence, already prevalent in the state, increased sharply with the advent of the Reconstruction Convention. It was not uncommon to see visitors at the convention carrying concealed weapons in the halls and lobbies. In order to rectify this situation, Ralph Long presented a resolution that the "convention do order that no person shall . . . be allowed in this hall, who carried belted on his person, rivalous or other offensive weapons." [25]

Shortly after the above resolution was approved, the convention took note of the race riot in Millican, Texas. Stephen Curtis, the black delegate from Brazos County in which Millican is located, moved that a special committee of three be appointed by Edmund Davis, president of the convention, to go to Millican to investigate the causes of the riot and to report back to the convention. The motion provided for an appropriation of five hundred dollars to defray the expenses of the committee and requested that General Joseph J. Reynolds, assistant commissioner of the Texas Freedmen's Bureau, provide protection for the members. After a motion by Ruby, the rules were suspended to allow the resolution to reach the Senate floor; and it subsequently passed on July 22, 1868, by a vote of thirty to eight.[26] The next day, Edmund Davis appointed to the committee Stephen Curtis of Brazos, Fred Summer of Sherman, and P. P. Adams of Henderson. To the surprise of many, Curtis declined and gave no reason for his decision, at which time W. Thomas of Fannin was named to replace him.

Violence in Brazos County was nothing new. From June 19, 1865, to the convening of the constitutional convention in June 1868, a virtual state of war existed between the two races in Millican. However, the two major confrontations, which attracted public attention, took place in June and July 1868. On June 7, while many blacks were worshipping in one of their churches, a party of five Ku Klux Klansmen rode through their community. As soon as blacks returned from church and found these white horsemen in the community, they commenced firing upon them with pistols and muskets. The Klansmen immediately dispersed, leaving behind masks, sheets, and two revolvers. After this incident, blacks began to prepare for open warfare by arming themselves and by forming drill teams. When whites heard of the actions taken by blacks, they charged the blacks with forming a military organization and requested that the local Freedmen's Bureau agent forbid the bearing of arms by people of color. The response of the Bureau agent was that if the Klansmen would halt their warlike activities, then, blacks would do likewise. Thus, an agreement between the two parties was reached prohibiting any armed bands, organizations, or secret societies not authorized by law.[27] This pact lasted only six weeks, at which time the two races clashed again over the hanging of a black Union League leader, Miles Brown.

On July 17, 1868, after the news of the hanging soared through the black community, blacks armed themselves again and set out to vindicate the death of a fallen comrade. En route to find the killer, seventy blacks were met by forty whites who had been deputized by the sheriff of Millican to stop blacks in their pursuit of the killer. When whites fired into the blacks gathering, a confrontation ensued. The next day federal troops were called out. The troops did quell the disorder, but in the melée that followed, according to one report, five blacks were killed; according to another, as many as fifty may have died, including the two black leaders, Harry Thomas and George E. Booker.[28]

It was in response to this July incident that the convention committee subsequently was sent to Millican. Yet, there is no record to indicate that the committee reported its finding to the convention. Instead, the committee concluded that a report was *never* intended to serve any purpose. The ironic thing about the whole situation was that while white radical delegates dropped the riot issue, no black delegate spoke out against the committee's action or inaction, nor did they attempt to bring this matter before the convention again.[29] The only action taken in response to this incident was a resolution introduced by Charles Bryant, which restricted an individual from holding office "who [had] taken the life of another person outside of the law."[30]

As has been stated earlier, the spirit of violence was prevalent in the convention, and altercations among members were not uncommon — neither black nor white was excepted. It appeared that August 1868, raised temperatures, as well as tempers. On August 3, two Galveston delegates, G. T. Ruby and R. K. Smith, fought on the floor of the convention, only to be stopped by the Sergeant-at-Arms. The fight started when Smith, a white physician who had come to Texas with the

Federal army, made insulting remarks about Ruby's ancestry.[31] On the same day, Arvin Wright of Ellis County, at sixty-nine, the oldest man in the convention, and sixty-four-year-old A. A. Bledsoe of Dallas had a physical confrontation while the convention was in session. The fight between the two whites erupted over a railway charter and ended up with physical harm coming to Wright, who was struck on the head with the cane of Bledsoe.[32] Three days later, two black delegates, Ralph Long and Wiley Johnson, had a fistfight outside of the convention hall. Johnson called Long a Rebel and got thrashed for it. They were immediately taken into the custody of the Sergeant-at-Arms; and a committee of which B. F. Williams was a member was appointed to investigate the incident and to examine the charge that these men had violated the rules of decorum. The committee's finding was that since the fight had occurred outside the convention hall, these members should be released for a lack of jurisdiction.[33]

Throughout the second session, which began in December 1868, and ended in February 1869, physical and verbal clashes among delegates continued. For example, in February 1869, an altercation occurred between G. T. Ruby and Scipio McKee, the black doorkeeper of the convention. The incident was precipitated by Ruby, who had tried to remove McKee as doorkeeper because he believed that McKee had slandered another black delegate, Bryant (who was involved in a rape case). McKee, a black who would later campaign for Andrew Hamilton, assaulted Ruby outside the convention hall and left him unconscious in the gutter. Ruby reported the incident to the convention and asked that McKee be punished. The next morning the committee to which the incident had been referred reported that the attack was, indeed, without cause. It then, recommended that McKee be dismissed from the service of the convention; however, by a narrow vote of twenty-nine to thirty-three, McKee was retained.[34]

Charles W. Bryant received considerable notoriety while a delegate because of a criminal charge brought against him. A few days before the convention adjourned, Austin authorities arrested Bryant on charges of raping an eleven-year-old mulatto girl. Radicals at the convention asserted that Andrew Hamilton had fabricated the entire incident to destroy Bryant's reputation. There might have been some validity to this assertion, for even after the charges were dropped, Conservatives assumed Bryant's guilt and expelled him from the convention by a vote of thirty-three to thirty.[35] Furthermore, prior to Bryant's expulsion, he had raised the eyebrows of many Conservatives when he responded to the editor of the *Houston Telegraph* who told blacks that they should "not vote because it would be taken away from them." Bryant's response came in an article entitled "Good Advice But

We Decline to Take It." In this article, Bryant succinctly told the editor: "If a free man can live so well in a free country without a voice in government, why not try it yourself?"[36]

On the other hand, the treatment that Bryant received was not metted out equally to white members who were convicted on similar charges. During the debate on the Bryant case, James P. Butler of Huntsville attempted to expel Judge Colbert Caldwell of Harrison County. According to the *San Antonio Express*, Caldwell, while attending a party in Houston, had demanded a "girl and bed." Butler tried to amend the Bryant expulsion resolution to include Caldwell on the basis that his alleged "conduct, was unbecoming a gentleman." But Andrew Hamilton saved Caldwell by moving to take up the previous question, that is, Bryant's expulsion, thereby avoiding a vote on the amendment.[37] So, even the closing scenes of the convention were marred with conflicts, ill will and physical violence among its delegates.

These aforementioned encounters did not prevent the delegates from drafting a constitution, nor did the incidents weaken or diminish blacks' contributions to this document. Thus, when the question of division of the state came up at the convention, blacks again took an active part. From the end of the war until the end of the convention, the question of dividing Texas into three states boggled the minds of many Texans. In the constitutional convention, it became a sectional as well as a racial issue. East Texans complained that other people of the state did not understand their problem with blacks, and, therefore, the only feasible solution would be to create a new, compact state in that area of the state where blacks resided. West Texans argued that the creation of a new state was necessary to prevent them from being discriminated against by the majority of Texans who were opposed to Unionists. Blacks supported the West on this issue, though not in a solid bloc. The five casting their votes for division were Bryant, Ruby, Kendall, Curtis, and Long. Those opposed were Johnson, McWashington, Watrous and Williams.[38] While the division bill finally passed by a vote of 42 to 28, its passage merely meant that a committee would be sent to ask Congress to divide the state into convenient parts. As it turned out, the anti-divisionists won, because Congress turned a deaf ear to the divisionists and the state of Texas remained intact.

It should be noted that the convention was extremely dilatory in drafting a constitution. It was not until after one session of dealing with *ab initio*, listening to resolutions and declarations, and another of discussing the issue of division that the convention got down to work on drafting the constitution, that is, January 27, 1869. After that date, the convention moved rapidly with each section and each article because various acts and provisions of the constitution had been worked over in committee. Only the question of suffrage provoked any real discussion. Radicals and blacks supported a provision that established a system of registration and disfranchisement that would exclude all federal and state officers, ministers, and newspapermen who had favored and openly supported rebellion. But the Conservatives who managed to get moderate Republicans on their side offered a substitute motion that allowed all men to vote, except those disqualified by the Constitution of the United States.[39] Rather than accept defeat on this issue, Davis and the Radicals attempted to adjourn the convention instead of finishing its work. After the majority refused to adjourn, both Ruby and B. F. Williams submitted their resignations. Ruby protested, saying that "the action of convention disgraced the entire country." [40]

When the convention completed its work February 6, 1869, only forty-five delegates willingly signed the Constitution. Edmund Davis, president of the convention signed only upon the orders of General Edward R. Canby. Along with Davis's signature, there were only those of two white Radicals, W. Frank Carter and William R. Tyle, and five blacks, Stephen Curtis, Mitchell Kendall, Wiley Johnson, Benjamin O. Watrous and James McWashington. Other individuals who signed included four Conservatives and thirty-four white Republicans who can be classified as moderates.[41] The blacks who did not sign objected to the constitution on the grounds that enfranchising ex-rebels might cause them to become strong enough to regain political control of the State, to violate the will of Congress and to suppress the rights of blacks. Thus, Ruby and Wiley Johnson signed a protest saying that "not only the rights of loyal blacks and whites are imperiled by this constitution, but that the will of Congress has been ignored." [42] In the same vein, B. F. Williams wrote, "I was under the impression that I voted for a substitute that would include the future, not the past; I protest against the past." [43] Ralph Long joined in written protest with Edmund Davis, stating that he was opposed to the constitution "except only that part which charges deception and intimidation on the part of its members." [44] Unhappy with the constitution largely because it did not disfranchise all ex-rebels, Ruby joined forces with Edmund Davis and Morgan Hamilton of the Radical group in sending a commission to Washington to lobby against acceptance of the document. When Congress turned a deaf ear to their plea, this dissident faction accepted the constitution as a *fait accompli,* and fielded a slate of candidates to be elected at the same time as the constitutional referendum.

Despite the fact that the Texas Constitution was the least radical of the state constitutions drawn up at that time, the delegates to the 1868 Convention established a workable structure of government which many authorities regard as the "best constitution" the state has ever had. As for blacks, this document recognized the equality of all persons before the law; proposed that officeholding and jury service be open to blacks; and that equal educational opportunities and general civil rights be accorded to the freedmen. The educational article provided for the opening of state-supported schools on an equal basis, regardless of color or previous condition of servitude. Despite the delegates leniency on the suffrage section, they granted the right to vote to "every male citizen of the United States of age twenty-one and upward." More importantly, the delegates were able to accomplish their primary goal — to draft a constitution which was ratified by the electorate on November 9, 1869, and which was subsequently accepted by Congress.[45]

After helping to write a constitution which would serve as the organic law of Texas for six years, the black delegates would return to their organizational work in the hinterlands, towns, and cities. They would help prepare the way for themselves as well as for scores of others who would be elected to state and local offices under both Republican and Democratic regimes. This constitutional convention not only gave black delegates experience in politics, but the biographical and political profiles of these delegates also provide one some indications of the makeup of the black leadership cadre as well. If one were to judge the future cadre based on the backgrounds of these constitutional delegates, it would be safe to say that the leadership cadre would come from the ranks of the ex-slaves; that the average age would be somewhere in the mid-thirties; and that the majority would not be native-born Texans. Indeed, this seems to have been the norm in Reconstruction and postReconstruction legislatures in Texas. Out of a total of forty-one black lawmakers who sat in these legislatures, all except five had been slaves, seventeen were mulattoes, and only five were native Texans. Moreover, the majority of them served for only one term in the legislature. The same analogy holds true for the majority of these black delegates. The larger percentage of them did not run for the legislature in 1869. As a matter of fact, most of them did not seek public office after they left the convention. However, it was their hope that the constitution that they helped to draft would be implemented (with the help of black lawmakers) in the Reconstruction Legislature.

[2]

The Reconstruction Legislature

The election held on November 30, 1869, after the ratification of the Constitution, elevated blacks to public office for the first time in Texas history. Whites, not yet recovered from having blacks assist in the framing of the Constitution, now had to turn their attention to the legislature where eleven blacks were elected to the House and two to the Senate. Whites seemed not to be concerned with the fact that blacks were in the minority in both houses or that they would continue to be. What concerned them most was the false perception that the bottom rail had reached the top. To be sure, the bottom rail had not reached the top, but it had moved up.

Despite their apparent upward mobility, the majority of the black Reconstruction legislators were political novices when they first arrived in Austin, February 8, 1870. Being drawn largely from the ranks of slaves freed by the Emancipation Proclamation, they had no opportunity to gain experience in partisan politics. Unlike some white members, and in future years black members, who would avail themselves of an introduction to partisan politics through service in county and city offices before their election to the legislature, this was not the case for most blacks who served in the Twelfth Legislature. Only four had served in the Reconstruction Convention and only one was freeborn. As regards the majority, they had to learn the art of politics, either on the job or under the auspices of nonpolitical institutions. Like other freshman legislators, they were unfamiliar with the legislative routines and were uncertain of their jobs. But they were quick learners — ones who expressed a desire early to share in determining their party's direction. Their interests were complex, however, and cannot be considered as constituting a single group. Although interested in public schools and in protection of the ballot, person, and property, they were also concerned with such issues as emigration and boundaries.

Who then were these men on the move? They included three blacksmiths, three ministers, one contractor, one laborer, one teacher, and four farmers. The leaders of the delegation were the two senators, George T. Ruby and Matthew Gaines. George T. Ruby, Benjamin F. Williams, Mitchell Kendall, and Sheppard Mullins had served in the Constitutional Convention, therefore, biographical information on them is not necessary at this point.[1]

On the other hand, a great deal can be said of Matthew Gaines, admittedly the most colorful black to sit in the Texas Legislature. However, since a whole section will be devoted to him in Part Four, it will suffice here to make only the following comments. Matthew Gaines was born August 4, 1840, on the plantation of Martin G. Despallier in Pineville, Louisiana. He came to Texas via a slave trade in 1854, at which time he was taken to Robertson County. He remained in Hearne, Texas, until 1863. In that year, he made an attempt to escape, but was caught and forced to spend his last two years of bondage in Fredericksburg, Texas. After the emancipation of slaves in Texas, Gaines returned to the Brazos area and settled in the small community of Burton, in Washington County. Having developed his natural oratorical abilities as a slave preacher, it was not difficult for Gaines to assume a leadership role in the community, both as a minister and a politician. Thus, at the age of thirty-three, Gaines was elected for a six-year term to the Senate. Gaines served only four years because his seat was challenged when he was convicted on the charge of bigamy in 1873. Leaving office as he did, Gaines continued to be active in politics and made his political views known in conventions, public gatherings and in his pulpit. He died in Giddings, Texas, on June 11, 1900.[2]

Another black lawmaker was Richard Allen, who was born a slave in Virginia, in 1826. Fragmentary sources do not indicate in which year Allen was taken to Texas, but evidence does reveal that upon his arrival he settled in Harris County and was owned by J. J. Cain. While a slave, he acquired the skills of carpentry and demonstrated his talent on many crafts in Houston. In 1870, the *Houston Union* stated that,

The finest and most elegant mansion that once graced our city — [that of] Mayor J. R. Morris — was the handiwork of Hon. Richard Allen while he was a slave; not the mere mechanics only, but the design, the draft and all.

Combining his talent of carpentry with that of engineering, Allen became a bridge builder after he was emancipated June 19, 1865. The result of which was the construction of the first bridge over Buffalo Bayou in Houston.

While experimenting with freedom, Allen also became an agent for the Freedmen's Bureau and a controversial registration supervisor in the Fourteenth District in 1868. Such a job served as a catalyst for his interest in politics. An orator who could sway an audience to his will, Allen was elected to the Twelfth Legislature to represent Harris and Montgomery counties in 1869; he was forty-three years of age. Though he served only one term in the Texas Legislature, Allen remained active in politics for all of his adult life. From 1872 to 1900 he could be found as a delegate at nearly every Republican convention — local, state and national. Coupled with his political activities, Allen held several public offices which included Street Commissioner of Houston, member of the Board of Directors of The Gregory Institute and first Grand Master of the Colored Masons of Texas. Allen died in Houston in 1911.[3]

Hailing from Bastrop County was Jeremiah J. Hamilton. Hamilton was born a slave July 1838 in Tennessee and arrived in Texas in 1847. As early as 1866, Hamilton had emerged as a spokesman for black workers of the Bastrop community. His leadership role was due in part to the fact that he had acquired a great deal of land and served as a land trustee for the black community. Having become literate as a slave, Hamilton established a school for blacks shortly after Emancipation. In 1867, he was selected to the board which registered voters in Bastrop County. A laborer by trade, at thirty-eight years of age Hamilton was elected to the legislature to represent Bastrop County.[4]

Less biographical information was found on Henry Moore, John Mitchell, Silas (Jiles) Cotton, and Goldstein Dupree. The exact state in which Henry Moore's slave birth took place is unknown. Likewise, Moore's slave occupation is unknown, but according to oral sources, Moore was regarded as one of his master's choice men and probably occupied a managerial position as a skilled worker. Because of scrimpy evidence, one cannot confirm the date nor the year that Moore settled in the Lone Star State, but according to an interview with his grandson, Moore purchased his freedom before coming to Texas. After the Civil War Moore became involved in politics and was listed as a farmer, fifty-two years of age, when he was elected to the legislature.[5] Representing Harrison County along with Moore was John Mitchell. A farmer by profession, Mitchell became involved in politics in 1869, when, at thirty-two years of age, he was elected to the Twelfth Legislature. Remaining active in politics after he left the House, Mitchell became a delegate to the Constitutional Convention in 1875, and ran unsuccessfully for a seat in the United States Congress in 1878.[6]

As previously mentioned, two of the less noted figures of the Twelfth Legislature were Silas Cotton and Goldstein Dupree. Born a slave, Cotton practiced the trade of farming and lived in Limestone County during the antebellum days. After Emancipation, he moved to Robertson County where he accumulated considerable property. In 1869, he was elected as the first black to represent the said county in the legislature. Cotton was the tallest black and also the one with the largest number of children among those who sat in the Twelfth Legislature.[7] A less popular figure than Cotton was Goldstein Dupree. Dupree, who represented Harris and Montgomery Counties, was thirty-eight years old when he was elected to the legislature. Having failed to receive the nomination for reelection from his district in 1872, Dupree's tenure in the House was limited to one term. He died in Montgomery County in 1873.[8]

Two blacks, who have been ignored by J. Mason Brewer, as well as by other historians who followed him, for not having belonged to that group of blacks who sat in the Reconstruction Legislature, were Richard Williams and David Medlock. Richard Williams was born a slave in South Carolina, where he acquired a skill as a blacksmith. He was fifty years old when he won a seat in the House to represent Walker County.[9] The other forgotten black was David Medlock, a black slave minister from Limestone County. Medlock's only recorded statement in the legislature was a request to have a photographer take the picture of the General Assembly. Had his resolution been accepted, there would have been no doubt as to his identity.[10]

Blacks' first experiences in the Twelfth Legislature came in the provisional session, which began in February 1870. The responsibility of the General Assembly at this session was to ratify the Fourteenth and Fifteenth Amendments and to elect two senators to represent the Lone Star State in Congress. Without much discussion, the legislature approved these two amendments and selected Radicals Morgan Hamilton and James W. Flanagan as United States Senators. With these matters out of the way, General Joseph J. Reynolds then transferred civil authority to Governor-elect Edmund J. Davis and in March 1870, Texas was readmitted to the Union.

When the regular session convened on April 28, 1870, the legislature began immediately to deal with the programs of the Governor.

While Governor Davis wanted legislation to provide for public schools, internal improvement, and frontier protection, as well as adequate financial support to implement his package, outrages committed by whites against freedmen made law and order the primary concern of his administration. Racial turmoil which began prior to 1865, appeared to increase after Davis took office. Thus, "Radical Republicans" responded to this untenable racial climate by proposing to create a state police force and to reestablish the state militia. It is well to note that the state had operated a police agency (The Texas Rangers) during the antebellum years, but it was restricted to the frontier. The state police bill that was being introduced in this legislature called for an integrated force of 258 men to deal primarily with civil law, and to be placed under the Governor's control. The militia bill as proposed was nothing more than a complement of the state police legislation. It did not differ significantly from the prewar militia, but it did appear to some that it enlarged the power of the governor. It not only gave the governor power to activate this force in the event of resistance to civil law, and to declare martial law where lawlessness obstructed justice, but also to make the citizens in the "lawless" locale pay for the militia's expense. Also, where martial law was declared, the governor could suspend civil law for the length of the emergency.

Needless to say, when introduced, the above bills created a furor both within and outside of the General Assembly. Some critics charged that the "real purpose of these bills was not to preserve law and order, but to perpetuate Negro and Carpetbaggers' rule." [11] Others argued from concern for "constitutional rights and the plan of governmental abuse of power." [12] Still others complained about the fact that both forces, militia and police, would be racially intergrated. Moreover, opposition to these bills was further encouraged by the self-serving interest of railroad promoters.[13] Yet, despite these criticisms and obstacles, these measures did not have any trouble passing the House, respectfully, on May 21 and June 7, 1870. However, the situation in the Senate would be quite different. After some legislative wranglings, the police bill passed the Senate on June 12, 1870, but passage of the militia bill was an uphill battle.

The two black senators, George T. Ruby and Matt Gaines, not only gave hearty support to these measures, but also played an instrumental role in pushing them through the Senate. Their positions are best seen in the debate on these bills. Fortunately for the student of history, one of the few debates still preserved from the Twelfth Legislature is that of the police and militia acts. It is probably this debate, more than any other issue of this legislature, which showed the thinking of both Ruby and Gaines, their mannerisms, styles, and concerns for blacks. In a polished and well-defined manner, Ruby based his favorable argument for the militia bill on the centralization of power inherent in the state and federal constitutions. Responding to the criticism that the militia bill would give the Governor too much power and reacting to the substitute bill which was designed to curb the governor's authority, Ruby argued that the militia bill as originally proposed, would only give the chief executive power already delegated to him by the constitution.

Using the tactics of the shrewd politician to get this bill through the Senate, Ruby told Conservatives and moderate Republicans that the militia bill had its origin in the violence which existed in Texas, but he was quick to add that these acts of violence were not committed by peaceable residents of the Texas counties. Rather, Ruby contended that such violence was committed by anarchists, who, because of rigid law enforcement in such states as Arkansas, North Carolina, and South Carolina, were forced to remove to Texas.[14] Still, anyone who had lived at least one week in the Lone Star State knew that Ruby's argument was far from accurate. Violence committed by native residents was just as common as were the Longhorns of Texas.[15]

Whereas Ruby was cautious, judicial and rarely referred to race in his argument for the original militia bill and against the substitute bill, Matt Gaines's argument was presented in a different light. In rejecting the substitute bill, Gaines gave his reasons as follows:

> I owe a duty to my constitutents whose interest I have at heart and that duty compels me to cast my vote against that resolution . . . In my own county there are men today riding around stealing horses and shooting blacks, and yet I am told that we do not need a militia system in this state. I also know that bands of men are in my country not only ready to kill the niggers, but to shoot down the damned hated Yankees, and still we have no business for the militia in this state . . . And I know if some of our democratic friends had seen the Ku Klux Klan as I have seen them, there would be less opposition to the [original bill][16]

Gaines argued that if the opposition to the original militia bill had come only from Conservatives and Democrats, he could understand, but for such opposition to come from Republicans "who were sent [to the Senate] by a colored majority" was an abomination; something that made Gaines furious. To the charge that these bills, state police and militia, placed too much power in the hands of the Governor, Gaines contended that racism, not centralization, was the reason for the opposition. In his own words: "It is not so much the idea of placing such great power in the hands of the executive, but it is the idea of gentlemen of my color being armed and riding around after desperadoes."[17] Among three of many reasons cited by Gaines for his support of these measures were: (1) these bills did not contemplate any injury to Democrats, Conservatives or Republicans; (2) they gave protection to blacks; and (3) they allowed blacks to vote without intimidation from the Ku Klux Klan.[18]

While the above debate was a factor in delaying the passage of these measures in the Senate, it was not the only one. Railroad promoters were equally guilty in employing dilatory tactics. Railroad men wanted a generous program of subsidies, but Radicals were opposed to such grants. So, in an attempt to force the Radicals to approve subsidies, the railroad supporters in the Senate tried to fasten the militia bill and railroad subsidies to the same legislative log and not allow one to pass without the other. Hence, when the militia bill came up for a vote, thirteen senators intentionally broke a quorum in an attempt to stop the bill. They were later arrested and forced to return to the Senate where four of them were released from arrest to restore a quorum. The militia bill then passed the Senate by a vote of 15 to 5 on June 16, 1870.[19]

Notwithstanding this resounding defeat, railroad advocates would persist in their efforts. Consequently, the first railroad subsidy was approved by the legislature soon after the passage of the militia bill. Davis, who urged Radicals to be hostile to railroad subsidies, immediately vetoed the bill. But in order to successfully maintain an anti-subsidy policy, Davis would have to get enough support in the legislature to prevent subsidy bills from being passed over his veto. In this regard, Senator Gaines led the Senate debate to sustain the veto, but to no avail. In the House, Davis's veto met with more success. By a vote of 55 to override to 29 to sustain, the bill failed to receive the two-thirds needed to override the Governor's veto.

It is interesting to note that twenty-two of the twenty-nine representatives who voted to sustain the veto were men who belonged to the Radical Republican Association. This organization of white and black Republicans was established June 4, 1870, for the purpose of "supporting the present administration and of successfully carrying party measures through the legislature." The members swore an oath of secrecy not to divulge anything the association said or did. According to their constitution, "the action of the majority of the members . . . in any political matter whatever would be binding . . . and would control their votes in the House of Representatives." The members were also instructed to vote in the House against any suspension of the rules except on bills involved with school, immigration, taxes, judiciary, apportionment. Likewise, they were to vote against all bills on their third readings, except those dealing with internal improvement.[20] Blacks who were members of this association included Benjamin F. Williams,

David Medlock, Richard Williams, Goldstein Dupree, Richard Allen, Sheppard Mullins, Silas Cotton, John Mitchell, Henry Moore, Mitchell Kendall and Jeremiah J. Hamilton. Richard Allen was elected vice-president of the Association, while Jeremiah Hamilton was rejected on two occasions before being accepted. On the other hand, Kendall and Moore were called before the committee twice and were eventually expelled from the association. The reason was they voted not to sustain the Governor's veto.[21] A careful review of the bills passed during the Twelfth Legislature reveals that blacks usually voted according to the dictates of the constitution of the Radical Republican Association.

It should be noted that the passage of the police and militia bills was no panacea for the lawlessness which existed in the state. Cognizant of this fact, blacks introduced a number of measures to complement the said bills. For example, Gaines introduced a successful resolution requesting the Governor to submit a report to the Senate on the number of murders and assassinations committed in the Sixteenth Senatorial District for the year of 1870–1871, and also the number of convicts sent to the state prison from that district.[22] Similarly, Gaines, was also responsible for the passage of a bill authorizing his own district to levy a special tax for the construction of a jail.[23] So bad was violence and so concerned about it was Gaines, that he offered a motion to suspend the rules to take up an act "to regulate the keeping and bearing of deadly weapons." This bill enabled the gun legislation to become law on the third reading.[24] Gaines's colleague, Ruby, also expressed concern for and awareness of lawlessness and crime which existed in the State of Texas. This was evident from his unsuccessful endeavors in initiating a bill to define the powers of the criminal district courts in Galveston and Harris counties.[25]

In addition to legislation which dealt specifically with violence and criminal acts, blacks introduced other bills that were designed to protect the civil and political rights of the freedmen. In the House, Richard Allen introduced an act to enforce Section 21 of Article I of the 1869 Texas Constitution,[26] which called for "equality of all persons before the law." When it appeared that it was going to take an unusual amount of time for this bill to reach the Senate, Gaines called up the House version of the bill and on October 25, 1871, it became law;[27] that is, enforcement took effect at least on paper. Concomitant with this bill, Gaines was also cosponsor of a resolution, which was referred to the Committee on Judiciary, "that any person or persons that may attempt to bribe or defraud any other person(s) of their vote and force them to vote for any person for any office whatever by denying them employment of any kind, land or property, and refusing to renew leases shall be deemed guilty of an offense and shall be fined in the sum of five hundred dollars or two years imprisonment." [28] Unfortunately, this bill was never reported out of committee.

Like many of their white colleagues, blacks demonstrated an interest in bills promoting the general welfare of the state, and as such, placed a great deal of emphasis on internal improvement. Ruby's interest in acquainting Texans with the mineral and agricultural resources of the state at a time when cotton and stock raising were the chief sources of incomes led him to propose "an act to provide for the Geological and Agricultural Survey of the State." [29] As a result of this survey, some of the vast mineral deposits in the state were discovered, and the agricultural possibilities of underdeveloped sections of the state were made known. In the House, with Richard Allen as Chairman of the Road and Bridges Committee, blacks would have an even greater impact on internal improvements. As chairman, Allen was able to bring about greatly improved transportation facilities. In order to encourage construction of bridges, Allen recommended the incorporation of the Belton Bridges Company and introduced legislation to the effect that Howard and Associates be authorized to construct a toll bridge across the Sabine River at Lake Fort in the southern part of Wood County between present day Mineola and Tyler. Likewise, numerous other bridges were started and a number of ferries were put into operation while Allen was chairman of this important legislative committee. As a result, lower East Texas was connected with Jefferson; Hillsboro and Corsicana; Waco with Corsicana; Dallas with Corsicana; and other areas of the state also profited in a similar way.[30]

Congruent with internal improvement, early in the first session B. F. Williams suggested that if the people of the state were anxious to see the resources of the state develop and were desirous of encouraging the building of railroads and increasing immigration, then a tax should be levied to raise revenues. In order to effectuate this idea, he introduced the following resolution.

> Resolved: That it is the sense of this House, that an act be passed to levy a tax of five percent per acre on all land above two hundred acres which shall be exempt from taxation as a homestead. The said tax to be set apart as an internal improvement fund and to be loaned to railroad companies on two percent bonds to encourage the building of railroads. When any companies shall have completed any part of the railroad and put the same in good running order, there shall be donated out of said fund three thousand dollars for every mile completed.[31]

This resolution was read twice and laid on the table. Yet the idea of immigration did not die, for the simple reason that one of the main concerns of the Twelfth Legislature was the development of unsettled land.

Just as white politicians encouraged immigrants from foreign shores to come to Texas to cultivate the unsettled land, black lawmakers also expressed an interest in this regard. But they would differ on who the immigrants would be and where they would come from. Nowhere was this more evident than in the Senate. Senator Ruby introduced an act to encourage the emigration of communities of persons from several cities in Alsace-Lorraine, who were skilled in the art of spinning and weaving cotton and wool, and in dyeing and printing fabric.[32] On the other hand, when an act to organize the Bureau of Immigration came before the Senate, the bill was amended to include not more than one agent for recruitment purposes from the United States and two from Europe. Gaines offered an amendment to that amendment to include one agent from Africa.[33] When Gaines's amendment was defeated by an eighteen to fourteen vote, he returned to his home district and attacked the immigration policies. Complaining about the introduction of white foreign settlers into the state, Gaines said: "They pay a man a salary of $3,500 per year to bring Dutch here to work the land that we cut the trees from and pulled the stumps out of. They sell the land to the Dutch on credit with ten percent interest, but a colored man cannot buy it on four months or forty months at fifty percent interest." [34] Disheartened by the immigration policy, but not discouraged in his quest to get more blacks into the Lone Star State, one month later Gaines introduced another immigration bill. This act was aimed at recruiting the mobile free black population in other states of the Union, but it met an untimely death in committee.[35]

On another issue — that of the protection of the frontier — Gaines and Ruby seemed to have been somewhat more in agreement than they had been on immigration. In regard to placing a border patrol against the Indians, both senators were in accord. Gaines argued that if Republicans would not pass the frontier bill which would protect the people of Texas, destruction would come to the party; and that "the price of property and lives of our people were more valuable than the cost of maintaining a patrol." In an ironic twist of events, Ruby appeared to be the more liberal of the two on this issue. He contended that he depreciated the fact that the Senate had to deal with the Indian in a different manner than it dealt with other classes of people who live in Texas; that the policy of the United States government in dealing with the Indians had been wrong from the beginning to the present and that this was the reason why the United States was forced to protect the frontier.[36]

In contrast to the fact that only the two black senators and one black representative voiced an opinion on the frontier issue, black lawmakers would exhibit a more avid interest in education. Accordingly, the first session was barely under way when Henry Moore offered the following resolution:

> Whereas, we are aware of the deffficiency and total want of public school for the masses of people throughout the state of Texas. Resolve: that the committee on Education be required to report back bills or otherwise for the establishing of public schools throughout the state in compliance with Sections 5 and 6 of Article 9 of the Constitution.[37]

After this resolution was laid on the table, Richard Allen offered a similar resolution asking the committee to report a bill on public education as soon as practicable.[38] When the bill was finally introduced, it called for a Superintendent of Public Education to be approved by the Governor and the Senate until the general election was held; for children of both races to attend classes at least four months of the year, and for establishing a permanent school fund in which blacks would share equally with whites. As introduced, this bill touched off a lively debate in the House on the question of integration. S. H. Miller of Bell County wanted the bill amended to specifically forbid any mixture of races. But no sooner had he made this amendment when Richard Williams, representative from Walker, moved to lay it on the table.[39] Williams's amendment to the amendment was lost by a vote of 33 to 32.[40] However, after much legislative wrangling, Miller's amendment was eventually laid on the table. Afterward, the original bill was passed by both Houses and was approved August 13, 1870.

Still, the advocate of segregation would not lay the issue to rest. When Governor Davis submitted the name of Joseph W. Talbot as Superintendent of Education, the Senate refused to confirm him because the majority of the senators did not want to create a racially mixed school system and Talbot had not declared himself opposed to integration in all cases. The rejection of Talbot's candidacy was the first indication that the Free School Bill of 1870 would not stand the test of time. Thus, when the second session convened in 1871, the advocates of segregation were set on repealing the Free School Bill, and repeal they did. Senator Albert J. Fountaine of El Paso presented a bill which was designed to change the old act. While Fountaine's bill did not specifically authorize or prohibit segregation in public schools, it did give school directors in each district the authority to make "any separation . . . that the peace and success of the school and the good of the whole may require."[41] Without a doubt, this bill, which passed both Houses to become the Free School Bill of 1871, was interpreted by the directors as justification for segregated schools. Needless to say, all black legislators in the House, except B. F. Williams, voted against the Fountaine bill. Williams's posture in this regard angered Richard Allen, who accused his colleague from Fort Bend, of being a Democrat in disguise. Williams, who countered that he "was old enough to know how he wanted to vote," [42] is but one clear-cut example of the differences that existed among black legislators.

Despite their differences, blacks remained steadfast in their desire for education. Shortly after passage of the first Free School Bill, Richard Allen introduced an act to incorporate the Gregory Institute of Harris County. After being referred and stalemated in the Education Committee, John Mitchell moved to suspend the rules to take up the bill, so as to allow it to pass on the third reading.[43] Thus, incorporation became a *fait accompli*. The Gregory Institute, which was first established by the Freedmen's Bureau in 1866 as a grade school for the express purpose of training teachers, now derived its *raison d'être* from the state. After the Institute's incorporation, all of the schools established by the Bureau in Harris County were abolished, and the pupils attending each were transferred to the Gregory Institute. It was largely due to the Institute's new status that in 1871 Harris County had the largest number of blacks enrolled in the public school system in Texas — 734 males and 760 females.[44]

Interest in higher education was also manifested by black lawmakers. In trying to safeguard the integrity of Texas colleges, Sheppard Mullins introduced a bill to prohibit the sale of ardent spirits within two and one half miles from the Greenwood Institute of McLennan County.[45] Likewise, Gaines introduced a resolution to keep liquor stores at least six miles away from any college.[46] Ruby also had the same idea in mind when he introduced an act "to prohibit the sale or distribution of spiritous or other intoxicating liquids, or the establishment of any drinking saloon, gambling house, or house of ill fame within certain districts." [47]

Even though all of the above bills passed without difficulty, blacks realized that if the Governor's programs, especially those affecting education, were to be successful, they would require a great deal of money. With this in mind, B. F. Williams introduced a bill which stated that all laws in regard to taxes in cities and towns which came in conflict with the general statutes "should be relegated to the general laws of the state." [48] On the other hand, Matt Gaines reasoned that if the educational endeavors were to be realized, there was a need not only for money, but for tax exempt status as well. In the interest of encouraging educational and religious groups to do what they could for the educational betterment of their own localities, Senator Gaines was first to voice a proposal for exempting such organizations from taxation. On May 12, 1871, he proposed that "all buildings with their furniture and libraries designed and used for the purpose of education or religious worship, together with the land owned by said institutions of learning or churches . . . are hereby exempted from taxation." [49] Buildings, facilities and other equipment used for charitable or literary associations were also exempted. This bill became law June 12, 1871.[50]

While black lawmakers were very aggressive in introducing and pushing educational measures which would have an impact either directly or indirectly upon their constituents, the same could not be said of them on the issue of labor. Not only was the Twelfth Legislature unfriendly to labor, but only two blacks introduced bills that dealt with the subject. Richard Allen introduced a bill "to exempt the wages of laborers and others from the writ of garnishment." [51] It was referred to the Judiciary Committee, but was never reported back. B. F. Williams presented an act for the protection of agricultural labor, but it was reported back from the committee unfavorably.[52] Given the fact that the majority of their constituents were rural workers, one is sometimes tempted to agree with the assertion W. E. B. Du Bois makes in *Black Reconstruction* when he argues that even though black lawmakers of Reconstruction were in the minority and had obstacles in their path, "they were not at all clear in their economic thoughts."

In contrast to their apparent lack of activity and/or interest in labor, blacks were very active and successful on the issue of incorporation. Among the items that were proposed, passed and incorporated were Mullins's Waco Light and Gas Company; Allen's Houston Manufacturing and Furniture Company, as well as the Mutual Aid Society of Houston; Mitchell's town of Lexington in Burleson; Kendall's incorporation of the town of Marshall; and Ruby's Galveston Mutual and Life Association, as well as Galveston's Horticultural Society.[53] By contrast, when the Texas Homestead Bill came up for incorporation, it was reported back from the committee unfavorably. Richard Allen charged that the action taken on the part of the committee had something to do with the fact that all the incorporators were blacks.[54]

At this point, it should be noted that blacks were not only concerned with racial matters, but also with supporting measures of broad social reform which would benefit whites as well as blacks. For example, many blacks introduced relief measures to aid white constituents. A case in point centered around Richard Allen, who introduced a petition for an ex-Confederate veteran concerning his pension. Out of this petition grew the Texas Independent Veterans Bill, which became law on August 13, 1871.[55] By its provision, Texas veterans were granted two hundred and fifty dollars per year, with an additional like amount for those wounded in service. Similarly, Gaines's successful proposal "to levy a special tax for the support of the lunatic institution in the state" [56] was designed to benefit whites as well as blacks.

Despite their performance, blacks of the Twelfth Legislature were politicians, and like politicians at all levels of state and local government, they were concerned with securing their own political turf. Thus, the changing county boundaries was a matter of principal importance to some of the black lawmakers. Their probable motive was to prevent a predominantly black district from being absorbed by a predominantly white one. This is what B. F. Williams had in mind when he presented a resolution from the citizens of Colorado County protesting against the formation of a new county from a portion of Colorado County.[57] Similarly, Goldstein Dupree presented a petition from citizens of Montgomery County protesting against "taking any territory from the said county to create a new one."[58] On the other hand, Richard Allen and Silas Cotton recommended that the County seat of Robertson be changed from Owensville to Calvert, which had a majority black population.[59] However, when this bill reached the Senate, Gaines, who wanted to play the game fairly, offered a resolution that the committee on Counties and Boundaries be more fully informed by the permanently located citizens of Robertson County as to the general desire of the said citizens regarding the removal of the county seat from Owensville to the town of Calvert.[60] When the citizens made their desire known, this bill was approved and the county seat was changed to Calvert, the newly incorporated town.[61]

When the legislature adjourned May 31, 1871, blacks could breathe sighs of relief that they had fought a good fight. Yet, the demands from blacks of the Twelfth Legislature were generally not revolutionary in nature. They did not fight for nor did they envisage any radical change in the political or economic structure of the Texas Government. Still, it has been alleged by some major and minor writers, historians and laymen, that Reconstruction in Texas was a time of radical and black rule. While it was neither radical nor black, there is ample evidence to suggest that blacks did exert an influence in the legislative process — influence that they would never again possess within the period of 1872–1900.

A proper evaluation of this evidence depends upon the context in which it is considered. Political power relationships can be most appropriately dealt with in an institutional context, that is, through conventions (as will be dealt with in Part Two), and through the legislative process. Of extreme importance is the role that black leaders played vis-à-vis whites in each of these settings. Thus, the question that comes to mind is one centered around the legislature process; that is just how was black influence felt and exerted in the Twelfth Legislature? This question can be answered by looking at three variables: (1) the numerical strength of blacks in this legislature vis-à-vis other legislatures; (2) their association with white radical allies; and (3) blacks relationship to and with the governor.

To be sure, black influence in this legislature was minimal when comparing its 13 members to 107 of its white counterpart. But when comparing the number of blacks who sat in this legislature to blacks who would sit in future legislatures, it soon becomes clear that never again would blacks have eleven members in the House and two in the Senate at the same time. Moreover, never again would blacks be assigned as chairmen of the standing and special committees. For example, in the Senate, George T. Ruby was chairman of the powerful Engrossing Bills Committee, while his colleague Matt Gaines was named chairman of the Special Committee on Contingent Expense. In the House there was a least one black committee chairman, Richard Allen, who chaired Roads and Bridges.

Black influence in the legislature was also enhanced or shown by the alliance of black and white Republicans. This does not mean, however, that white Republicans support of blacks was one hundred percent or even eighty percent. What it did mean it that during this period, there were more whites for whatever reason — self-serving or otherwise — who would support a piece of legislation that was favorable to blacks than would be the case in future years. The Radical Republican Association is a good example. Through this association, a little more strength was added to this fragile coalition between white and black Republicans. Consequently, blacks were able to present, introduce and have more of their bills passed (though these were few) than would be the case in subsequent legislatures.

By contrast, one's power and influence might depend upon one's personal affinity and contact with the governor. Such influence was exercised through letters, informal meetings and conversations. The best example of such a relationship with the governor was that of George T. Ruby's. Ruby was considered the chief spokesman of the administration and seldom did his councel go unheeded. Ruby was also the chief patronage broker of Galveston County, and as such literally ran the country. For example, it was upon Ruby's recommendation that Victor McMahan, a moderate Republican, become mayor of Galveston over Radical Republican William Sinclair.[62] Like wise, H. G. Sprague received the clearkship of the District Court of Galveston over the opposition of Judge Samuel Dodge, because he had won the support of Ruby. Moreover, it was Ruby who was instrumental in securing Norris W. Cuney's appointment in 1870 as the first assistant to the Sergeant-at-Arms of the Twelfth Legislature.

The governor was potentially the single most powerful person in Texas since he had the power of manipulating local politics through appointive offices; and black leaders did not fail to recognize this fact. It is save to say that most blacks who would become "somebody" in politics would write the governor, seeking an appointment for themselves and their constituencies. For instance, in 1870 Goldstein Dupree and Matt Gaines wrote the governor and recommended that J. M. Thornmenheimer be appointed as weigher of cotton in Harris County.[63] Nathan Haller, who would serve in the Twenty-fourth Legislature, asked for and was appointed as Hide Inspector of Barzoria County, while Walter Burton, who would become a senator in 1874, recommended Llyod H. McCabe as Registrar of Fort Bend County.[64] Observedly, letters written to Davis were not restricted to appointments. Many were centered around violence and the removal of individuals from office. Thus, Sheppard Mullins wrote Governor Davis asking him to send troops to Brazos County for the protection of blacks from mob violence in 1871.[65] Gaines and R. J. Moore sought the Governor's support and advice in the removal of the Treasurer of Washington County because of "his attitude towards blacks."; [66] Given the above contact with the Governor, one can argue that local politicians were to some degree dependent upon the governor for their survival and, in turn, he was dependent upon them to deliver the votes for his election. Being members of the same party, one can argue that with some exceptions, Governor Davis and black lawmakers shared a fairly good relationship.

In sum it can be argued that the legislative program offered by blacks in the Twelfth Legislature was similar to their demands in the constitutional convention. They were concerned with the civil, political and educational rights of blacks, and in promoting the tranquillity, as well as the general welfare of the state. Their performance was marked by success and failure. Yet it can be characterized as a mixture of idealism and realism. Blacks secured their greatest trimuphs with the passage of the State Police, Militia, Election, and Educational Bills. The State Police and Militia Bills gave blacks more protection for their property and their lives than they had previously enjoyed. The Election Bill, at least temporarily protected, their right to vote. Education bills allowed them equal, though segregated, participation in the state's first public school system. To the contrary, black lawmakers failed in their endeavor to enact legislations that would benefit blacks economically. Still, even though they did not accomplish all that they had sought, they had made a beginning. Despite the fact that the elections of 1872 and 1873 would alter somewhat their influence in the Thirteenth and Fourteenth Legislatures, this setback would not cause them to change their demands significantly.

[3]

Blacks at the Crossroad
1872–1875

Conservatives, Republicans and Democrats, who in 1870 formed a political alliance to wrest control of the state from the "undesirable" radical and black forces, achieved their objectives in 1871 and 1872. In the election of 1871, "Radical Reconstruction" for all practical purposes came to an end. Notwithstanding the campaign efforts of the Republicans, Democrats captured all four of the Congressional seats. They captured both houses of the state legislature. Needless to say, blacks lost ground in the number of elected state officials, as well as in the territories represented. While the two black senators, Ruby and Gaines, returned to the Senate to finish their terms, only eight blacks secured seats in the House in the Thirteenth Legislature. The election of 1873 was almost a carbon copy of that of 1872. The Democrats maintained their control in the legislature, while at the same time they captured the prime prize, the governorship. Again, blacks would see a decline in their numerical strength in the Fourteenth Legislature. There were six blacks elected to the House, and only one secured a seat in the Senate.

When the Thirteenth and Fourteenth Legislatures convened, the Democratic majorities clearly outlined the political philosophy of their party in several enactments. These lawmakers repealed the state police and militia acts and replaced the personnel of these agencies with an all

Members of the Thirteenth Legislature.
— Courtesy of Texas State Archives.

white Texas Ranger force. Also eliminated from the militia and police act was that part which gave the Governor extra control over those forces in cases of emergency. In addition to these actions, the Democrats modified the election bill so as to return to a one-day election to be held in local precincts rather than in county seats. The Democrats also attacked the Republican school system as being too centralized, and they replaced it with a weaker substitute which left many children without adequate school facilities for years to come. During this same period, the legislature converted monetary aid for railroads into grants of public land. Finally, they called for a constitutional convention to meet in 1875.

Given the actions taken by the Democrats, the question that arises is, how did blacks fare under the circumstances? Did they simply react to the negativism of the Democrats or did they still try to enact legislation which would benefit their black constituents? Before these questions can be answered, it is necessary to take a look at the backgrounds of these men who sat in the Thirteenth and Fourteenth Legislatures.

The eight blacks who were elected to the Thirteenth Legislature were Shack Roberts, James H. Washington, Henry Phelps, Allen Wilder, Henry Moore, Richard Williams, Richard Allen, and Edward Anderson. By far, the most colorful of these legislators was Shack Roberts. Roberts, a Methodist minister, was born a slave in Arkansas, but was brought to Gilmer, Texas, in 1844, by his master, O. B. Roberts. While Roberts's master served in the Confederate army, Roberts was charged with the responsibility of protecting his master's property and family. Apparently, Roberts did a good job, for before the war was over Roberts's master not only gave him his freedom, but also deeded him some land and furnished him with material to build a house for his family. Shortly after he became free, Roberts was attacked by the Ku Klux Klan in Gilmer, and was left for dead along the roadside. Surviving this ordeal, he moved to Marshall, Texas, where he became active in politics. He was elected to the Thirteenth Legislature to represent Harrison County in 1872, at the age of fifty-one. For two successive terms afterwards, he represented Harrison County and remained active in Republican politics for years to come. After he lost his bid to return to the Texas Legislature, Roberts became a pastor of a Methodist church in Marshall. While there, he and his congregation bought 200 hundred acres of land, divided it into lots, sold them for a great profit and with the money helped to establish Wiley College. Roberts took pride in the above accomplishment and usually referred to Wiley as a college which was "open to both sexes and all races." [1]

Another black lawmaker of the Thirteenth Legislature was James H. Washington. Washington was born in Fredericksburg, Virginia, (to free parents). He acquired his elementary and secondary school training in the public schools of Virginia, before entering Oberlin College. Upon completion of his studies at Oberlin, Washington returned to Washington, D.C., to live with his mother, sister, and brothers. In the early 1870s, he decided to come to Texas, and to settle in the town of Navasota, in Grimes County. There, he organized a chapter of the Union League and worked on his first job as principal of the city schools. In 1872, he entered the political arena and was elected to the state legislature to represent Grimes County. After serving this county for one term in the legislature, Washington moved to Galveston. There, his interest in politics continued as he ran for and was subsequently elected to the city council. When his council term expired, he was appointed Inspector of Customs for the City of Galveston. Afterward, he returned to community service and to politics. In 1879, he attended the National Conference on the Exodus to Kansas. In 1891 he was the keynote speaker at the Tenth Annual Conference of Colored Teachers. Still very active in politics, his last appearance at a Republican national gathering came in the late 1890s. On December 23, 1916, Washington died in LaMarque, Texas.[2]

From Fort Bend County came another black legislator, Henry Phelps. Phelps, born a slave in Virginia, was a farmer by trade and was forty-two years old when he was elected to represent Fort Bend County in the Thirteenth Legislature. It is not known in what year he arrived in Texas, but he became a charter member of the Union Loyal League of Fort Bend, in 1869. He was also appointed to the first Board of Appeals of Fort Bend, in 1869, a board which supervised the registration of voters, as well as tallied votes on election day. No doubt his early entrance into politics was a plus for him, because in 1872, Phelps was elected to the legislature by a large margin. After completing his term, Phelps returned to Fort Bend County where he was appointed Inspector of Hides. Although never again elected to the legislature after 1874, Phelps remained active in politics until his death.[3]

Hailing from Washington County was Allen Wilder. Contrary to J. Mason Brewer's assertion that Wilder was elected but didn't serve in the Thirteenth Legislature, research has shown that Wilder was an active participant in the House of Representatives. Wilder was born in North Carolina, where he acquired the skills of an engineer while still a slave. Exactly when he came to Texas is uncertain, but after arriving in the Lone Star State, he became a teacher and was also an attorney-at-law. He was twenty-nine years of age when he ran successfully for the legislature in 1872. Wilder ran again for the House in 1876, but was defeated in a contested election. In 1878, he made another unsuccessful bid for public office, but this time for a Senate seat. Afterward, Wilder retired from politics and devoted his time to two professions — teaching and practicing law. In the late 1880s, Wilder ran afoul of the law by fraudulently signing school vouchers and committing perjury. After these last incidents, any record of Wilder's activities appears nonexistent.[4]

Another black elected for the first time, but for whom very little information is available, was Edward Anderson. Anderson was a thirty-eight-year-old farmer when he was elected to represent the Fourteenth District. Where his slave birth took place and in what year he came to Texas are unknown.[5] Unlike Anderson, biographical information exists and profiles have already been given on Henry Moore, Richard Williams, Richard Allen, as well as on the two black senators, Matt Gaines and George Ruby.

It is interesting to note that of eight blacks who were elected to the House in 1872, four were involved in contested elections. Their tenure in office was, therefore, abbreviated — inasmuch as they did not take their seats in the House until late in the session or were unseated before the session was over. Richard Williams and James Washington won their seats in a contested election after it was discovered that the discrepancies in the votes were due to a mistake made by the clerk in the numbering of names on the registration list.[6] So, Williams and Washington, (along with Henry Phelps, who was late because of illness), did not take their seats until February, one month after the legislature had convened.[7]

On the other hand, Richard Allen and Edward Anderson were unseated in March 1873, after being sworn into office. Both were from the Fourteenth Senatorial District, which consisted of Harris and Montgomery Counties, and both charged racism as cause for their dismissal. According to the Majority Report, many blacks who voted for Allen and Anderson either did not reside in the said counties or their names did not appear on the registration list. The most damaging testimony came from Goldstein Dupree, who was not nominated by the Republicans for reelection. Dupree testified that he knew some of the people who were not residents of Harris and Montgomery Counties, but who had nevertheless voted for Allen and Anderson. It was alleged in the Minority Report that Goldstein was paid for this testimony. Whether or not this allegation is true, it can however, be argued that blacks (especially Dupree) contributed to the demise of their own numerical strength in the Thirteenth Legislature.[8]

Members of the Fourteenth Legislature seemed very similar in background to those of the Thirteenth Legislature. These were three farmers, David Abner, Thomas Beck and John Mitchell, and three skilled men, Shack R. Roberts, Edward Brown, and Jacob Freeman. As a result of their having served in the previous legislature, the pedigrees of John Mitchell and Shack R. Roberts are not necessary at this point. On the contrary, not only is the personal data on David Abner more intriguing, but is is also more abundant. David Abner was born in Selma, Alabama, in 1820. He was brought to Texas in 1843 by the daughter of his master, who with her husband settled in Upshur County. Abner remained in this county until after the Civil War. In 1866, he moved to Marshall, Texas, and rented a place known as the Nathan Smith Plantation. Like many other blacks in Texas, Abner came into freedom wanting land, a home, and a good family life. So, after settling in Harrison County, he became a prosperous farmer and after a few years of hard labor and economical living, he managed to buy the place which he was renting. By 1876, he was easily worth between thirty-five to fifty thousand dollars and was signing notes, bonds, and securities for thousands of dollars for whites, as well as blacks. According to oral sources, Abner was a natural politician. This statement was substantiated by the fact that within a few years after settling in Marshall, Texas, Abner was elected as Harrison County Treasurer. In 1874, at fifty-four years of age, he was elected to the Texas Legislature. The following year, he was also elected as member of the 1875 Constitutional Convention of Texas.[9]

Abner was a part of every movement for the improvement of blacks in Harrison County. He helped to organize Bethesda Baptist Church and became one of its first deacons. He also helped to establish the first elementary school for blacks in Harrison County. As a member of the Texas–Louisiana Association, which he helped to organize in 1869, he became one of the great spirits behind the organization of the Centennial Academy. After leaving the legislature, his interest in education continued. Thus, he was at the forefront of the movement to establish Bishop College and as such became one of the two original black trustees. When Abner retired from the legislature he became the sole proprietor of an ice industry and continued to speculate in land which totaled over 300 acres of land in East Texas.[10]

The three other blacks about whom less biographical information is available were Jacob Freeman, Edward Brown, and Thomas Beck. Jacob Freeman, a slave mechanic, was born in Alabama. He was brought to Waco, Texas, at the age of eleven. During the Civil War, he served with his master in the Confederate Army for twelve months. After Emancipation, Freeman entered politics and at thirty-three years of age, he represented Fort Bend County in the Fourteenth Legislature. Doing a good job in either pleasing or getting the ear of his Fort Bend constituents, Freeman was reelected to serve in the Sixteenth Legislature in 1878.[11] Like Freeman, Edward Brown was born in Alabama, where he acquired the skills of a carpenter. He was thirty-four years when he was elected to the Legislature to represent Harrison County.[12] Hailing from Mississippi was Thomas Beck, a farmer of thirty-four years of age. He represented Madison and Grimes counties.[13]

As far as the senators are concerned, whereas, two were elected in 1873, Walter M. Burton and Matthew Gaines, only Burton served out part of his term. Walter Moses Burton came to Texas from North Carolina in 1850, at the age of twenty-one. He was brought to the Lone Star State by a wealthy planter, Thomas Burke Burton. While a slave, Burton was taught how to read and write by his master, skills which served him well in later years. Burton was a farmer by trade and also was owner of a plantation and several large farms in Fort Bend County. Contrary to the findings of many sources, Burton's master did not deed him any land, but rather sold him large plots of land for the small sum of nine hundred dollars. No doubt this land made Burton one of the wealthiest and most influential blacks in Fort Bend County.[14] Consequently, Burton got involved in politics as early as 1869, at which time he was elected sheriff and tax collector, as well as president of the Union Loyal League of Fort Bend County. During his tenure as a sheriff and tax collector from 1869-1873, the white people of Fort Bend respected Burton, because he did not annoy or "antagonize" them. It is not known whether Sheriff Burton was allowed to arrest white people of the town. What is known is that he had a white deputy who was specifically authorized to arrest all whites who broke the law. When Burton left office, many whites became disturbed because in their opinion, now would arrive a "different class" of blacks in office. Because Democrats were so pleased with Burton, he was endorsed by them to run for Senator on the Democratic ticket in 1873.[15] However, Burton preferred to remain in the Republican camp and subsequently won his bid for the Senate on the GOP ticket. Thus, Burton became the only black to serve in the upper house for seven years — from 1874 to 1875, and from 1876 to 1882.

Burton's first term in the Senate was interrupted and shortened by a contested election, as well as the calling of a constitutional convention in 1875. In January 1874, Burton was granted a certificate of election from the Thirteenth Senatoral District, but his seat was contested by a white Democrat, whose reason for contesting was that Burton's name was listed three different ways on the ballot, W. Burton, W. M. Burton and William Burton. Consequently, each name received votes in various counties in the district. The Senate committee on election had at first recommended the seating of the Democratic candidate, but later it reconsidered its decision and based the outcome of the election on "intent" of the votes cast for the different Burtons. The Senate then confirmed Burton's election in March, 1874.[16] By the time Senate confirmed Burton's election in March 1874, over half of the first session of the Fourteenth Legislature was over, and the second session was abbreviated because of the call for a constitutional convention. Still determined to serve his people, Burton ran and was reelected to the Senate in 1876. Burton left the Senate in 1882, and upon the request of a white colleague, he was given a golden cane for his service in that chamber. Even after leaving office, Burton still remained active in state and local politics until his death in 1913.[17]

The other black who was elected to the Senate in 1873 but did not serve was Matthew Gaines. He, like Burton, was involved in a contested election, but unlike Burton, Gaines lost his right to be seated. Seth Shepard, a white Democrat, contested the election on the following grounds: (1) that he had received more votes than Gaines; (2) that Gaines was not a resident of the Sixteenth Senatorial District at the time of the election; and (3) that on December 9, 1871, the District Court of Fayette County had indicted Gaines for the crime of bigamy and that on July 15, 1873, Gaines was tried, found guilty and was sentenced to one year in prison.

In overturning Gaines's election, the committee failed to take into consideration two important facts: (1) On November 24, 1873, the Texas Supreme Court reversed the finding of the District Court, and (2) Gaines ran for reelection in his home district four weeks after the decision of the Supreme Court, thus making him a legal resident. Gaines was not given an opportunity to testify or to have his lawyer defend him before the committee. Without access to the full report of the committee, one can only speculate that Gaines's lack of an appearance at this hearing had something to do with the fact that the chairman of this committee was J. E. Dillard, who adamantly detested Gaines's political philosophy.[18]

To be sure, the backgrounds of these black officials had not prepared them for the political battles that lay ahead. But like their predecessors, they soon realized that they would have to invent ways and means of coping, dealing with obstacles and handicaps, and of trying to introduce and push measures that were in the interest of blacks. Likewise, they knew that they would have to support Governor Davis, who himself was baffled over the actions of the Democrats. Thus, when the Thirteenth Legislature convened, Davis, recognizing the opposition to his program, began to speak in favor of reconciliation and compromise. Accordingly, he agreed to make the following concessions: (1) to allow each county to elect its own school board of directors; (2) to maintain, but change portions of the militia and state police acts; and (3) to distribute taxes more equally. Despite these conciliatory gestures, the

Democrats still did not buy Davis's program and began almost immediately to dismantle it. Their first efforts were directed toward free public schools, a very combustible issue and one which affected blacks dearly. Hence, the Democrats passed a new school law which abolished the centralized system and returned the powers to local communities. No sooner had this bill passed than Shack Roberts introduced an act "amendatory to an act approved November 29, 1871, to organize and maintain a system of public free schools in the state of Texas." [19] Needless to say, Roberts's bill died in committee. Disheartened but not undaunted over what was happening to public schools, Ruby championed the cause for education in the Senate, but in a different light. He proposed, but lost, a resolution "that the board of any school district may at their option make arrangement with any established school library to open its collection of books, educational apparatus, scientific and art collections, free of charge to teachers and scholars." [20] According to Ruby, payment for this service would come from individual districts, and the sum would not exceed five percent of the tax collected. Despite his failure in the above endeavor, Ruby did not give up the struggle for education. He next introduced an act favoring teachers. Realizing the need for good teachers in the state, the Senator from Galveston presented a bill to "ascertain the amount of money due teachers of public free schools prior to March 1, 1873, and to provide for the payment of the same." [21] This bill was referred to committee, but was never reported back. Despite these and similar setbacks, black legislators' concerns for education remained unshaken. This point became evident as Richard Williams introduced a bill to establish a normal school at Harmony in Walker County, despite the odds against its passage.[22]

It is interesting to note that while Democrats made substantial cuts in the educational budget, they incorporated sixteen railroads and gave away sixteen sections of public land to the respective railroad companies. The only thing the blacks could do to stem the tide of granting these subsidies was to vote against the bills, which they did, but to no avail. Their unanimous vote was predicated on three of several reasons: (1) Governor Davis had urged blacks not to support railroad interests; (2) blacks believed that it was unconstitutional to grant railroads public land in the manner that the Democrats were doing; and (3) blacks were forced to sit in separate coaches on railroad cars, even though they paid first-class fares.

Because of a federal law of 1872 which made no distinction in race, color, or creed in public facilities, blacks repeatedly defied the segregation policy of the railroads. So, in an effort to get back at railroads and in accordance with blacks' grievances, Henry Phelps and Matt Gaines introduced bills in both houses of the legislature to prohibit railway companies from making a distinction in the accomodations of first class passengers.[23] As was the case so many times before — same song, same verse — these bills died in committee.

Not only did the Thirteenth Legislature aid and abet the illegal practices of the railroads, but it turned a deaf ear to social reform. This meant that any social reform affecting blacks would have to come from black initiative. Thus, early in the session, blacks pushed for prison reform. It was not unusual, then, that Richard Willams, coming from Walker County where the state penitentiary was located, would champion this cause. The first session was barely underway when Williams introduced a resolution asking the legislature to aid the town of Huntsville in restoring jobs to its citizens which had been taken by prisoners. He also complemented this resolution by reading petitions and memorials from the citizens of Walker County. One petition asked for "relief against convicts" in and around Huntsville. Another memorial was more precise in its demand. It asked for the passage of a law authorizing certain apartments in the penitentiary at Huntsville to be used as a common jail. With such evidence in hand, when William introduced a bill to authorize the County of Walker to levy a special tax to repair the jail and the courthouse, the bill passed without any difficulty.[24] Likewise, in the Senate, Gaines took up the cause to establish a jail in Walker County. His bill urged inspection and a report not only on the conditions of the jail, but also on the condition of the prisoners.[25] The bill also passed and became law June 27, 1873.

Gaines's concern for social reform did not stop with prison reform. Working very closely with his rural constitutents, Gaines introduced an amendment designed to aid and protect the masses of black tenant farmers. His amendment to the Landlord and Tenant Act provided that:

> Any person or persons [˙who˙] shall rent or lease land to any persons of the state and either fail or refuse to furnish supplies as provided for in the written contract or lease made and entered into between the tenant and landlord or persons owning the said land shall be responsible to the said tenant for all damages that he may sustain and tenant shall have a lien on the crops so rented for damage adjudged against landlord and landowners.[26]

To the surprise of no one, this amendment lost by a wide margin. Why more blacks in the House did not attempt to sponsor similar legislation on labor is not at all clear, since all of them represented rural constituents. Perhaps some of them felt it best to expend their energies on legislation for incorporation where they were surer of success. For example, Allen Wilder and Matt Gaines were responsible for the incorporation of the town of Giddings. Henry Moore called up Senate Bill Number 97, which passed on the third reading, and provided for the incorporation of the Hallsville Masonic Institute of Harrison County; Richard Williams led the fight for the incorporation of Texas Wells and Irrigation Company.[27] In a word, it can be argued that outside of incorporation, blacks had very little success with the passage of bills that they introduced in the Thirteenth Legislature.

However much the black and white Republicans tried to hold on to the Edmund J. Davis regime, the Thirteenth Legislature set the tone for the final unfolding of the radical *denouement* on March 31, 1873, when it approved an act to set the first Tuesday in December of that same year for a statewide general election. Senator Ruby protested, and all blacks voted against the measure, but to no avail. When that election occurred, it showed a rise in Democratic strength and a simultaneous decline in the numerical strength of blacks. Moreover, ex-Confederate Richard Coke was victorious in his bid for the governorship. Because Democrats believed that Davis was going to use the constitutional issue to remain in power until April 28, 1874, their party leaders decided to assemble the Fourteenth Legislature in January 1874, and to inaugurate Richard Coke immediately. Davis, being placed on the defensive, decided to challenge the Democrats by seeking federal intervention from Washington; but when President Grant turned a deaf ear to his request, Davis capitulated and resigned on January 19, 1874.

The Fourteenth Legislature then proceeded with the regular business. After they had taken care of the routine of electing officers, Governor Coke set the tone and theme of the legislature, warning and advising the General Assembly that the end of an era was over, that "radicalism" was no longer the order of the day. In a manuever designed both to appease and to demonstrate to whites that a "new day" had dawned, Coke urged the legislature to get rid of the "worst features of the old constitution by amendments" and if this would not work, to rewrite the constitution. Coke went on to explain that the social and labor systems, and, to some degree, the political system of Texas had changed fundamentally in the last ten years. As he put it; "We have 40,000 unenlightened black voters . . . in some portions of Texas outnumbering whites and having equal privileges with them at the ballot and jury boxes." [28]

In order to alter or change the labor system that Governor Coke spoke of, the legislature first took up the argument on the Landlord and Tenant Act that they had left unfinished in the last legislature. When discussion on this subject came up, David Abner countered this measure by introducing an act to prohibit the hiring of minors without the consent of parents or guardians.[29] This bill quickly died in committee and the legislature went on to pass what became known as the Landlord and Tenant Law of 1874 — a law designed to protect both parties. The landlord was given a first lien as was the tenant. The landlord had a lien on the crop which prohibited the tenant from leaving the land before paying the landlord for everything for which he [the tenant] had been furnished during the year. Similarly, the tenant had a lien upon property and rent due if the landlord failed his part of the contract.[30] But even a cursory examination of this law will reveal that it was weighted heavily in favor of the landlord. In effect, the law gave more protection for the white landowners. Shack Roberts was vehemently opposed to this act and did not make any bones about stating his position on the floor of the House. Speaking as an experienced tenant, Roberts said that this bill "is oppressive on the downtrodden race; whatever honorable gentlemen might say . . . the landlords have the land, the corn and the house and could make any contract with the workman he liked. If the [black] man failed to make a crop, he must have no food provided or left for his subsistence [and if this bill passed, the same spirit would rise up again]"[31] The history of the tenant system in Texas has shown that Roberts was correct in his assessment.

After having made some gestures, (though not always successful) toward changing the labor system, the Democrats decided that they would heed the advice of Governor Coke to change the political and social system. In order to undertake this task, they would first have to redraw the county boundaries. Hence, redistricting became a *cause célèbre* in the Fourteenth Legislature. As blacks saw their voting strength being diminished by boundary changes, they did not sit idly by. Thus, Edward Brown and David Abner voiced opposition to and voted against a bill to make a new county out of Panola, thereby, diminishing black strength in the Fifth District.[32] Similarly, when an amendment came up to consolidate the Fifteenth and Eighteenth Districts, Blacks violently objected. This amendment originated from a resolution introduced into the House on January 15, 1875, by Charles A. Culberson which called for a constitutional convention. The resolution also called for the election of three delegates from each of the thirty senatorial districts. Tillman Smith of Grimes County amended the resolution so as to combine the Fifteenth and Eighteenth Districts into a large one with a total of six delegates. The purpose of this amendment was to ensure the election of a majority of Democratic delegates. Smith's rationale for the amendment was that the Republican majority in the Fifteenth District was over 300, while in the Eighteenth District the Democrats had a majority of 1306. In Smith's opinion, the Fifteenth District needed consolidation to protect it from black rule. He argued that the white people of that district would be denied representation in the upcoming convention unless consolidation took place. Then, in a manner designed to appease the black representatives, particularly those of populous Harrison County, Smith ended his speech on the amendment by saying that Harrison was represented by conscientious blacks. In a remarkably frank exposition, David Abner countered Smith's argument by saying that he didn't care about the amendment and that Smith's complimentary remarks of him would not make him untrue to the interests that he represented. Abner went on to add that Smith spoke from both personal and collective ignorance of whites; that the "Democratic party wanted too much and may kill itself in the effort." Abner's worst fear was that if the Democrats were given their way, they would make, as had been the case in 1866, "another constitution that will require overturning." [33] Abner's colleague from Harrison, Shack Roberts, came to his aid by voicing objection to the amendment. Roberts asked Smith why he had run for Representative of the Fifteenth District if district had been controlled and left to the influence of black Republicans. Roberts made it emphatically clear that he was not only going to oppose the amendment, but that he was going to vote against a constitutional convention.[34]

The House at first refused to allow the amendment, but three weeks later, it returned to the Culberson Resolution and voted 30 to 12 to approve a constitutional convention. The twelve dissenting votes came from all Republicans (including the six blacks). In the Senate, Burton opposed the majority plan for a convention but refrained from voting. After this vote was taken, the legislature adjourned *sine die* so as to allow for time for campaigning and for the election of delegates to the constitutional convention.

The election of delegates to the Constitutional Convention was held May 1875, at which time six blacks were elected. They were M. H. Goddin, Bird Davis, William Reynolds, Lloyd Henry McCabe, David Abner, and John Mitchell. One can argue, and rightly so, that M. H. Goddin had been the forgotten member of this black cast. The reason is that major studies such as Brewer's *Negro Legislators of Texas*, listed Asa Holt as one of the six black delegates rather than Goddin. In reality, Holt was a former white Confederate. On the other hand, extinct records prevent one from knowing anything about M. H. Goddin who was elected from the Fifteenth District, except for the fact that he submitted his resignation one day after the convention convened. Almost equally extinct is the record on Bird Davis. Davis was born a slave in North Carolina. Exactly when he came to the Lone Star State is not Known, but he was thirty-three when he represented Wharton County in the constitutional convention.[35]

More relevant data can be found on William Reynolds and L. H. McCabe, who, unlike their colleagues John Mitchell and David Abner, had not served in previous legislatures or conventions. William Reynolds was a freeborn fair-skinned Negro from Baltimore, Maryland. After receiving both public school and college training in Maryland, Reynolds moved to Texas. He taught school at Hempstead for a number of years before becoming involved in politics. His first appearance in politics came when he was elected as a delegate to the Republican National Convention from Liberty, Texas, in 1872. In 1873, he represented Waller County, and also served as secretary to the Republican County Convention held at Richmond, Texas, in Fort Bend County. In 1875, he became Waller's representative to the Constitutional Convention.[36]

The other black at the convention was Lloyd Henry McCabe. Although J. M. Brewer, as well as the *Convention Journal,* listed this individual as Mac McCabe, further research has proven that he was indeed Lloyd Henry McCabe. Contemporary newspapers, as well as a document signed by him at the convention substantiate this fact. Born to free parents in Troy, New York on December 21, 1847, McCabe was a basketmaker by trade. He received a solid education in the schools of Troy before coming to Texas after the Civil War. His first job in the state was not in the public schools, but rather in the Customs House at Galveston. Upon leaving this position, he taught school somewhere along on the Brazos River and later entered politics. He made his first successful bid for public office when he was elected to represent Fort Bend County at the constitutional convention. After the convention, McCabe served as District Clerk of Fort Bend County from 1876 to 1880. The individuals who examined the minutes written by McCabe were usually impressed that they were so well written. McCabe resided in Fort Bend County for sixty years until his death on March 24, 1930.[37]

When the Constitutional Convention convened September 6, 1875, the stage was set for an uphill battle for blacks, as they would have to struggle with Democrats who stood for white supremacy, states' rights and decentralized government. Cast into such an atmosphere, William Reynolds, the most active of the first black delegates, proposed that the following be added as a new section of the constitution: "that no form of slavery shall ever exist in this state and involuntary servitude of any character whatever is hereby forbidden except as punishment for crime when the party shall have been duly convicted."[38] Reynolds was told by his colleagues that his motion was unnecessary and, consequently, it was tabled by a vote of 35 to 32. Continuing in his drive to secure rights for blacks, Reynolds voiced opposition to land and property qualifications for voting. To be sure, no greater threats to the future of blacks arose in the convention than did acts against their suffrage. In order to counteract the abridgment of black suffrage rights,

Reynolds offered the following resolution: "that all elections in the state shall be free and open and no power, civil or military, shall at anytime interfere to prevent the free exercise of the right of suffrage." [39] This resolution was referred to the Bill of Rights Committee, but it met an untimely death there. Immediately following this resolution's defeat, a majority report was introduced, proposing the payment of a poll tax as a prerequisite for voting. This bill, however, was defeated when black delegates joined forces with Republicans and Granger Democrats to bring about its demise. Prior to the defeat of this poll tax bill, Democrats had tried to induce the Republicans into voting for it by proposing generous provisions for education. While this issue was under discussion, Reynolds seized this opportunity to try to get the convention to reserve one-sixth of 180 acres of Texas public land for an Agricultural and Mechanical College for black youths of Texas.[40] Needless to say, Reynolds's efforts were exerted in a losing cause.

Another controversial issue which affected blacks at this convention was gerrymandering of the judicial, congressional, representative, and senatorial districts. As one contemporary editor put it, one of the main purposes of this reapportionment was to disfranchise blacks "by indirection." [41] This being the case, one would think that all black delegates would have been standing or sitting with both hands raised in the General Assembly, but this did not happen. There is no record that indicates any activities on this issue on the part of blacks. Moreover, after this convention was drafted, black delegates failed to voice their opposition to this new anti-black document. If they did, their objections were not printed in the newspapers or journals. In response to the charge (leveled by the press), that blacks of the convention were controlled by white Republican Robert Mills, delegates McCabe, Reynolds and Abner issued a written statement indicating that "such assertions were untrue, unjust and unfair." [42] But while one can argue that blacks were not puppets of Mills, one can only speculate about their actions and/or inactions as they relate to the drafting of this constitution.

That black delegates were not more assertive in this convention might have had something to do with their inexperience, the atmosphere of hostility into which they were cast, and the defeatist attitude that they adopted once they realized they could not win. Yet, despite what might appear to some as a dereliction of duty, black delegates did vote on crucial issues. And these issues helped blacks escape, at least for the time being, disfranchisement by constitutional means; to retain provisions already made for public education; and, despite gerrymandering, to maintain control over some Black Belt counties. On the other hand, the actions taken by whites in this convention served as both a lesson for future black politicians, as well as an indication of things to come. In short, blacks could now expect future legislatures to be controlled by Democrats who were anti-black; blacks could not depend on the organic laws of Texas to protect their interests; and blacks would have fewer and fewer white allies. Indeed, then, blacks were at the crossroads.

[4]

The Post-Reconstruction Legislatures

Although some parts of Texas were redeemed by force as early as 1867, others by the elections of 1872 and 1873, and still others with the drafting of the Constitution of 1875, this was not the case in the Black Belt counties. By virtue of their numerical strength, blacks exercised political control and were consistently elected to the state legislature from 1876 to 1896. Contrary to published reports that the Twentieth Legislature was all-white, two blacks sat in that august body. Altogether, two senators and seventeen representatives sat at various times in the legislature during post-Reconstruction. With the exception of the Sixteenth Legislature, which had ten black members, all successive legislatures showed a decline in black members; numbers varied from five to one. Small in numbers, black lawmakers could not be considered as constituting a bloc vote of any significance. Still, they were a force to be reckoned with; a force which helped to safeguard the rights of blacks where possible, to support the welfare of the state where necessary, and to move the state along an equalitarian course when the opportunity presented itself. It is well to remember that these black legislators would make this uphill battle under tremendous odds, and in hostile Democratically controlled legislatures, at a time during which Texas politics was undergoing a transition. The backgrounds of these

54 THROUGH MANY DANGERS, TOILS, AND SNARES

Composite Picture of Black Legislators. 1870–1898
— Courtesy of Representative Paul Ragsdale's office.

men, which did not appear to be significantly different from blacks of previous legislatures, did not prepare them to deal with Democrats any better than their backgrounds had prepared them to deal with Republicans. Understandably, these men were reputable members of their local communities, but this status did not derive from the fact that they came from the upper class.

The Fifteenth Legislature consisted of three black representatives and two black senators. Five blacks were elected to the House, but two of them Allen Wilder and Patrick Francis, did not serve because they were involved in contested elections. Wilder actually took the oath, but was unseated when it was alleged that fourteen votes were cast for him illegally.[1] As for Patrick Francis, the Secretary of State did not even acknowledge his claim to election. Of the blacks who actually sat in the General Assembly, two had served in previous legislatures, Shack Roberts and Senator Walter Burton. The other three included two native Texans, Henry Sneed and William H. Hollard, and one native Alabamian, Walter Ripetoe. Of Sneed, very little is known except that he was a farmer by trade and was twenty-seven years of age when he was elected to represent Waller County in the Legislature.[2]

Like Sneed, William H. Holland was born a slave in Marshall, Texas, in 1849. Holland was the son of a white planter and a slave mother. Though the claim has yet to be authenticated, Holland probably was the son of Captain Boyd Holland or J. K. Holland. While still very young, Holland, along with his two brothers, was purchased by Captain Boyd Holland, the man who was responsible for the education that they received at Oberlin College. Upon returning to Texas from college, Holland taught school in several counties and also in the city of Austin. One of his first jobs in the capitol city was as principal of a high school in the Doublehorn community. While in Austin, Holland was a member and Superintendent of the Sunday School of the African Methodist Episcopal Church, where Reverend C. W. Abington was the minister and where B. F. Williams had once served as pastor.[3]

Exactly when Holland became involved in politics is uncertain, but his first recorded appearance came in 1875. In that year, when the Democrats made a bid for black votes by inviting them to a nonpolitical barbecue meeting, Holland took issue with them and charged them with capitalizing on the political ignorance of blacks. It is not known when Holland moved to Waller County, but he was appointed to a position in the post office of that county in 1876. He served in that capacity only a few months before he declared his candidacy for a seat in the House and was successful in this venture. Even though Holland did not return to the legislature in 1878, his interest in politics remained high. According to local newspaper accounts, Holland entertained the idea of running for mayor of Austin in 1880, but changed his mind after holding several rallies in various black churches of the city.[4]

In addition to politics, Holland was also interested and actively involved in the economic, social and educational welfare of blacks. He was at the forefront of the movement to establish the Agriculture and Mechanical College for black youths at Prairie View. In addition, Holland was selected as the first Superintendent of a Deaf, Dumb, and Blind Institute for Colored Youths, a position which he held for ten consecutive years. After vacating this office for an eight year period, Holland was reappointed to the same post for three more years. When making his initial application for the above position, Holland wrote Governor James Stephen Hogg, stating that he was well-known among the best citizens of Austin.[5] One of those individuals whose name he used as references was J. K. Holland. This fact leads one to believe that Holland's father or first master might have been J. K. Holland. The notes of J. K. Holland, found at the Texas Historical Association, raises further speculation on this subject. In these notes, the latter Holland contended: "On adoption of the constitution . . . my old body servant decided to run for a place in the legislature . . . as a member of the House. He served his race as well as he knew how . . . I now have in my possession a bill-of-sale executed in the days of slavery for this member of the Texas Legislature."[6] Whether or not the individual referred to was W. H. Holland is secondary to the fact that Holland's slave birth did not prevent him from making a contribution to his race, as well as to the state of Texas. In like manner, his previous condition of servitude did not prevent him from developing a good relation with members of both races. Thus in 1898, when Holland returned to the Capitol after being away for a few years, Representative J. D. Child of Tarrant County presented a resolution to the House, asking that a welcome be extended to him.[7] After being accorded such an honor, Holland left the city and moved to Mineral Wells, and subsequently died there in 1907.

The other black serving for the first time in the state legislature was Walter Ripetoe (sometimes Riptoe). Ripetoe was born in Montgomery, Alabama, March 30, 1838. He came to Texas in January 1850, and lived in Rusk County until the end of the Civil War. Afterwards, he moved to Harrison County and on October 1, 1871 he began teaching school. At the time that he was elected to the Senate, he had spent nineteen years in the state and had lived eighteen months in Precinct Five of the City of Marshall, Harrison County. Interestingly enough, Ripetoe was elected to the Senate on February 15, 1876, by a majority of 2,600 votes, at a time during which plans were being made to establish a white man's party in Marshall.[8]

The Sixteenth Legislature was very reminiscent of the Twelfth

Legislature in terms of numbers. Eight blacks were elected to the House, while the two senators returned by virtue of the fact that their terms had not expired. Of the eight representatives, three — B. F. Williams, Thomas Beck, and Jacob Freeman[9] — had served in previous legislatures. The others deserving attention at this point are R. J. Evans, Harriel G. Geiger, B. A. Guy, Elias Mayes, and Andrew Sledge. R. J. Evans was born a slave in Louisiana in 1853, and was brought to Texas in 1857. In the absence of evidence, one cannot state with certainty, how or where Evans received his education, but the record does indicate that he became a teacher prior to his involvement in politics. His first entrance on the political scene came during Reconstruction when Evans was elected alderman of the City of Navasota. A very ambitious young man at the age of twenty-five, Evans left the latter post to seek election to the House of Representatives from Grimes County. In 1881, he made another successful bid for the House and was reelected to represent the said county. Contrary to J. Mason Brewer's assertion that Evans's absenteeism in the Seventeenth Legislature was due to a feeling of inferiority and inability to discharge his duty, Evans proved to be one of the most vigilant guardians of the rights of blacks to serve in the Texas Legislature. He never failed to represent the interests of blacks, either through sponsoring an outright bill or proposing an amendment or a rider to an amendment. Falling out of favor with the Regular Republicans in 1884, Evans was chosen by the Straight-Out Republicans to run as their nominee for Commissioner of the General Land Office. Losing the election, Evans said farewell to public office, but remained very active in Republican politics until his death.[10]

Harriel G. Geiger was a one-eyed fair complexioned black man from South Carolina. He was a blacksmith and was forty years of age when he represented Robertson County in the Sixteenth Legislature. Taking advantage of the split in white votes, in 1878 Geiger won the above post by running on the Greenback ticket. Geiger was somewhat of an opportunist, who, while registered as a Republican, was by no means a "diehard" Republican. He sought out every opportunity possible to win elections. Therefore, he was sometimes a Republican, sometimes a Greenbacker, sometimes to the right and sometimes to the left. For example, he was the only black who voted to sustain the veto of Governor Oran M. Roberts on an appropriations bill which included six hundred dollars in back pay for black Senator Burton, who had been involved in a contested election in 1874.[11]

To be sure, though, many whites were offended by some of the postures that he took on racial issues. For example, when Geiger asked for a few days leave of absence from the Sixteenth Legislature, one of his white colleagues said he voted against Geiger's request because Geiger was opposed to whites from Robertson County, running for office. While this assertion might have been true, what really happened was that Robertson County had an eighty percent black population which made whites' chances of winning office very slim. In another incident, whites accused Geiger of inciting a race riot when a black man was shot in the courtroom in Hearne, of Robertson County. While Geiger had not actually incited the riot, he did give moral support to blacks who had protested the shooting. That Geiger was popular, and that he represented a fairly large district in the Calvert–Hearne area made him a force to be reckoned with, by both the whites and blacks of Robertson County.[12]

In 1880, Geiger sought reelection to the House, but he lost to E. C. Mobley by 624 votes. After this election, Geiger was tried and convicted for accepting a bribe, but he never served a jail term. Meanwhile, after serving in the first session of the Seventeenth Legislature, Mobley left Robertson County. An election was then held to fill his seat in the House, and Geiger was selected as Mobley's replacement. In 1882, Geiger sought reelection but was defeated by a white, P. F. Pier. Later, Geiger decided to run for local office. He ran successfully, in 1884, for Sheriff of Robertson County against T. B. Jones. However, he lost in his second bid for the same office in 1888.[13]

It should be noted at this point that while Geiger served in the legislature, he secured a license to practice law. So, after he left politics in the late 1880s, he devoted all of his time to challenging the system by practicing law. In 1900, Geiger, who had had many arguments with whites in Robertson County, went before Judge O. D. Cannon, a staunch racist Democrat, to defend a former slave. While the trial was going on, Geiger is reported to have made some insolent remarks, whereupon Judge Cannon shot him five times in the chest. Geiger died instantly.[14]

Other blacks of the Sixteenth Legislature were Elias Mayes, Andrew Sledge, and B. A. Guy. Mayes was born in Concehuce, Alabama, February 18, 1831. He had come to Texas in 1863, and settled in Montgomery County, but in 1866 he moved to Grimes County where he obtained an education. A farmer, a Methodist minister and a student of law, Mayes moved again in 1877 — this time to Brazos County. There, he ran and successfully won a seat to represent Brazos County in the Sixteenth and Twenty-first Legislatures.[15] Andrew Sledge, like his colleague Mayes, was also a minister. He was born a slave in Chapel Hill, Washington County, Texas, on August 15, 1854. As a Baptist Minister, Sledge served as pastor at Caldwell, for eighteen years; at Temple, for two years, and in his hometown of Chapel Hill for twenty-five years. He also served for a number of years as President of the State

Baptist Convention and was frequently a delegate to the National Baptist Convention.[16] Thus, when he ran for office, he had a ready-made constituency. But while one might assume that he was active in politics prior to his election to the legislature, the record does not indicate such. In contrast to Sledge, very little is known of B. A. Guy, except for the fact that he was born a slave in Virginia. He was a farmer and thirty-seven years of age when he was chosen to represent Washington County in the legislature.[17]

The Seventeenth Legislature saw a decline in the numerical strength of blacks. There was one black senator and there were four representatives. The four black members of the House were Thomas Beck, R. J. Evans, Robert A. Kerr, and Doc Lewis. Blacks who were not incumbents in this legislature were Doc Lewis and Robert Kerr. Information on Doc Lewis, being very limited in scope, reveals that he was a farmer from Wharton County and was thirty-seven years of age when he was elected to the House.[18]

Bastrop County sent Robert A. Kerr to the legislature in 1881. Kerr was born on December 23, 1833, in New Orleans, Louisiana, to a black mother and white father, Major A. Kerr. In 1855, Kerr was brought to Port Lavaca, Texas, by his white father. Before the Civil War, he moved to San Antonio where he earned his living as a professional barber. But Kerr's tenure in the Alamo city was not very long; he was soon accused of writing passes for slaves to escape into Mexico, and, as a result, had to leave the city. During the Civil War, he returned to Port Lavaca and worked as a shipping clerk for his father. Shortly thereafter, he moved to Victoria, where his father's sister was responsible for the education that he received.[19] During Reconstruction, he was appointed as election judge for the counties of San Patricia, Refugio, Calhoun, and Victoria. From his initial entry into politics, Kerr was active in Republican circles. In 1872, he was selected as a delegate to the Republican National Convention, and in 1881, he won a seat in the House of Representatives. After leaving the legislature, he was elected again as a delegate to the Republican National Convention in 1892.[20]

Kerr was more than a politician; he was also a community leader. He was largely responsible, along with other blacks, for establishing Bastrop's first black high school. Credit is given to him because it was Kerr who used his influence to get concessions from whites in order to bring this idea to fruition. When he was asked by whites of Bastrop to help them pass a bond issue, Kerr told them he would do so, if they would build a five thousand dollar high school for colored youths. They agreed, and Kerr reciprocated by helping them get a twenty thousand dollar bond issue passed. Not only was the black high school built, but *more* than five thousand dollars was spent. As a result of his action, Kerr was elected as one of the six members of the school board of Bastrop County; there were four whites, and two blacks.[21]

By the time the election for representatives for the Eighteenth Legislature was held, the White Man's Party in the Black Belt counties had taken its toll on black voters. The White Man's Party (as will be discussed later) had as its primary objective the elimination of blacks from the franchise and stipulated that only whites could vote in the Democratic primary. The result of which was that by 1881 only two blacks would sit in the House and none in the Senate. The two blacks, R. J. Moore and George W. Wyatt, had many things in common. They were both natives of Texas, both were teachers and both were elected to state office for the first time. Moore represented Washington County, while Wyatt represented Waller and Fort Bend counties. R. J. Moore, a mulatto, was born in Navasota, Texas. He received his education at the Hearne Academy and taught school for a number of years at the Old Washington-on-the-Brazos. There, he was also a postmaster and a county commissioner before being elected for three consecutive terms to the legislature from Washington County.[22] On the other hand, George Wyatt was born in Waller County, Texas; where he received his education is not known, but he was listed as a teacher of thirty-five years when he was elected to represent the Fifty-third District.[23]

The Nineteenth Legislature saw an increase of one additional black member producing a total of three. Since B. F. Williams and R. J. Moore had served in previous legislatures, the only black political novice in the House was James H. Stewart. Born a slave in Caddo Parish, Louisiana, in September 1857, Stewart came to Milam County, Texas, in 1868. After attending elementary and secondary schools in the state, Stewart entered Prairie View A&M College, where he received a bachelor's degree. He later earned a Doctor of Divinity degree at Yale University. Before becoming involved in politics, Stewart taught school in several cities of the state, namely, Houston, Dallas, and Hempstead. He also served as principal of the Brenham Negro School for nine years. During Reconstruction, he attended various Republican functions in Hempstead and Houston. In 1885, he moved to Robertson County where he was elected to represent that county in the House. Upon leaving the legislature in 1887, he decided to return to his first love, education. From 1912 to 1914 he served as Superintendent of the Deaf, Dumb, and Blind Institute for Colored Youths. Also, on two occasions, Stewart was secretary of the Baptist Sunday School Association. Moreover, he played a leading role in the establishment of the Black Fraternal Order of the National Woodmen of Texas, and served as sovereign commander of that organization until his death in 1924.[24]

The Twentieth Legislature, formerly known as the "lily-white legislature," had two blacks, R. J. Moore and H. A. P. Bassett. Moore was an incumbent, while Bassett was a novice. Bassett was sworn into office fifteen days after the General Assembly convened because he was involved in a contested election. Upon being accepted, Bassett took the occasion to thank Democrats for their decision. He praised the Governor for placing men on the committee "who will do justice to a man regardless of politics, race, color or previous condition of servitude." Lack of data prevents one from knowing anything about Bassett until his first recorded appearance in politics, which came at a Republican meeting held in Navasota on August 6, 1882. At that time, Bassett was appointed secretary of the local Republican organization. After Bassett left the legislature in 1888, he remained active in politics and became a delegate to the Republican state convention as late as 1892.[25]

Elias Mayes, a former legislator, and Alexander Asberry, a newcomer, represented black interests in the Twenty-first Legislature. Alexander Asberry was born on November 1, 1861, at Wilberville, Fall County, Texas. After attending elementary and secondary schools, he furthered his education at Hearne Academy. A businessman, a landowner and a devout church man, Asberry ran for the legislature in 1884, but was defeated.[26] He met with success when he ran again in 1888. In the year that Asberry was chosen to represent Robertson County in the House, he was also elected as a delegate to the 1888 National Republican National Convention. Even though Asberry did not win a bid for reelection in 1890, he continued to take an active part in Republican politics. Thus, in 1896 he became a candidate for the House again. He lost by twenty-four votes in a contested election and decided to seek redress for his defeat through the District Court office. When he took his complaint to Judge O. D. Cannon, who was serving as District Judge, Cannon shot him in the arm. This incident, however, did not prevent Asberry from taking his case to the legislative Committee on Privilege and Elections. When Asberry's case reached the said committee, it ruled against him on the grounds that he had not followed the right procedure in filing his case. In other words, the Majority Report stated that: (1) Asberry's statement of contest was not filed with the District Court office, and (2) the statement of contest, as well as a certified copy of the record of each precinct, was not received by the Speaker of the House. But it was impossible for such documents to be sent to their respective places because Judge Cannon steadfastly refused to release them. Despite this setback, Asberry continued to remain active in Republican politics until his death.[27]

The lone black in the Twenty-first Legislature was Edward A. Patton. Patton was born in San Jacinto County, Texas. Where he received his education is unknown, but when he represented Polk and San

Jacinto counties in 1891, his profession was listed as a teacher and farmer; he was then thirty-two years of age.[28] Prior to becoming a representative, Patton had run unsuccessfully for the House in 1878. There are conflicting reports as to what happened to Patton after he left the legislature. According to oral sources, Patton was shot by the Sheriff of San Jacinto County when he decided to run for office again. Conversely, according to an article written by Monroe Work, Edward Patton was living in Washington, D.C., and was working in government services as late as 1920.[29]

Nathan Haller of the Fortieth District, which consisted of Brazoria and Matagorda counties, became the only black to serve in the Twenty-third Legislature. Haller, a blacksmith, was born a slave in Charleston, South Carolina. Before the Civil War was over, his master took him to Walker County, Texas. After living in Walker county for a number of years, Haller moved his family to Brazoria County, where he became active in politics. His preoccupation with Republican politics dates back to the Davis regime. As a matter of fact, he wrote Davis concerning several appointments. Yet, despite his active involvement in politics, he did not win a seat in the legislature until 1892. He ran for reelection again in 1894 and won, but only as a result of a contested election. Retiring from politics in 1895, Haller moved to Houston and died there some years later.[30]

Serving with Nathan Haller in the Twenty-fourth Legislature was Robert Lloyd Smith. Like his colleague Haller, Smith, too, was born in Charleston, South Carolina. Unlike Haller, however, he was born in 1861, to free black parents, one of whom was a schoolteacher. Smith attended the public elementary schools in Charleston; then, he matriculated for his high school diploma at Avery Institute for four years. In 1875, he entered the University of South Carolina and remained there until 1877. Leaving the University of South Carolina when it shut its doors to black students, Smith entered Atlanta University, where he graduated in 1880 with a bachelor of Science degree in English and Mathematics. After teaching for five years in the Georgia and South Carolina public schools, Smith moved to Oakland, Colorado County, Texas, where he became principal of the Oakland Normal School. Later, he became a member of the County Board of School Examiners. In order to help blacks economically, Smith founded the Oakland Village Improvement Society and the Farmer's Improvement Society. In 1895, Smith became involved in politics and ran successfully for the legislature in predominantly white Colorado County. He was reelected in the same county in 1897, making him the only black to serve in the Twenty-fifth Legislature and the last black to sit in the Texas Legislature until Barbara Jordan was elected to the Senate in 1966.[31]

If the backgrounds of these legislators were no higher or lower than those of legislators in previous legislatures, the task which they faced was more formidable, the fight more tenacious and the problems more numerous. Throughout the period 1876–1900, the Democratic party, which controlled the legislature, maintained strong support from the evangelical majority by identifying itself with southern states rights and white supremacy traditions. Also, the Democrats passed laws which reduced blacks to the status of economic peonage, restricted their suffrage, legalized Jim Crow, and dragged their feet on education. If the black leadership read these events as ominous, then one would expect them to defend themselves, as well as their constituents, against such onslaught. It is not surprising, then, that during post-Reconstruction, black lawmakers would address themselves to such issues as school funds, higher education, the convict lease system, and civil and penal codes.

In the main, one could argue that in the postwar years, the state of Texas was undergoing tremendous changes, changes that were all-encompassing — the industrialization of the state, the commercialization of agriculture, the urbanization of rural areas and the advancement of education. The people of Texas approached these changes as opportunities or problems, depending upon their economic and cultural interests, the personalities of their leaders and the historical tradition from which they came. For example, the issue of the railroads, which would affect almost every facet of life in Texas, would be approached differently by whites than it would by blacks. A brief look at the railroad industry might shed some light on this subject.

When the Civil War ended, Texas had very few railroads, but as time progressed, the interest in railroads skyrocketed. In order to satisfy this demand, the Texas government liberally granted public land and bonds to investors in exchange for new rail lines. Because it was fairly easy to receive a grant of land or a bond, a large number of individuals entered the railroad industry. This massive influx into this industry resulted in widespread abuse — rebates, drawbacks, higher charges for short hauls than for long hauls, and discrimination in rates between places and persons. In order to curb such abuses, individuals as well as groups petitioned the legislature in the late 1870s and early 1880s for railroad regulations.

In 1876, the Fifteenth Legislature passed an act declaring common carriers subject to rate regulation. But without enforcement, such an article proved useless. Railroad regulation was taken up again in the Sixteenth and Seventeenth Legislatures. When the bill to that effect came up in the Seventeenth Legislature, it gave black representative R. J. Evans the opportunity that he had been looking for, that is, the chance

64   THROUGH MANY DANGERS, TOILS, AND SNARES

to attach an amendment to it concerning public accommodation. This amendment, which was designed to change the passenger tariff on railroads from five to three cents per mile, stated:

> That each railway company shall be required to class their coaches to be known as first and second class coaches and select tickets as such first and second class: the first class tickets to be sold at a rate of three cents per mile; provided any person desiring a first class ticket shall be entitled to the same by paying three cents per mile and entitled to passage in which will be known as first class coaches; and any person buying a second class ticket will be entitled to a passage in what will be known as the second class coach and any railroad company failing to comply with the provision of this act shall be liable to the person or persons so refused in the sum of not less than two thousand dollars ($2,000) nor more than five thousand dollars ($5,000).[32]

Energized because Evans's amendment was tabled, and equally encouraged by the provision of the Civil Rights Act of 1875, blacks in 1879 began to press even harder for equal accommodation. The wife of Senator Walter Burton, who in 1871 had defied a separate coach law, was thrown off a moving train when she refused to leave the white coach.[33] Moreover, blacks defied the plea made by Governor John Ireland to the Colored Men's Convention of 1883, not to discuss the railroad issue. Instead, the Convention denounced separate accommodation in no uncertain terms.[34] Unable to convince blacks not to press the issue, Ireland than went to the railroad companies and asked them to provide separate but equal coaches for black and white passengers. Some heeded his advice but others did not.

Ireland's action was but a prelude to a separate coach law. Five years later, in the Twenty-first Legislature, a bill was introduced in the Senate calling exactly for such provisions. To the surprise of no one, when this Senate Bill reached the House, it was met with strong opposition from the two black members, Elias Mayes and Alexander Asberry. It was their feeling that "the idea of separate facilities would not stop with railroads, but rather would spread to streetcars, omnibuses, sidewalks, and everywhere."[35] Asberry, who presented a petition from citizens of Dallas against this measure, opposed it on the grounds that it affected blacks directly and adversely, and argued that it lacked black input when it was drawn up.[36] Mayes felt that it was a dangerous bill "that conferred authority not yet existing."[37] Mayes and Asberry were right. The idea of "separate but equal" did not stop with railroads. Five years later, in 1895, Robert L. Smith found himself attacking a bill which called for separate waiting rooms.[38] Needless to say, the efforts of these lawmakers were nothing but an exercise in frustration. While one might have expected them to react in the way that they did, they were fighting a losing battle from the beginning. As recent research has revealed, segregation in Texas did not wait for the Supreme Court decision in *Plessy vs. Ferguson* before it began to solidify.[39] Rather, it began prior to, and during, Reconstruction.

Aside from problems of public accommodation, blacks had other problems with the railroad industry. Representatives R. J. Moore and George Wyatt, in 1885, supported a bill to end abuse evident in routes between long and short hauls, while Asberry took up the cause of the cattle industry against the railroad in 1889.[40] Since cattle ran wild over unfenced prairies and into streets of rural villages, they were likely to be struck by the trains. Asberry assumed the responsibility of preparing a law to make the railroad companies liable for damage in such instances.[41] This bill, which became law, also called for the court to award damages whenever a suit was brought against the railroad.

As far as railroad regulation *per se* was concerned, blacks were mixed in their reactions toward it. A bill for regulation was introduced in the House in 1879, but it died in committee. In 1881, another act for regulation was called up, but this bill did not even get as far as committee. Eight years later, a similar measure reappeared in the House. Alexander Asberry voted against the bill to establish a railroad commission, stating: "I am opposed to delegating to any one set of men the power to say what prices or incomes of any feature of business shall be. I think this bill kills a great enterprise instead of building it up." [42] As was the case before, the bill did not pass, but it came up again in the Twenty-second Legislature. Contrary to the action taken by most blacks, Ed Patton not only endorsed the bill, but offered an amendment to complement it: "That it shall be the duty of the commissioner to require railroad companies operating in the state to prepare and keep suitable stations at the nearest point of all state institutions provided they do not exceed three miles." [43] The bill died again in committee, but subsequently passed in the James Stephen Hogg administration in 1892.

Closely akin to railroads on the priority list of blacks was that of education. In the same manner that the state had used public unappropriated land to promote railroads since 1845, it would use public land to enhance education. In keeping with this the Constitution of 1876 reserved one-half of the state's unappropriated land for the benefit of public schools. That one-half of the state's land would actually be used for the stated purpose was a question that blacks would of necessity have to deal with in years to come. The issue of education, as it relates to land and taxes, began to surface in 1879, when fiscally conservative Governor Oran M. Roberts vetoed an appropriation bill which would have devoted the constitutional maximum of one-fourth of the state's *ad valorem* tax to maintain the public schools. In the special called session, the legislature cut appropriations to one-sixth of the *ad valorem,* despite opposition from Republicans, especially blacks. In order to provide additional funds for public schools, the legislature passed a bill to sell unappropriated public land at a minimum of fifty cents an acre (in unlimited amounts) and to sell land classified as farming in blocks up to 640 acres and grazing land up to 1,920 acres at one dollar an acre.

Blacks' response to the action of the legislature was immediate. In the Senate, Walter Burton offered an amendment to the previously mentioned act "that money arising from the sale of said land shall not be used for any other purpose than for the benefits of public free schools." [44] In addition to this amendment, Burton also introduced two resolutions on this subject. In the first one, he asked the Committee on Finance to report on House Bill Number Nine (#9), "an act making an appropriation for the support of free public schools for the scholastic year ending August 31, 1879." This resolution was adopted, but Burton was still not satisfied. Hence, he introduced a joint resolution to amend Section I of Article 7 of the Constitution so that it would read as follow:

> It shall be the duty of the Legislature of the State to make suitable provisions for the support and maintenance of free public schools for the gratuitous instruction of all inhabitants of the state . . . ages 6–18. Money should be equally distributed to all schools of the state and a poll tax of one dollar shall be collected to raise revenues.[45]

While Burton was defeated on the latter resolution, his fight to gain adequate support for public education would be taken up by some of his black colleagues in the House. In the debate on the House floor, Hal Geiger held that poor people would not pay taxes if one-fourth of the taxes were not given back to them. Benjamin Williams argued that it was the constitutional duty of the legislature to provide for one-fourth of the revenue to be used for free education and that poor people would no longer have faith in the legislature if this act was changed.[46]

As a result of this small appropriation, public school enrollment decreased and did not reach the level that it had been in 1879, until 1884. In the latter year, the legislature increased the school appropriation again to one-fourth of the *ad valorem* tax revenue. Black legislators, elated over this act, did not fail to take advantage of it. Hence, R. J. Moore introduced "an act to compel parents and guardians to send their children to school for four months." [47] No sooner had blacks rejoiced over the *ad valorem* tax than they were forced to deal with the new school law of 1884. This act did away with the yearly community school systems, which allowed the county judges to appoint three school trustees from the community each year.[48] By the same token, this bill established the district system, which called for an election of trustees who almost always were white. Thus, blacks' demands for control of their school were led by Robert L. Smith. In order to remedy this situation, in 1895, the freshman representative from Colorado County presented an act before the House "to provide for a more efficient system of public free schools of the state of Texas by providing for the election of colored trustees for colored schools [and] conferring upon such trustees the right to manage and control colored schools and for other purposes." [49] This bill became law on March 21, 1895.

Not content just to have access to elementary and secondary schools, blacks launched a campaign in 1876 to establish an agricultural and mechanical college for black Texans. Since 1866, Texas had been placed under the Morrill Act; the purpose of which was to establish an agricultural and mechanical college in the state. Because of the provisional status of the Texas government, formal acceptance of the grant was delayed until 1870, when Texas was readmitted to the Union. Once the grant was accepted, the state had five years in which to put the act into effect. So, in 1875, Texas Agricultural and Mechanical College was established. One year later, black representative William H. Holland questioned its legitimacy stating "the federal government had given aid to land-grant colleges without stating this money should benefit any one race and yet A.&M. College is for whites only." [50] Because Holland knew that protest without action was like criticism without correction, (ultimately useless and contemptible) at the earliest opportunity in February 1876, he introduced an act "to establish an agricultural and manual school for colored youths of the state." [51] While this bill was being scrutinized by the Committee on Education, Walter Burton took up the cause in the Senate and introduced the identical act.[52] In both houses, the bill followed the same route; that is, it was reported favorably out of committee, won approval and became law in April 1876. So, contrary to the assertion made by Lawrence Rice in *Negro of Texas* that Alta Vista Agricultural College (as Prairie View was first called) was established when white authorities came to the conclusion that the Morrill Act intended for provisions to be made for the agricultural and mechanical education of colored youths, this was not the case. Alta Vista was, in point of fact, established at the urging of black legislators. Holland monitored almost every aspect of this bill until it was finally engrossed. And at that time, he got a hundred copies of this document and distributed some to his friends and kept the others as souvenirs. His efforts to pass this bill won him the title "Father of Prairie View." [53]

On March 11, 1879, under a great deal of adverse circumstances,

Alta Vista College was opened to students. Only eight black males enrolled, making them the first blacks in the history of Texas to attend the state-supported college.[54] Because enrollment was down at the beginning of the 1879 Spring Semester, Governor Oran Roberts appeared before the legislature and advised the General Assembly to rent out the land for the remainder of the year. When this happened, Senator Burton rose to the occasion. Because he knew that many blacks who had grown up on the farm would not be interested in any kind of agriculture, scientific or otherwise, and because he knew that some blacks were opposed to an agricultural school inasmuch as they saw in it an effort to hinder their intellectual and social progress, Burton, on February 22, 1879, introduced an act "to establish a normal and manual school for colored youths." [55] This bill was reported favorably out of committee on March 12, 1879, and was passed on April 14, 1879. Thus, in the spring of 1879, Alta Vista was converted into a normal school for the training of black teachers. The legislature then appropriated $6,000 for the school's operation and, accordingly, the school was reestablished as Prairie View Normal School.

In 1881, the House adopted a concurrent resolution offered by R. J. Evans that a committee be appointed to ascertain and report on the damage to Prairie View that had resulted from a storm. When the House appeared to be moving too slowly on House Bill Number 6, "an act to make and pay for repair made by the storm," Evans moved to suspend the rules and to take the bill out of order. His amendment was passed and subsequently House Bill Number 6 passed also. But Evans didn't stop in his drive to improve Prairie View. When a resolution which called for an education committee to investigate the management, operations and condition of Texas A.&M. College was introduced, Evans attached an ammendment to it that the investigation should include the normal school for colored youths. Evans's amendment also called for two black representatives and one black senator to become members of this committee. It was his feeling that the normal school needed inspection, but "that colored members would be better fitted to make this [investigation] than those of a less pronounced complexion." After Representative John McComb of Montgomery accused Evans of being racist for offering such an amendment which "discriminates on account of race, color or previous condition of servitude", Evans withdrew the amendment; but he let his colleagues know that he deprecated such a charge.[56]

The existence of Prairie View was threatened in 1882, when the State Comptroller refused to issue warrants and to approve financial accounts for its support. Thus, the lack of appropriations prompted black representative, Thomas Beck in April 1882, to introduce a bill so that Prairie View would receive its necessary state funds:

> Section (1) That the Agricultural and Mechanical college for the benefits of colored youths of the state, established by an act of April 14, 1876, is an integral part of the A.&M. College of Texas established by an act approved in 1871 and now established at Bryan.
>
> Section (2) That the sum of $2000 be granted and the same is hereby set apart out of any fund in the treasury of the state not otherwise appropriated for the benefit of the said school and the same be drawn by the Board of Directors on vouchers audited by the Board or approved by the secretary and on filing such vouchers the comptroller shall draw his warrant on the treasurer for the same, from time to time as the same may be needed.
>
> Section (3) That the failure of the legislature to set the appropriation heretofore granted Prairie View has embarrassed and created an emergency that this act take affect after its passage and as it is so enacted.[57]

While this bill was being examined in the Education Committee, Governor Roberts moved to save the school from financial decay by accepting donations from businessmen. Meanwhile, everyone concerned with the fate of Prairie View, could breathe a sigh of relief on June 4, 1884, when the legislature passed the necessary appropriation to keep the school alive. In order to make sure that Prairie View would remain a viable institution, in 1891 Ed Patton, the lone black in the Twenty-first Legislature, took up the funding cause. In that year, he went before the legislature and asked for a two-year appropriation in the sum of $98,000, and he was successful in securing it. After this date, Prairie View, though economically deprived, was able to survive.[58]

At this point, it should be noted that while blacks were proud of Prairie View and worked hard to maintain it, they never considered it as the "branch university" referred to in the Constitution of 1876. The Constitution explicitly stated that "the Legislature shall also, when deemed practicable, establish and provide for the maintenance of a college branch university for the instruction of colored youths of the state, to be located by a voice vote of the people." [59] Almost from the time that this clause was inserted into the Constitution, Texans — both white and black — argued over its implementation. When Prairie View College was established, this issue became even more complicated. Some individuals took the position that with the establishment of Prairie View, the above provision of the Constitution had been fulfilled. Others argued that Prairie View was only a normal school and could not be classified as a "classical university." [60] Still others felt that if blacks were to receive a liberal arts education, a separate university similar to that of The University of Texas was needed. Most black legislators were in favor of a branch university. On September 28, 1882, W. H. Holland, a former lawmaker, wrote Governor Oran M. Roberts and asked that the city of Austin be placed in nomination for the location of the branch university.[61] Several years later R. J. Moore submitted a resolution that "the Board of Education be requested to make arrangements for a building site and lay such plans before this legislature for raising funds as they may think best." [62] This document was simply referred to committee and died. In 1893, Nathan Haller introduced a bill "to establish and put in operation a branch university for colored youths of Texas." Haller also presented a petition from the colored citizens of Brazoria asking for the establishment of the said university.[63] Two days after Haller introduced his bill, a large delegation of colored men went before the House to urge establishment of the branch university. Haller's bill was favorably reported to the committee, but subsequently met its death there.

Contrary to the published literature, which states that R. L. Smith of the Twenty-fifth Legislature introduced a bill to set aside 50,000 acres of land for the creation of a separate branch university, it was Representative John D. Pitts of Hill County who introduced a bill to set apart 50,000 acres of public domain for Prairie View. The only thing that Smith did was to make a motion to take out of order House Bill 226, which gives the Land Commissioner authority to set apart public domain for the benefit and use of common schools and universities of the state. But even this bill was amended and finally died in committee.[64] When the branch university bill was taken up again in the Twenty-sixth Legislature (which had no blacks), the legislature passed a bill setting aside 100,000 acres of the remaining unappropriated public domain as a specific endowment for the colored branch university. The Supreme Court prevented this bill from taking effect by declaring that no unappropriated public domain was left. So, from 1899, when a concurrent resolution was passed by the Twenty-sixth Legislature condemning the action of the Supreme Court, to the present time, the issue of a branch university has not been resolved.[65]

Along with railroads, state lands and education, the question of prohibition developed into a major political issue in 1870s and 1880s as the prohibitionists sought political allies in order to get a prohibition amendment written into the constitution. They gained enough support in the legislature in 1879 to pass the Bell Punch Law, a tax which called for two cents on each alcoholic drink. In 1881, a prohibition amendment passed the State Senate but failed in the House after considerable debate. It should be added that prohibitionists' strength and/or influence increased over the years not because of black support, but rather in spite of it. Except for Walter Burton, most black lawmakers shared Evans's views on this issue — that prohibition should be submitted to the people for a vote rather than be legislated in Austin. While Thomas Beck presented a petition from citizens of Travis County on the whiskey law, he voted against prohibition of alcoholic beverages. On the other hand, Burton not only presented a petition from citizens of Texas in favor of prohibition, but he asked the Senate for a constitutional amendment prohibiting the importation, manufacturing, and sale of intoxicating liquor as a beverage in Texas.[66]

While Burton fought a losing battle on prohibition, other black legislators had too many more exigent problems than prohibition with which to concern themselves. Of extreme importance to black lawmakers was labor, both agricultural and skilled. Despite the emphasis placed on industrialization, Texas was still very much an agricultural and a rural state in the postwar years. In 1876, Texas led the nation in cotton production. It is not surprising, then, to find that the majority of blacks were engaged in tenant farming and that white planters would take advantage of the situation. It was largely due to the efforts of large white planters that the Landlord and Tenant Law of 1874 was amended in 1876 to prohibit tenants from sub-renting land without the consent of the landlord. As had been the case before, Shack Roberts was the lone black voice in the legislature speaking out on this bill, but all to no avail. Similarly, black men meeting in convention in Houston in 1879, denounced the Landlord and Tenant Act.[67] Despite this protest, in 1885, efforts, though unsuccessful, were made by white lawmakers to make it a felony to sell mortgage crops with the intent to defraud the mortgagee. In response to blacks' action and reaction to the oppressive Landlord and Tenant Act of 1876, R. J. Moore introduced an act "to prohibit any person from taking a bill of sale on personal property when the same is in fact designed for a mortgage or other lien upon the property named therein and to secure an existing lot or to be credited for and to provide adequate penalties thereof." [68] Like many bills before it, this bill got only as far as committee. When the Landlord and Tenant Act came up again in 1894, Robert L. Smith presented an amendment to the bill: "to provide that no claim in favor of the landlord by a tenant shall be valid for any amount in excess of the value of the crop produced." [69] It seemed strange that in a period during which the economic and political condition of blacks reached a nadir, that not more than two black representatives attempted to introduce legislation which would alter the Landlord and Tenant Act, in asmuchas a large number of them were farmers and all represented farming constituencies. Based on the available data, one can understand clearly the obstacles that black legislators faced in trying to introduce any kind of legislation. Too, one would not expect them to address all issues affecting blacks. Not to attempt a bill, an amendment, a rider, or a resolution on this latter issue, certainly suggests a lack of urgency in acting on the critical needs of their constituents.

Outside of agriculture, the only other areas where a sizeable number of blacks were employed in the 1870s and 1880s, were the wharves and ports of Texas, and the railroad industry. Still, blacks fought an uphill battle in these occupations. White legislators were concerned first and foremost with securing longshoreman jobs for whites. Thus, when a House bill to limit foreign workers came up in the Eighteenth Legislature in 1883, B. F. Williams had to remind his colleagues that it was the duty of the legislature to protect both whites and blacks on the wharves of Texas.[70] As far as railroad work was concerned, while it did employ a large number of blacks, blacks were not always secure in their work, because many times they were replaced by prisoners under the convict lease system.

It is interesting to note that during the period of post-Reconstruction (1875–1900), blacks accounted for fifty percent of the individuals incarcerated in the state penitentiary, despite the fact that they constituted only twenty-five percent of the total population. Because of the paucity of prisons, which resulted in overcrowding at the existing ones, numerous convicts were hired out under both private and contract lease system. In 1875, the Fifteenth Legislature expanded the county convict law by allowing all commissioners' courts to employ for public work any convict guilty of a misdemeanor of petty offense. As in the days of slavery, the individual offering the highest bid, that is, paying the highest monthly rate, would secure the services of the convict until the fine and the court cost of the prisoner were paid. Needless to say, this act drew reactions from black lawmakers as well as laymen. While Shack Roberts voiced opposition to the bill in the House, Walter Burton presented a petition in the Senate from Fort Bend citizens who protested against employment of convicts in that county. Simultaneously, laymen began petitioning the legislature, complaining of the inhumane treatment accorded county convicts, and the Colored Men's Convention of 1879, aired complaints that the convicts were subjected to barbaric conditions.[71]

Disturbed at the situation in 1879, R. J. Evans introduced a bill, "to amend an act to provide for the employment and hiring of county convicts and prescribing the duties and fees of officers charged therewith." Since this bill was referred, Evans prepared himself for the fact that it would probably die in committee. So when the next legislature met in 1881, Evans decided to offer another amendment to remedy the existing convict lease law. In the special session of the Seventeenth Legislature, Evans rose to the floor and said that even though he did not believe that convict labor should be in competition with free labor, he was going to offer an amendment that "no county convict shall be hired for less than one dollar per day." [72] Hal Geiger, believing that the amendment did not go far enough, said that a distinction should be made between the "convict sent up for a felony and the convict sent up for playing a game of cards." Geiger believed that every man should be given his due, but he was opposed to discriminating against the poor. In describing the discrepancies which existed in administering the law, Geiger said:

> A man comes in court and the judge sentences him . . . the sharpers and the scalpers are there to take his scalp and he receives for his labor twenty cents a day. The law provides that he shall not work over 12 hours and not less than eight, but I tell you, he puts in fourteen and he does not fail to receive the strife upon his back when he fails to do his duty, let him be white or colored. The county needs to protect the white as well as the colored. When the law stands up for us, when it is a feasible law, it must be obeyed. I claim this law [is designed] to get any man who rides on mules and horses but not [one who rides] on railroad cars.[73]

Sharing a similar view was Robert A. Kerr, who said that the convict lease system was nothing but a long step toward the restoration of slavery. This analogy was evident, he said, by the fact that young men in his county were hired to work sixteen months for trivial offenses.[74] In the Senate, Burton took the same position as that of Evans. Realizing that there were not enough votes in the upper house to do away with the convict lease system, Burton sought to change it through an amendment which stated "that no person shall be employed as a guard who is not a qualified voter." [75] A. P. McCormick of Brazoria County, offered an amendment to Burton's amendment that "no person shall be used as a guard over such convict who is not a qualified voter of the county wherein such resides or is so employed." [76] It should be added that aside from this change, no other reform was made in the convict lease system bill in the Seventeenth Legislature.

The convict lease issue came up again in 1885. This time, Senate Bill Number 45 called for the hiring of a convict for twenty-five cents a day, part of which was to be used for his fine and the cost of court assessed against him. H. A. P. Bassett of Grimes County countered this bill by offering an unsuccessful amendment, to raise the allowance to fifty-cents.[77] Bassett's colleague R. J. Moore presented a petition from citizens of Washington County against the convict lease system of penitentiaries, but this was done to no avail. Again in 1889, legislators would have to face the issue of convict lease. This time black lawmaker Asberry went on record as favoring the passage of a bill introduced by Scott Fields of Robertson County, asking for the appropriation of two hundred thousand dollars with which to purchase a state convict farm upon which to place all state convicts now employed outside of the walls of penitentiaries upon the expiration of the contract. It can be argued that the passage of the above bill was the only measure taken by any legislature to change the status quo of the convict lease system in Texas during the last half of the nineteenth century.[78]

In light of the fact that blacks were not receiving equity at the law and the the convict lease system was not improving their conditions, these lawmakers of color sought to amend various penal codes. In 1876, Holland unsuccessfully introduced a bill to repeal an act of November 1866, which established part of the penal code of Texas.[79] In 1877, Thomas Beck and Walter Ripetoe introduced an act to amend Chapter 6, Title 15 of the Penal Code "to prohibit the hiring, or harboring of minors against the consent of parents and guardians." The bill passed on the third reading. In commenting on it, Ripetoe added that "this bill is of special interest to colored people, but beneficial in general application to others." [80] As author of the bill, Ripetoe was very pleased with its passage, but because of a lack of enforcement, the bill did little to stop the hiring of minors. In that same year, Burton offered an amendment to an act for the suppression and punishment of tramps, opining that this act "should not be so construed as to shift the burden of proof on the accused." His reasons for this amendment was that the act should not apply to any person who had ever worked on the railroad.[81] In 1885, R. J. Moore was successful in amending Section 2, Chapter 3, of the General Law of Texas of the Nineteenth Legislature relative to a writ of *habeas corpus*. This amendment made sure that the liberty of an individual was not taken away without due process.[82] Nathan Haller and Robert Smith of the Twenty-fourth Legislature were also concerned with penal codes. They made their position known when they voted against a House bill which called for punishment by hanging. In their stated opposition against this act, they argued that the bill made no distinction in punishment between crimes of murder, rape, and robbery, and that it was "simply barbarious to use hanging as a deterrant for these crimes." [83]

Along with amending penal codes, blacks were interested in revising some of the civil statutes. A logical starting point for such reforms was the constitution. Thus, Burton offered a joint resolution to amend Sections 5 and 24, of Article 3, of the Constitution of 1876. Following the lead of Burton, Evans introduced the same resolution in the House. These sections, if amended, would have changed the time of convening the legislature from every two years to every year. Likewise, in a losing cause, Walter Ripetoe tried to amend the constitution to relegate the governor to a six-year term in office.[84]

In attempting to revise some of the civil codes, blacks were careful not to exclude the judiciary. In 1879, Andrew Sledge offered a joint resolution that the Judiciary Committee report a bill to establish county courts in each county and have them open at all times for trials of respective individuals.[85] Thomas Beck of the same legislature was responsible for calling up Senate Bill Number 225; "an act which would diminish the civil and criminal jurisdiction of the district court and would give local courts more control." [86] While both of the above bills failed, in 1883, Wyatt was more successful in introducing an act to amend Article 2400, Chapter 3, Title 42, of the Revised Civil Statutes of Texas, regarding the fees of constables. This act was important because most of the black elected officials between 1870–1900 were constables and worked very closely in the black community. In like manner, in 1889, Mayes was concerned with the fees of another group of individuals who worked directly with the black community; that is, the justices of the peace. In a losing cause, he tried to amend the Revised Civil Statutes so as to make sure that these individuals would be paid regardless of whether the case was moved out of their jurisdiction as a result of an appeal.[87]

In their fight to change or remedy problems in the judiciary, blacks naturally turned to the question of the selection of jurors. The Constitution of 1876 had left it up to the legislature to determine the eligibility of jurors. In keeping with this provision, early in the Sixteenth Legislature, Burton introduced an act prescribing the qualifications of jurors and also an act to give positive effect to Article VI Section 1 of the 1876 Constitution. Both bills died in committee.[88] In 1883, the Seventeenth Legislature took up the issue once more. It prescribed the following qualifications for jurors "that no person shall be qualified as a juror in a civil or criminal case unless he was a legal voter or a citizen of the state . . . a freeholder in the state or household in the county in which he may be called to serve; of sound mind and good moral character provided that an inability to read or write shall be sufficient cause to challenge [the qualification]." [89] The last clause of the above act was a "go" signal for local white officials to exclude blacks from jury duty. Because of the tenor of the latter clause, the entire bill was challenged by R. J. Moore, who introduced an act to repeal the law relative to requiring jurors to read and write.[90] Notwithstanding the efforts of the black representative from Washington County, this amendment did not pass and blacks continued to be excluded from jury duty. This setback, however, did not prevent blacks from expressing an opinion about the individuals who should be exempted from jury duty. Concomitant with this concern, in 1889, Elias Mayes was successful in introducing House Bill 500, which categorized the individuals and occupational groups who should be exempted.[91]

Jury selection, exclusion or exemption went hand in hand with voting. Needless to say, one of the paramount concerns of blacks in the post-Reconstruction legislatures was the issue of suffrage. While blacks had escaped many restrictions on their voting rights when the constitution was drafted in 1876, all male citizens between the ages of twenty-one and sixty were required to pay a poll tax of one dollar to support education. Shack Roberts subsequently introduced a bill to exempt from payment of a poll tax, all soldiers who had lost a limb or had been permanently disabled in any way in the Wars of Texas, the United States, or the Confederate States.[92] Though the above bill was passed at the urging of black legislators, it can be argued that in general, blacks did not object to this poll tax for educational purposes, but when it was imposed for other reasons, they were quick to make a protest. Such was the case when Shack Roberts, Henry Sneed, W. H. Holland, and J. M. Swisher, a white of Travis County, objected to House Bills 292 and 298 because they required an extraordinary poll tax on certain items, which in these legislators' opinion was "an unjust and unusual method of raising revenue."[93]

For about two years after the drafting of the Constitution of 1876, the issue of poll tax for suffrage purposes lay dormant. In 1878, the idea began to surface because Democrats believed that fusion on the part of Republicans (mostly blacks) and Greenbackers would wrest control of the state government from them. That year had already brought about an increase in black representation in the legislature — two senators and eight representatives. So, in 1879, the Democrats introduced a joint resolution to amend the Texas Constitution to include a poll tax for voting purposes. This resolution barely passed the House, but was defeated in the Senate. According to the *Galveston Daily News,* the resolution would not have passed the House had not Elias Mayes, black representative from Brazos, changed his opposition to the bill. Mayes sided with the proponents when he was given assurance by the supporters of the amendment that before it could become law, the amendment would have to receive the approval of the people.[94] Given the state of affairs in Texas, that is, the violence and intimidation meted out to black voters, Mayes should have known that bringing the issue before the people would only mean that a poll tax law would be enacted. If he was not cognizant of this fact, at least he should have been aware of what and how his other black colleagues were saying or thinking on this issue. A look at the position of other blacks might shed some light on this critical issue.

Hal Geiger, first to voice opposition to this poll tax, held that suffrage was God-given and was the greatest right of the American people.[95] J. R. Evans argued that the amendment was "intended to oppress the poor and to give monied men a chance to control the election, as well as the poor man's vote." The right of suffrage, Evans said, "is the greatest right of the poor." [96] Andrew Sledge voted against the resolution of a poll tax for the following reasons:

(1) Because it is a violation of Section 19 of the Bill of Rights which declares that no citizen of the state shall be in any manner disfranchised except by due course of the law of the land.
(2) Because it is the entering wedge of the doctrine of a property qualification for right of suffrage.
(3) Because it is in opposition to the ideas that this is a government of the people, by the people and for the people.
(4) Because it is a direct stab at the liberation of the people.[97]

In support of these black legislators' effort, the Colored Men's Convention in 1879, issued a statement saying that not only was the poll tax bill unjust, but that it would not be equally applied to blacks and whites.

The above bill, having failed to be enacted, led to the introduction of another poll tax bill in 1883, but again it met with defeat. Similarly, it was reintroduced in 1889, failed again and was again reintroduced in 1891. Edward Patton, the only black serving in the Twenty-second Legislature, made his first speech in the House on the poll tax before it died in committee. Patton argued that the measure was aimed at his race and it was calculated to create and nourish race prejudice in the state. Patton argued that "this bill disfranchised many whites; and that white property holders, having the power, the wealth and intelligence should not disfranchise the young and poor white men through race prejudice." [98] Still, no one paid any attention to his appeal.

Tired, but not worried about their failure to get a poll tax bill through the Twenty-second Legislature, Democrats introduced a similar piece of legislation in the House in 1895. Because Robert L. Smith knew that the handwriting was on the wall for the passage of a poll tax law, one of his first acts as a legislator was to introduce a bill "to disseminate among qualified voters of Texas a better knowledge of a certain constitutional amendment as shall be at any election to be voted upon by them to prevent the holding of an election for such purposes before the expiration of one year from the time such amendment is approved by the legislature." [99] This measure was also defeated. Failing in his efforts, Smith did not give up the struggle to safeguard the suffrage rights of blacks. Thus, when a Senate bill was called up which was designed to "prevent illegal voting and false returns," Smith complemented it with the following amendment: "if any member of a political party shall endeavor to influence the primary election of another party or if a member of one political party shall vote at the primary election of the other he shall be fined in the sum of not more than five hundred dollars and not less than fifty dollars." [100] This amendment was referred, but when it was reported out of committee, it was watered down to such an extent that even Haller and Smith voted against it. Their argument was that: "The bill in its present form, instead of preventing fraud, might be a vehicle for unfair primary elections." [101]

Poll tax would not be the only tax that would trouble blacks. The dog tax, as well as tax exemption for certain individuals would also be a "bone of contention" for some of them. The dog tax, which fell heavily upon tenant farmers, was imposed upon families with more than one dog. In the Fifteenth Legislature, Henry Sneed and Shack Roberts tried to alter this law through amendments, but they were unsuccessful.[102] Attacking this bill from another angle was Senator Ripetoe, who opposed the law because of its loophole, that is, if a family had more than one dog, they simply had to allow each member of the family to claim one in order to dodge the law.[103] As far as exemption was concerned, H. A. P. Bassett was not concerned with farmers, but rather with manufacturers. Thus, he proposed (but lost) an amendment to the constitution calling for exemption of taxation for merchants of Galveston.[104] Evans held a similar view on exemption of Ministers of the Gospel from occupation tax. Like Bassett's bill, Evan's bill died an untimely death.[105]

In deliberating on taxes and appropriations, the postwar legislatures were almost forced to deal with the issue of pensions. As for black legislators, they were mixed in their reactions to pensions. There were some, such as Shack Roberts, who voiced outright opposition to an act to provide an annual pension for surviving soldiers and widows of soldiers of the Texas Revolution and Signers of the Texas Declaration of Independence.[106] On the other hand, there were other blacks who would go along if it would include blacks. For instance, when the pension bill came up in 1881, "to provide pension for veterans who lost a limb in one of the wars," Kerr offered an amendment to include in this bill as beneficiaries, slaves who had lost limbs while serving their masters in the army.[107] B. P. Paddock of Tarrant County, who had sponsored the bill, claimed that he supported Kerr's amendment, but he later withdrew the motion. The bill was then reintroduced in the special called session in 1882. This time, Evans offered an amendment to include "all who acted in the capacity of teamsters and servants," namely, slaves.[108] The House refused to adopt the amendment.

The fact that the majority of blacks were not recipients of pensions did not prevent black lawmakers from being concerned with equal distribution of pensions. As such, Evans voted "no" to "an act to repeal an act granting land to persons who are permanently disabled." His reason for voting "no" was that he did not believe it "was fair to repeal the law and shut off many who were entitled to what others had received previously to that act." [109] Walter Ripetoe and Walter Burton took similar positions in the Senate in 1879, when they voted "no" to a bill which would raise the interest rates on pension certificates for individuals who would purchase them on or after July 1879. They argued that such a bill discriminated against the present holders of pension certificates and would deprive them of the interest on the same.[110]

Pension for veterans came up again in 1891, this time in the form of the establishment of a Confederate nursing home. Edward Patton, the lone black in the legislature, not only voted for the bill, but glorified it with the following remarks: "There may be some doubts as to the constitutionality of the bill, but I vote "aye" because I believe it is right that when a man lays down his life for a principle or country and is only fortunate enough to take up after combat a fraction of the life he laid down, he should be cared for by the state or country which he had sought to protect." [111] These remarks may have been distressing to many of Patton's constituents, most of whom were black. Such remarks were typical of Patton who was probably the most conservative black who sat in the legislature. If the above remarks struck some of his black constituents unfavorably, his position on interracial marriage was even more shocking as he introduced a bill to amend Chapter 1, Title 10, Article 326 of the Revised Statute of Texas. This amendment called for punishment of any white and black persons who shall inter-marry . . .[112]

Not many blacks were as conservative as Patton, and subsequently they took into consideration the rights of women. In 1879, Thomas Beck offered an amendment to a bill which called for paying workers to do extra clerical work. This amendment stated that one-half of these workers "may be females." [113] To a bill to prohibit women from being employed in liquor stores, Robert Kerr offered the following amendment: "The wife, daughter and female members of the dealer may be permitted to work in the store of the owner." [114] On the lighter side of things, Nathan Haller of the Twenty-fourth Legislature offered an amendment concerning "fallen" women. To the Senate Bill, "an act to establish an industrial home for fallen women and young women in danger of falling and to make necessary appropriation," Haller's amendment was to insert the words colored and white alongside the word fallen in this bill.[115]

Blacks exhibited a surprisingly modern cast of mind on such issues as health codes, gun control, and the commemoration of historic events. For example, in an attempt to do something about the plague which affected all Texans, black politicians gave their hearty support to the Quarantine Law. Andrew Sledge went so far as to propose that the whole financial burden of this health law should not be left entirely to the state, but should be shared by local towns and cities.[116] On gun control, Burton led a fight in the Senate to pass a law to that effect, because in his own words: "I have seen so many persons acquitted of carrying a gun until I would be in favor of a fine and imprisonment for such offenses." [117] As to the celebration of historic events, R. J. Evans took into consideration the historic importance that June 19, 1865, held for black Texans, when he introduced the following resolution:

> Whereas this is the 19th day of June and the fourteenth anniversary of the emancipation of slaves in the United States and whereas, a large number of citizens including members of the legislature desire to participate in the celebration of the day.
>
> Resolve: that the House stands adjourned until tomorrow June 20, 1882, at 9:00.[118]

This motion, as written in its original form was lost, but its concept was soon revised when William Johnson, of Leon County, was successful in presenting a motion to the effect that any member of the House desiring to attend the Juneteenth celebration should be excused until the following day. Thus, contrary to the belief of some individuals that Al Edwards, representative of the Eighty-first District, originated a novel idea in 1980, when he proposed to make the nineteenth day of June a state holiday for black Texans, Edwards was only looking over the shoulders of his predecessor who had come up with the idea almost a hundred years previously.

By 1898, blacks who served in the post-Reconstruction legislatures could look back over the preceding twenty-two years to a few accomplishments and many misgivings. These accomplishments centered around the establishment of Prairie View Normal School, the enactment of a law to put black trustees over black schools, the establishment of the Deaf and Dumb Institution for Colored Youth, and the passage of a bill to make railroads liable for damages to cattle. The misgivings were many; to name only a few, there was the creation of a convict lease system, the prevention of the branch university, and the enactment of an oppressive Landlord and Tenant Law. It should be noted that rather than spending most of their time advancing measures to further social, economic, or political changes, blacks found themselves struggling — most times unsuccessfully — to defeat the socially reactionary legislative initiatives of their white colleagues. Even when they were successful in presenting measures designed to assist the economic or political conditions of their constituencies, their bills were either bottled up in committee or were so compromised as to render them ineffective. No doubt blacks introduced bills that were forward-looking, but still most failed. More obvious was the fact that these measures in the direction of reform went unappreciated by their white colleagues amidst the rising social turmoil gripping the state. That black lawmakers failed to achieve many of their goals was not always because of their ineptitude, ignorance or divisiveness. They failed in part because they could not successfully surmount an opposition to white racism.

Part Two
The Snares:

White Over Black In Party Conventions

[5]

A Thorn In The Side

It is time to look at the great power we possess . . . It is a sin to have power and not to use it.
— Matthew Gaines
Houston Weekly Telegraph
June 29, 1871

Attempts were made by prewar Unionists to establish a Republican party in Texas soon after the Reconstruction Acts were imposed upon the South. In this regard, the Union League played an instrumental role. This secret organization, which urged blacks to remain loyal to the Union and instructed them on their political rights, was first introduced into Texas by Judge James H. Bell in March 1867. Shortly after the inception of the Union League, a number of meetings were held between blacks and whites to discuss the political situation of the state. Thus, on April 27, 1867, Union men held a meeting in Austin, to formulate plans for holding a state convention in July to establish a party which would embrace the Congressional Plan of Reconstruction. In keeping with the purpose of this conference, these individuals passed resolutions which supported the civil rights of blacks, as well as internal improvement in the state. After taking care of routine matters, they adjourned, returned to their homes and began canvassing to recruit new members for the new party.[1]

During the recruitment period, Union men discovered that they were not the only ones who were vying for black support. Conservatives were also. For example, when the two black leaders, Jacob Raney and Anderson Scroggins, came out in favor of the establishment of the Republican party, the Conservatives did not sit idly by. As a matter of fact, Governor James Throckmorton was the first to react. He summoned Raney and Scroggins to his office and told them to consider voting for the Conservative party because in his opinion, the Conservatives held the interest of blacks at heart. Probably thinking that these black gentlemen could not read, and if they could, they were inept, Governor Throckmorton gave Jacob Raney and Anderson Scroggins copies of his inaugural message, as well as copies of laws passed by the Eleventh Legislature, so that the two could see the concern of Conservatives for blacks. As if this action was not enough, he asked these gentlemen to call a meeting of blacks so that the freedmen could be lectured to by his men, who were sure to tell the freedmen about all the good things that the Conservatives had done and would do for blacks. When this meeting ended, these gentlemen thanked the governor, returned home and addressed a letter to him in which they expressed their true feelings. In their letter, they denounced Throckmorton for his opposition to the Congressional Plan of Reconstitution, his failure to protect Union and black men before the law, his approval of the School Bill of 1866, which discriminated against blacks, and his veto of a voting bill proposed at the Constitutional Convention of 1866, which would have included blacks.[2]

At this point, not only did it become clear that blacks were going to support prewar Unionists, but also that Union men had been far more successful in mobilizing black voters than had been the case of the Conservatives. Consequently, when the convention assembled in Houston July 4, 1867, to establish the Republican party, there were 150 black delegates in addition to twenty whites. The irony of the blacks' presence at this convention was that their number was not reflected by the convention officers nor committee appointments. Only four blacks received honor. George T. Ruby and Scipio McKee were named as vice-presidents, while Sheppard Mullins and Stephen Curtis were placed on the Platform and Resolutions Committee. It is well to remember that even though they failed to be elected or appointed to many offices, blacks did support and help to draft a platform which favored their interest. Of particular importance was a proposed plank which endorsed a homestead bill — an act which would have made provision for all citizens, without distinction of race or color, to secure a portion of the unappropriated public domain.³ According to the *Galveston Daily News,* blacks at this convention were in favor of the above plank which also called for the confiscation of the properties of plantation owners, but Judge James Bell, who was presiding, kept the issue from the floor.⁴

After drafting a compromise platform, the convention adjourned with the Republican party firmly established. Yet, the work of the organizers was incomplete. There was a need to create a state central committee to coordinate Republican efforts at the local level. Once established, the operation of the party was set in motion through an alliance between blacks and whites. The viability of such an alliance was untested in the annals of Texas politics. The question that naturally comes to mind is, when tested, what would be the position of blacks? The answer to this question depends on two of several factors: (1) how well blacks would be treated and (2) what role black leaders would play; that is to say whether or not these leaders would capitalize on opportunities presented, accept without protest that which was given to them or demand an input in the coalition.

The first test of the above coalition came in October 1867, when a split occurred within the administration of Governor Elisha Pease over the validity of the Constitution of 1866 and legislation passed after that date. Pease, who was appointed provisional Governor of Texas after Throckmorton was removed August 7, 1867, took the position that with some exceptions, the constitution and laws of 1866 should remain in effect. Morgan Hamilton, Pease's Comptroller, held the exact opposite view. This controversy between Pease and Hamilton reached an impasse when Hamilton decided to move it outside of the administrative circle and to take this battle to blacks through the Union League. Starting from this point on, blacks would become a "thorn in the side" of their fellow white Republicans. Not only did blacks support Hamilton, but through the Union League, they would attempt to make their voices heard in the coalition. Hence, shortly after the Hamilton–Pease controversy escalated, the Union League of Galveston opposed Pease's appointment of Major R. H. Perry as Chief of Police because of his attitude toward blacks.⁵ Moreover, it was largely due to the efforts of the League that George T. Ruby could boast as early as September 1867, that he would be elected as a delegate to the constitutional convention from a predominately white district.

Despite blacks' efforts to assert themselves on the above issues, Governor Pease and his supporters did not take them seriously. They took such a position for three of several reasons: (1) Pease and his cohorts did not feel threatened by the numerical strength of blacks, because they held the false notion that since they helped to establish the Union League in Texas, they controlled black voters; (2) neither Pease nor his men viewed the League as a viable organization which could effect change. Rather, they saw it as a movement composed of "white fools, demagogues or worse . . . such colored men as they could induce to follow their lead;" (3) aside from voting, Pease's men did not believe that blacks were capable of playing a major role in the Republican organization. Rather, they saw blacks simply as junior partners in the coalition who were incapable of speaking for the Republican party.[6] What Pease and his men failed to realize was that blacks were no more comfortable in being junior partners in the coalition than they (whites) would be comfortable in having them as equal partners, and that it was only natural that blacks would exert themselves or at least ask for their fair share in the coalition.

As a result of Pease's posture, but more so because blacks expected to be treated fairly in this coalition, when the Union League met on June 25, 1868, black delegates asserted their power by removing Pease's man, James Bell, as president of the organization. These delegates defied the advice of their white leaders and voted for a black man, George T. Ruby, as their President. Blacks were in a position to take over all the offices of the League, but they had not made plans for such a change of command. Needless to say, Ruby's victory caused a great deal of unrest within the organization. It caused such an uproar because it removed the administration's chief mechanism for mobilizing black votes and placed it in the hands of a black man. After this convention, Democrats, who were *never* in favor of black suffrage, sarcastically commented that the action of blacks at this convention was becoming to Governor Pease "who had unchained [blacks] and now they had proved unmanageable."[7] Sharing a similar view was a Republican newspaper editor who wrote: "Unless Governor Pease, A. J. Hamilton and Judge James Bell are saved by the success of a better party than the one they have unchained, they will at least find themselves insulted and trampled upon by those who once seemed too proud to be called their political followers and servants."[8] While Pease's men had not been trampled upon, they certainly had been challenged.

To be sure, blacks held the ace card of the Republican party in their hand. They had the votes, that is, the power. But at this point it is necessary to distinguish between the sources, the bases of power, and the actual exercise of power. Voting, holding office, favorable population distribution, economics, and wealth may be sources of power; but they are only potential sources of power. In themselves, they are passive and inert. They may be converted into real power only when appropriate means for operationalizing them are available and utilized. With blacks commanding the largest single bloc vote within the party and George T. Ruby at the head of the Union League, blacks had the appropriate means available for harnessing and bringing pressure to bear upon the behavior of white Republicans, specifically in obtaining concessions from them. Without a doubt, they had the ace in their hand. How well they would play their cards would depend to a large extent on Ruby, as well as other black leaders. That is to say, whether they would stand firm in their conviction or be manipulated by whites; whether they would push to get other blacks into office or whether they would look out only for their own well being.

Answers to these questions began to unfold when blacks tried to seize control of the Republican party at the state convention held August 12, 1868. One of their plans was to prevent James Bell, former Union League President, from becoming chairman of the convention. Unfortunately, blacks had not done their homework in precinct conventions. When they arrived at the convention, they found that the majority of the delegates were white. The result of which was that the Pease administration filled most of the committees with their own men. The only blacks who received positions were B. F. Williams and Benjamin Watrous who were placed on the Platform and State Central Committees, respectively.[9] When it became obvious that blacks would not be able to take over the convention, their leader, G. T. Ruby, decided to meet with those whites who had expressed dissatisfaction with the proposed platform. The men to whom Ruby spoke were Edmund Davis, James Newcomb, and Morgan Hamilton, all of whom wanted a strong plank on *ab initio*. Failing to get an *ab initio* plank, these men, under the leadership of Edmund Davis, bolted the convention.

A few days afterward, the Davisites formed their own Republican organization and called a convention to be held August 14, 1868. Blacks did not commit themselves to the Davis party at first, but waited until the platform was presented. Among the items that the platform included were *ab initio,* law and order, a free public school system, internal improvement and no proscriptive residence requirements for office holding. After analyzing this platform, blacks under the leadership of Ruby decided to join the Davisites. In return, three blacks were named to the State Executive Committee, Charles Bryant, B. F. Williams and G. T. Ruby.[10]

To be sure, the Republican party had split and all efforts to reconcile the warring factions had failed. The split was all sustaining because dissatisfaction among black leaders and black voters provided the ammunition needed to launch a successful attack against control of the party by Governor Pease and his men. Pease, who had always taken the League for granted, now realized clearly that with the efforts of Ruby and the Union League, he could be eliminated from politics. So, in order to remain in control of the Regular Republican party, Governor Pease, Andrew J. Hamilton, and Judge James Bell launched a crusade to break up the League. Their objectives were threefold: (1) to break up the Galveston chapter, that not only served as Ruby's power base, but that of many urban blacks; (2) to place the mobilization of black votes in the hands of whites again; and (3) to dispose of Ruby as a political leader. White Conservatives knew that the last task would not be easy to undertake, and therefore, they were mixed in their opinion as to whether or not to go through with it. Some argued that despite the difficulty involved, the troublemaker Ruby, had to go. Others, such as Ferdinand Flake, fearing the numerical strength of blacks, warned local officials not to confront Ruby directly. Instead, Flake suggested that Conservatives should withdraw their support from the League and, consequently, it would die a natural death, because neither blacks nor their white supporters had enough sense to run the organization.[11] Still other Republicans, such as Dr. Robert Smith, persisted that Ruby must go. In keeping with this view, Smith began a direct assault upon Ruby by first accusing him of not representing his black constitutents at the constitutional convention. Instead, Smith argued that Ruby was working for his own interest by supporting Conservative A. B. Slvonker in exchange for a bribe of $600. This hostility between Smith and Ruby, which goes back to their fight on the convention floor, came to a head on September 9, 1868, at a Galveston Republican Association meeting. On that night, a fight broke out between these two gentlemen and according to a reporter, had not the police been present, blacks would have killed Smith.[12] Thus, this fight left no doubt in the mind of the administration that blacks intended to control the Union League.

It is interesting to note that while Conservatives tried to destroy the League, the Davisites endorsed it as the backbone of their organization. James P. Newcomb wrote in his San Antonio paper, "the Union League had brought us one victory; it has the power to give us another and in its power the future destinies of our State are held."[13] The question that naturally comes to mind is whether or not blacks would continue to control the League now that they were being curried very closely by Davis's men. Only time would provide the answer to this question.

The year of 1869 was an important one for the Republicans. It was their opportunity to wrest control of the State. But in order to accomplish the previously mentioned goal, they would have to be unified and unity was not something that they were about at the beginning of that year. However, the idea of reconciliation began to surface when Andrew J. Hamilton proposed a compromise with the Democrats in return for their support of his candidacy as governor. He told a group of Democrats in Brenham not to be afraid of Republicans because the Republican Convention had prevented the disfranchisement of former Confederates and that he personally did not believe in the subordination of white to black rule.[14] Needless to say, Hamilton's flirtation with Democrats was a cause for concern among many Republicans who wanted to maintain the party in power. The end result of Hamilton's action was that John L. Hayes, Chairman of the Republican State Executive Committee, immediately scheduled a meeting of the said committee for April 20, 1869. As soon as Haynes issued a call for this meeting, Morgan Hamilton issued a call for a state convention of his group to meet at Galveston May 10, 1869.

As this internecine fighting continued within the party, many individuals from the rank and file came to the conclusion that to go into the election divided into two factions would be tantamount to political suicide. Thus, a compromise movement was launched by James G. Tracy, editor of the *Houston Union,* Ferdinand Flake, editor of *Flake's Daily Bulletin* and Edwin M. Wheelock, a former union army chaplin. The movement was strengthened when it received the endorsement of General Joseph J. Reynolds, Assistant Commissioner of Texas Freedmen's Bureau, who urged the organizers to eliminate the leaders of these two factions if they could not reconcile their differences. In order to bring reconciliation to fruition, Tracy and Wheelock scheduled a convention of all Republicans to meet in Houston May 24, 1869, and asked the Davis faction to cancel its convention so that harmony could prevail.[15] Morgan Hamilton, suspicious that Tracy's proposed convention was a plan to nominate Pease for Governor, rejected Tracy's appeal.

Hamilton's convention met as scheduled at Galveston May 10, 1869, with delegates from fifteen counties. Tracy and Wheelock somehow managed to become delegates to this convention. When they arrived, they found the convention packed with members of the Union League firmly in the hands of Ruby, who was presiding at the time. In a speech before the convention, Ruby urged his predominantly black audience not to support A. J. Hamilton because he did not hold their interest at heart; that he made a trip to Washington primarily to point out that blacks were not being killed in Texas. Tracy and Wheelock sat silent until Ruby called for the nomination for Governor in the upcoming election. At this point, Tracy interrupted the presiding officer and introduced a resolution not to nominate anyone, but rather to adjourn in order to consolidate with his upcoming convention. The delegates acquiesced to the will of Tracy and the convention adjourned.[16]

When Tracy's convention met in Houston June 7, 1869, the major theme among its sixty official delegates was compromise. Due to the large number of black delegates, the Davis faction was able to secure most of the convention officers, but still only two blacks were accorded honors, Richard Allen as vice-president and George T. Ruby as a member of the Platform and Resolution Committee. Blacks had very little input in the committee proceedings, due in part to their small number, but more because the spirit of compromise was too strong at this convention. While the platform endorsed Congressional Reconstruction and the Fourteenth and Fifteenth Amendments, it did not include a plank on *ab initio*. In the spirit of compromise, the delegates selected an *ab initioist*, Edmund J. Davis, as their gubernatorial candidate and a Conservative, James W. Flanagan as his running mate.[17] When the convention adjourned, the general concensus of that body was that in order to secure victory, the race issue should be played down. The Republican party, then, was unified and the blacks sacrificed.

Absent from the campaign was any clear statement from Davis and his supporters on the race question. While Republicans had given lip service in their platform to the Fourteenth and Fifteenth Amendments, in the campaign, they substituted their endorsement of these amendments with only one statement, "to secure the rights of blacks." In other words, their entire efforts were centered around the white voters. As for the black voters, they were treated like naughty children who had to stay in their room when company came. They were expected to produce the votes, but not to be approached publicly by white leaders. The irony about such posture was that George T. Ruby, the Union League President, accepted it. Ruby's misreading of white Republican party leaders' motives would not only indicate a flaw in his leadership, but would also cause him to act irrationally. This behavior became evident when a black man, John DeBruhl, attempted to secure the party's nomination for the legislature from the Twelfth District in 1869, and George Ruby made an attempt to block him. Ruby wrote to J. P. Newcomb to put a stop to DeBruhl's nomination because it "threatened to give credence to the story the enemy assiduously [*sic*] circulates of a black man's party."[18]

Despite the fact that Ruby had now accepted the tenets of white Republican leaders, and that the Union League under his leadership had delivered the votes for Davis, as well as for other Republicans in the election of 1869, blacks still remained "a thorn in the side" of white Republicans. For example, when Davis was inaugurated, none of the black Representatives were invited to the inaugural ball. They signed a protest, but it came to naught.[19] More troublesome to white Republicans was the fact that they were unable to play down the slogan that the Republican party was a "Nigger party" and also unable to attract more whites to the organization. Because the party was unable to cast this millstone from its neck, James Tracy, chairman of the State Executive Committee, and James P. Newcomb, Secretary of State, sought to reorganize the League in April 1870. In keeping with their objective, on May 15, 1870, a meeting of the Grand State Council was held and J. P. Newcomb was elected President of the League, replacing George T. Ruby.[20] Despite the fact that a white man was now at the helm of the League, Tracy was still uncomfortable with the organization. Consequently, one year later, May 1871, Tracy instructed Newcomb to use his position to send out messages breaking up local chapter of the League. Tracy's plan was to replace these chapters with simple county Republican clubs.[21] But before Tracy could get his plan off the ground, opposition to it came from both blacks and whites, politicians as well as laymen.

Many blacks took issue with Tracy because most of them who had risen to a position of power in politics had come via the Union League. The League was a power base for blacks at the local level where they operated from a position of strength and authority. Moreover, the thought of breaking up of the League upset the apple cart for many whites who had played important roles in establishing the League in various Black Belt counties. So, before Tracy could move the party in the direction that he wanted, he would, of necessity, have to deal with the dissatisfied faction of the coalition.

Angered over James Tracy's attempt to reorganize the League, George Whitemore, Louis Stevenson, Matthew Gaines, George Slaughter, and other dissatisfied blacks and whites, met in Austin May 18, 1871, and ousted Newcomb from the office of President of the League. George Slaughter was then asked to act as the Executive Director of the League until a convention was held to elect new officers. When this happened, Newcomb moved quickly to prevent the Slaughter faction of the League from being recognized by the national office. He called a meeting of a few League members whom he could muster and passed a resolution which he sent to the National Office stating that the Slaughter faction was nothing more than a group of individuals who wanted to overthrow the present leadership. In return, the national office promised to keep hands off.[22] But the Slaughter faction persisted. On July 3, they held their regular convention, approved Newcomb's suspension and elected a black man, Johnson Reed of Galveston, as President of the League.[23]

Faced with this bold step taken by these individuals, Tracy and Newcomb soon came to the conclusion that it would be best to back away (at least for the time being) from reorganization. In order to heal the wounds created by their unsavory actions, they sought to pacify dissatisfied blacks by parceling out jobs to them through two major employment agencies, the state police and public school system. But the method by which they went about this task left a lot to be desired. For example, Newcomb urged William Griffin, school superintendent of Galveston, to give two positions on the board to blacks. Griffin naturally chose two blacks who would go along with the program of Tracy and Newcomb. George T. Ruby and Norris Wright Cuney were obvious choices.[24]

Notwithstanding the efforts of Tracy and his cohorts to pacify blacks, many men of color still questioned the leadership of the Republican party. Among the most vocal was Matt Gaines. As Gaines looked at the Third Congressional District race which was to be held in 1871, he realized that this was the only district and probably the only time that blacks would get an opportunity to send a member of their race to Congress. Over 98,000 blacks lived in this district, approximately 41.5 percent of the black population in the state. Without a doubt, there was a great potential for black victory, especially if white voters were split. At first Gaines had thought about running for Congress, but later he decided to remain in the state legislature and to push other blacks to secure this seat, preferably a black local Judge, Richard Nelson.[25] It goes without saying, then, that if Tracy had been successful in breaking up the League, he would have lessened blacks' chances of victory in the Third Congressional District. Gaines was angry at Tracy's decision and was not hesitant in letting Tracy know that the Republican party under Tracy's leadership was not responsive to the needs of the vast majority of its constituents. Gaines argued that instead of breaking up the League, what was needed was a change in the Republican party leadership.

Also joining Gaines in his tirade against the Republican leadership were Lewis Stevenson and George W. Whitmore. Stevenson had organized the Union League in several Black Belt counties. He, like Gaines, was contemplating a Congressional District race. When Newcomb told Stevenson that the leadership of the party was going to support the white incumbent, William T. Clark, Stevenson replied that the Union League was still a powerful force and if it would become necessary he would take his battle "to Africa," Black Belt counties.[26] Similarly, Whitmore shared the views of Gaines and Stevenson because the former was the Congressman from the First District and his fate rested on the support of the Union League.

Disturbed over Tracy's aborted efforts to reorganize the League and also over blacks' dissatisfaction with his candidacy, William T. Clark rushed to the Third Congressional District before the nominating convention which was scheduled to be held on August 3, 1871. In contrast to his last election in 1869, one in which he took the black votes for granted, this time Clark would meet with black legislators and county officials, would solicit the support of George Ruby and would participate with blacks in the celebration of Juneteenth.[27] These gestures by Clark were made in the face of the advice from Gaines, who urged blacks to support a black man from their district for Congress, and to weaken the criticism of Frank Webb, black activist, who argued that Republican leaders were not giving blacks a fair share in the party. In Webb's own words: "We daily see subordinate offices that hundreds of colored men in our midst could fill credibly given to white men of very questionable republicanism and who cannot command a single vote besides their own or exercise the slightest influence among colored people, who after all are the Republican Party." [28] But Clark failed to take Gaines or Webb seriously. He knew that Louis Stevenson was a candidate for Congress with the possible support of the League, but he was shocked at the announcement of two other black candidates. A respected black minister, Israel S. Campbell, and a Galvestonian Justice of the Peace, Richard Nelson, entered the field in July 1871. Nelson, who was Gaines's choice, conducted a vigorous campaign based on black solidarity, causing *Flake's Daily Bulletin* to comment sarcastically that "Lord Nelson said England expects every man to do his duty, Judge Nelson says he expects every man to vote his color." [29] Both black candidates subsequently were sent as delegates to the Houston Republican Convention to continue their efforts to win the nomination.

Because, perhaps, of the fast-moving events of the time, probably because of differences they had among themselves, or possibly because of a snare in the existing leadership, when the Republicans met in Houston on August 3 and 4, 1871, the black leadership was divided. About one-third of the leadership was aligned behind Gaines in support of a black candidate, one-third sided with Stevenson, and the other one-third followed Norris Wright Cuney and George T. Ruby in their support of Tracy's candidate, William T. Clark. Whites did not fail to capitalize on this division. Thus, according to preconceived strategy, the Tracy faction, which included Governor Davis and those who supported Clark's renomination, denied admittance to some twenty to thirty legitimate delegates known to be in favor of the nomination of a black candidate. Ruby, who was presiding over this convention, asked the police to keep these delegates from reaching the floor until after the Credentials Committee had decided their case. While the committee was deliberating to reach a decision, Ruby went ahead with the election of permanent officers. The result of which was Tracy's election as permanent chairman, which virtually ensured Clark's nomination. Meanwhile, Gaines's choice, Richard Nelson, was ignored and his name was not even placed in nomination.[30]

After Clark was nominated, George T. Ruby was given the honor of a token nomination, which he modestly (and expectedly) declined. Then, in a surprise move from the convention floor, black Representative Richard Allen was nominated by a black delegate, Fred Lumpkin. But Allen, who was somewhat shaky because of his close ties with Tracy, stood up after receiving two votes to Clark's thirty-five and said that he had run because his people had a right to a seat, but now he was ready to make Clark's nomination unanimous. When the resulting vote overwhelmingly favored Clark, Lumpkin and Gaines denounced the convention for its arbitrary proceedings, as well as for its failure to nominate a black candidate. Gaines ended his protest by saying: "Irish and the Dutch are good in their places but [white folks view] blacks [as somebody who] is always there to vote for the white man. Expel me from the party, but I'll never be a Clark man." [31]

Meanwhile, Stevenson and six of the delegates who supported him walked out of the convention before it adjourned. Along with other delegates who were barred from entering the "Clark Padlock Convention," these dissidents called a convention in a nearby Hall. [32] In this rival convention, one of the black candidates, Israel Campbell, withdrew his name in favor of Lewis Stevenson, who the group then unanimously nominated for Congress. Nathan Haller, who would later sit in the Twenty-fourth Legislature, served as the secretary of this convention. When called upon to endorse Stevenson, he said that he was sure attempts had been made by the Clark men to buy delegates, because he had received an offer. Contending that he had never been "for sale since his shackles as a slave had fallen from [his] limbs," Haller urged blacks to stand true and support Stevenson. [33] But Haller was not the only black of note at this convention. Incumbent representative, Richard Williams, was also in attendance. When asked why he supported Stevenson, Williams said that he believed that nine-tenths of the masses of blacks were in support of Stevenson and that he could not go back on his people. [34] After the speech making was over, a Grant and Stevenson Club was formed and Richard Williams and Nathan Haller were named vice-president and secretary, respectively. [35]

One could almost draw a class distinction in this contest for the Third Congressional District, although the lines tended to be blurred by previous conditions of servitude. That is to say Ruby, Cuney, Allen, and Hal Geiger, all fair complexioned, all men of influence sided with the Clark faction; although Allen and Geiger had been slaves, while Ruby was freeborn and Cuney, who was born to a slave mother could be considered quasi-free, inasmuch as his white father had taken him under his wing and had given him a college education. On the other hand, those individuals who followed Matthew Gaines in support of a black man were usually very dark complexioned. Those persons who favored a black candidate, but would accept another white to run in the place of Clark, tended not to be as dark as the Gaines men in complexion. They included James H. Washington, Richard Williams, and Nathan Haller.

When the convention adjourned, Gaines returned to his home district and urged black Republicans to ignore the party's white nominee and to follow him in supporting a black man as their choice. Notwithstanding Gaines' rebellious action when the Clark ratification convention was held, party leaders called upon Gaines to do his bidding toward the nominee. Gaines attended the meeting, but when called upon to speak, instead of endorsing Clark, he denounced the Republican party for its neglect of blacks in their demand for office. Then turning to the predominantly black audience, he said, "We blacks are entitled to a candidate . . . shall we turn the mill forever and somebody else eat the meal." [36] When Gaines was interrupted by J. H. Washington, who attempted to speak in behalf of Stevenson, Gaines made it clear that he was in "favor of bringing both Stevenson and Clark down in favor of a black man." The fact that more blacks did not come to the aid of Gaines in support of a black candidate, or that Texas did not send a black to Congress in 1871, has to be laid at the steps of the black leadership. For blacks made up forty-four percent of the votes in the Third District; the League was not yet broken up; blacks were still in control at the local level and the white votes were split. Though no people is monolithic in views and opinions, it did appear that all signs were "go" for a black Congressman of the Third District if only the black leadership had been more unified.

Black division aside, the contest in the Third District placed the leaders of the Republican party in a precarious position. While they needed white support, they could not afford to lose the backing of blacks who were demanding that they themselves should be nominated and elected to more offices in the party. The result of such discontent was one of the reasons why the Republicans lost all four congressional seats in the election of 1871. After being defeated, the leaders of the party returned to the idea of reorganization. At this time, they did not try to break up the League, but rather they tried to undermine it by creating local clubs such as the National Guard and the Sons of Liberty. It could be argued that these organizations would not have the stigma of a "nigger" organization attached to them and as such would draw white support. Still, the function of these clubs was expected to be no different from that of the League — to deliver greater control over county politics to state officials. In other words, black voters would be delivered without black demands being made upon the party leaders. Congressman Clark probably expressed the sentiment of party leaders best when he said if Republicans would organize such clubs, they would hit "the infidel on the hip."[37] Yet, while these clubs looked good on paper, they were never really effective. These local clubs did not work for the same reasons that the attempt to break up the League had not been successful. Power was the spoiler. Blacks had been triggered into action by attempts to remove their power base at the local level; they would not sit passively by while white leaders worked toward that end.

Tracy, annoyed because he felt that the large number of blacks kept whites out of the party and also because blacks did not accept peacefully and passively their junior status in the party, soon came up with another plan to remove this thorn from his side. This time he sought to control county conventions by electing delegates who would keep whites at the head of the party. He was able to accomplish this task by appointing a large number of school officials at the local level who were able to get firsthand knowledge of what was happening in local politics and as such, were able to devise ways to manipulate county conventions.[38] Apparently, this strategy worked; for the administration had matters firmly in hand when the Republican state convention met in May 1872, to elect delegates to the national convention. Only three blacks were elected, G. T. Ruby, R. Allen, and B. F. Williams. Likewise, there were three members of the permanent organization — J. H. Washington, G. T. Ruby, and R. Allen.[39]

As the Republicans faced fragmentation of the black-white alliance in 1872, the Germans of the Twenty-fifth District challenged the blacks' desire for political control in this predominantly black district. The conflict started when blacks argued that they deserved two of the district seats in the House. In order to avert what appeared to be a split in the party in that district, Colonel J. R. Burns, Republican elector at large, informed James P. Newcomb, secretary of state under Governor E. J. Davis, that the German members of the party were ready to accept one black as a matter of policy, but not two. Burns went on to tell Newcomb that he should allow only one black to run, (with the understanding that this individual would later withdraw) so as to allow not the black constituents, but the district chief executive to nominate state officers who would be more acceptable to whites.[40]

What Burns had failed to realize was that blacks throughout the state were becoming disgruntled with white paternalism and were becoming more concerned with self-determination. A case in point was the action taken by blacks of the Sixteenth Senatorial District which Matt Gaines represented. At this convention, Gaines urged blacks to use their numerical strength to wrest control of the party from the whites. Adhering to the advice of Gaines and ignoring the counsel of

Jacob DeGress who said such a move would be destructive to the party, the black delegates, who outnumbered whites, selected a slate of officers composed entirely of blacks. Afterward, they moved to take over the party for themselves at the local level.[41]

Black leaders' disgruntlement and dissatisfaction with the Republican party could only spell disaster for everyone concerned in the election of state officials in 1873. So, with this in mind, black party faithfuls called the first convention of colored men in Texas in July 1873, to discuss the "moral, commercial and political interest of the black race." At this meeting — presided over by Norris W. Cuney — there were 156 delegates from twenty counties. Officers of the convention were as follows: President, Norris W. Cuney; Vice-Presidents, Matthew Gaines, Richard Allen and John Reed; Secretaries, John Cass and James H. Washington. The Committee on Address included W. C. Richer, W. A. Price, Jacob Freeman, G. T. Ruby, J. J. Hamilton, John DeBruhl, B. F. Williams, R. J. Moore, Coote Jenkins, L. A. Clope, J. J. Webb, Walter Ripetoe, N. W. Cuney, N. H. Haller, J. H. Washington, and Richard Allen, chairman. After discussing the political plight of blacks, the delegates at this convention endorsed the national Republican party. By the same token, they introduced resolutions which denounced men who bartered the rights of blacks and used power for personal gains, citing white Republican legislators and federal office holders as the villains. Even though these black delegates unanimously approved the program of Governor Davis in previous years, they steadfastly refused to endorse Davis for reelection. They did so for two of several reasons. Some felt that the convention had not been called for this purpose. Others were of the opinion that endorsement should not be given because their race had been denied office.[42]

Several Republican newspapers asserted that this convention of colored men had overthrown the "Radical Leadership" of the party. While the convention had not overthrown the leadership, it can be argued that it contributed to its demise. Blacks' aspiration vis-a-vis whites' created an unstable internal situation in the Republican party. Whites had preconceived ideas about the coalition. These misconceptions could easily be seen or shown by the permanent, subordinate, immobile status assigned to blacks. It is not surprising, then, that blacks were never fully satisfied with what white party officials offered them. Consequently, their discontentment would give rise to more black leaders who would demand an equal share of power in the coalition. On the other hand, such a situation would also open up the possibility of manipulation of these black leaders by other white leaders who would attempt to give them what appeared to be more than they gave to others.

[6]

Miscalculation Or Manipulation

Professor Alwyn Barr writes that "in the last quarter of the Nineteenth Century, the Republican party in Texas resembled an iceberg in a Democratic ocean, continuously in existence, [but] often in turmoil beneath the surface."[1] Concurring with Barr, one can argue that part of this turmoil stemmed from the fact that blacks were determined to be treated as copartners in the Republican coalition. The first evidence of this came at the Republican state convention which met in Brenham, on May 25, 1875. Not only did blacks prevent federal office holders from wrestling control of the party, but it was largely due to the support of blacks that the organization continued under the control of Edmund J. Davis until 1883. Concomitant with black demands, desires and efforts to take a more active part in party functions, Norris W. Cuney was appointed secretary to the State Central Committee; B. F. Williams and N. W. Cuney were named members of the Credential Committee and Richard Allen and N. W. Cuney were elected vice-presidents.[2]

Since this was not an election year, the specific purpose of calling this convention was to determine what position, if any, the Republicans should take regarding the proposed constitutional convention. To the chagrin of blacks, the convention did not take a stand on this issue.

Yet, despite this minor setback, as will be shown later, blacks were determined to play a major role in Republican politics. As experience provided knowledge and confidence, blacks pressed for increased recognition in party councils, in the allocation of public offices and in the implementation of public policies relative to the needs of blacks. A look at the activities of blacks in party conventions from 1876–1898 might shed some light on the subject.

When the Republican state convention assembled in Houston in 1876, there was cause for great concern among Republican leaders. Federal office holders and the ever growing influence of blacks in the party presented problems for the old leadership. Shortly after the convention was called to order by Chairman Edmund Davis, a floor fight erupted over the method of selecting delegates for the national convention. White Republican leaders wanted to vote for delegates by acclamation, while blacks wanted to vote for them by counties. In the end, it was blacks who emerged victorious. This was the first sign of an all out war that would be waged by blacks, (who out numbered whites three to one,) for the control of the party in the last quarter of the nineteenth century.

Still, despite the fact that blacks won the floor fight, they did not secure delegates which were commensurate with their number in this convention. There were only two blacks elected from individual districts, Richard Allen and Norris W. Cuney, and two alternates W. H. Holland and Frank Webb. Similarly,.there were no black at-large delegates and only three black alternates, W. A. Price, J. H. Washington, and J. J. Hamilton.[3] The irony about the selection of delegates at this convention was that the bulk of them came from the Davis wing of the party, a faction which relied heavily upon the support of blacks. Why, then, were there not more blacks elected as delegates? The answer to this question may lie in the fact that in many instances blacks were out-marshalled and out-generalled by the presiding officers at the convention who were more knowledgable about parlimentary procedures. A case in point centers around J. G. Tracy, the presiding officer at this and other conventions, who used his position to his advantage. That is to say, he either recognized or failed to recognize any individual he wanted and also in many instances used proxies rather than alternates as voting delegates.[4] By so doing, Tracy was able to manipulate the selection of delegates and thus ensure that there were more white delegates than blacks. On the other hand, it can be argued that in cases where blacks clearly understood the issue, they usually voted and supported measures which affected their destiny. For instance, it was largely due to the efforts of black delegates that this convention incorporated a plank in its platform which opposed the 1875 State Constitution. Likewise, it was because of the efforts of a black delegate and future legislator, W. H. Holland, that the convention supported a plank (although weak) on free public education.⁵

Throughout the post-Reconstruction era, blacks continuously asserted themselves in party conventions, sometimes more than others. For instance, in 1878, they appeared to have been less aggressive than they had been in the previous convention. Their actions were probably due to the fact that the Republicans did not nominate a slate of state candidates that year. Hampered by internal problems and fearing defeat in the election of 1878, Chairman Davis called a meeting of the Republican State Executive Committee and endorsed the Greenback candidate, George W. Jones, for governor.⁶ This decision naturally gave rise to schism within the party. Most federal office holders disagreed with Davis's action and argued that the only way the Republican party of Texas could strengthen its position with the federal government was by placing a ticket in the field. So in keeping with their belief, the federal office holders called their own convention, which met in Dallas in October 1878, and elected a state ticket with A. M. Cochran at the helm.⁷ While most blacks accepted Davis's decision to fuse with an independent candidate, Richard Allen, accepted the second spot on the federal office holder Straight-Out-Republican ticket. It is interesting to note that in both cases — the decision to put a Straight Out Republican ticket in the field and the decision to fuse with Greenbackers — blacks had very little input.

A lack of black participation in party policy could only mean a further schism within the party. Fortunately, the defeat of both the Greenbackers and the Straight-Outs in 1878, played an important role in unifying the Republican party in 1880. When the Republicans met in convention March 24–25, 1880, it appeared that harmony existed; the split between the two factions was healed. Dr. Cochran, Chairman of the Straight-Out Republican ticket, willingly relinquished his position to Edmund J. Davis, Chairman of the Republican Executive Committee. On the other hand, blacks showed up at the convention in record numbers. But despite their numbers, when Davis proceeded with the election of officers for this convention, again blacks would play an active, but not dominating role. Richard Allen and Walter Burton were elected vice-presidents, while Norris W. Cuney and Richard Nelson were made temporary and permanent secretaries, respectively.⁸ A committee of fifteen was appointed to the Platform and Resolution Committee, but only one black, Burton, was part of it. When the election of delegates took place, blacks did not fare any better. Only W. H. Holland was elected as an at-large delegate. N. W. Cuney was selected as a district delegate from Galveston, while Allen was chosen as an alternate delegate from Houston.

Although clearly in the minority, blacks who were elected delegates were not in the least hesitant about letting the convention know that they could not be instructed on how to vote at the national convention. No sooner was a resolution to that effect made than a black delegate took issue with it, stating that: "it is an insult to instruct me how to vote." Cuney agreed, by saying: "My district chose me, but not with any pledge." Allen contended that: "Instructing the delegates came from northern Texas where you have few Republicans. In our [Black Belt] counties we have Republican majorities." [9] The emotion expressed by these blacks was an indication of their growing frustration resulting from being manipulated and used by their white allies.

After the national convention, the State Executive Committee — a committee devoid of blacks — met in Hearne, Texas, on August 25, 1880, to discuss whether or not to place a ticket in the field. After much deliberation, the said committee nominated a state ticket headed by E. J. Davis.[10] As usual, no blacks were nominated for state office. Still, white Republicans expected and did receive the bulk of black votes in the election of 1880. Although Davis was defeated, he received 64,502 votes, which was the largest number of votes polled by a Republican candidate since the election of Democrat Oran M. Roberts.[11] To be sure, blacks had returned to the Grand Old Party after a short honeymoon with the Greenback party in the last election, but they had not returned in numbers equal to that in 1874. The reason was that there were still some blacks who were dissatisfied with the Republican party. Hence, blacks' disgruntlement would impact upon the party's selection of candidates at the next convention.

When the Republicans convened August 23, 1882, it appeared that blacks had come with the intention of taking a very active part in the deliberations and of securing party honors and concessions. They first took on the battle for chairmanship of the State Executive Committee when a black, W. H. Holland, ran unsuccessfully against C. C. Brinkley. Losing in this struggle, blacks turned their attention to the temporary chairmanship. Realizing the importance of this position, two blacks, W. R. Carson and N. W. Cuney, opposed the white candidate, Webster Flanagan. In the end, Cuney emerged victorious. Following the advice of former Governor Davis, the majority of blacks went along with the idea of not placing a ticket in the field. Instead, a committee headed by Cuney was formed to confer with anti-Bourbon Democrats to ascertain who would be the best candidate to support. This committee, of which Richard Allen was a member, chose George

W. Jones, an independent and former Greenbacker, as the candidate that the party would endorse.[12]

Since no nomination was made for a state ticket at this convention, there was a lot of time left for speechmaking and blacks did not fail to take advantage of this situation. Among those addressing the convention were R. J. Evans, John DeBruhl, and N. W. Cuney. Evans made a plea for the establishment of the colored branch university. Hence, his speech set a precedent which was to follow almost continually for the next twenty years on this issue. DeBruhl, concerned with segregation in schools, made a motion that the convention go on record for opposing the law which provided for segregation in public schools. When Chairman Tracy ruled the motion out of order, DeBruhl delivered an eloquent speech on this subject, but was voted down unanimously. Cuney, then, addressed the convention regarding the exclusion of blacks from the jury. But, however much blacks might have pleaded the cause of their constituents, when the platform was adopted, it was freed of any concessions to blacks except the one proposed by Cuney.[13]

Black failure in the above regard did not mean that blacks had been passive in this convention. It simply meant another case of blacks being outnumbered on the Platform and Resolution Committee, and out-marshalled by the presiding officer. To wit, blacks made a concerted effort to be seen, heard and accepted as copartners in the coalition. Nowhere was this attempt better evidenced than in the crisis that arose over the seating of the Dallas delegation. There were three delegations from Dallas at this convention, known respectively as the Cochran Wing, the Norton Wing, and the Colored Independent. After much confusion, discussion, and deliberation, the Cochran and the Colored delegations were seated. For blacks, the seating of their delegation was more than a victory. It was a test of their strength as well as an indication of things to come, that is, the drawing of the color line.[14]

Blacks and whites were in open opposition when the Republican state convention convened in Fort Worth on April 29, 1884. Among many issues on which they were divided was the replacement of Edmund J. Davis (who had died in February 1883) as party leader. This matter, however, was resolved early and quickly when blacks voted solidly for Norris W. Cuney. The two races were further divided when Cuney's delegation was seated over A. G. Mallory's. Mallory, who had been unable to control the Republican county convention in Galveston had bolted this county convention and held one of his own, at which time he selected a delegation to attend the Fort Worth meeting. Without knowing the reasons for the presence of Mallory's delegation, the Credential Committee recognized it on the first day of the convention. When Cuney heard of the decision of the committee, he presented a minority report to the General Assembly, explained how Mallory's delegation had been selected and asked that his delegation be seated over his opponent. His plea to his fellow delegates to follow the "dictates of fairness," eventually paid off. When the votes were taken, the minority report was adopted by a vote of 247 to 203.[15] To be sure, the color line had been drawn, even to the extent that blacks sat on one side of the convention hall while whites sat on the other.

Before the convention got down to its specific purpose of electing delegates to the national convention, blacks met in a secret caucus in a building near convention hall in order to devise a strategy to secure more delegates to the national convention, preferably twenty-two out of the twenty-six. Under the leadership of Richard Allen and Burriell Johnson, blacks threatened to bolt the convention if they were not given their fair share of delegates. When the election of delegates took place, blacks received nine out of the twenty-six: N. W. Cuney, Richard Allen, R. J. Evans, J. R. Ferris, H. C. Ferguson, W. H. Blount, J. R. Carter, Samuel McCoy and W. W. Davis.[16] This number was a far cry from the twenty-two delegates which they were seeking, but still it was more than anything they had received before. Such action on the part of the black leadership further illustrated their growing political sophistication, as well as their determination to dominate the party.

When the Republicans assembled in convention again in the fall of 1884 to discuss the ticket issue, black presence, strength and influence were again manifested. Black presence was clearly seen when seven hundred black delegates, as compared to seventy-five whites, paraded in downtown Houston at the start of the convention. Black influence was felt throughout the convention, but it was most especially demonstrated when blacks, adhering to the advice of their leader, rejected a motion by a vote of 80 to 308 to place a Republican ticket in the field in 1884.[17] Black leaders who favored rejection were N. W. Cuney, R. A. Kerr, C. M. Ferguson, John DeBruhl, and Willie Davis. By far, the most adamant on this issue was DeBruhl, who argued that placing a ticket in the field would be suicidal to the Republican party.

When the convention debunked the idea of nominating a state ticket, federal office holders, as well as dissatisfied blacks and whites bolted the convention and issued a call for one of their own. On September 23, 1884, this Straight-Out Republican convention nominated a slate of all white candidates, save R. J. Evans, who was chosen to run as land commissioner on the ticket. With the exception of Evans's candidacy, this convention did not show any particular interest in blacks. Still the majority of the followers were black, while the leaders were white. As was the case in the Regular Republican Convention headed by Cuney, blacks were given only a small number of offices within the organization. Melvin Wade and Robert Armstrong, both blacks, were made vice-presidents, while Richard Allen was appointed to the Address Committee.[18]

Having been defeated in the election of 1884, leaders of the Republican party decided to regroup. Accordingly, the state nominating convention which met in Waco, August 25, 26, 1886, saw a return of many bolters to the Grand Old Party. By the same token, the convention also saw continued disagreement between black and white delegates. Speaking figuratively about what happened at this convention, the editor of the *Dallas Daily News* said: "There was a square up and down fight between the colored and white and the latter went down on the first round."[19] This editor was referring to the floor fight which erupted over an attempt to fill three important positions at this convention — Texas National Committeeman, Chairman of the State Executive Committee and the Permanent Chairman of the convention. In the election of each of these posts, black numerical strength was the deciding factor. The first position, being the most prestigious and desirable was sought by Norris W. Cuney, who ran against O. T. Logans of Grayson County. Cuney, backed by African Americans, was able to capture the office of National Committeemen without any difficulty. Afterward, he maneuvered his forces into awarding the second place, Chairman of the State Executive Committee, to his friend, Judge J. B. Rector. As to the last position, it was Cuney who placed the name of A. J. Rosenthal before the convention as permanent chairman, and with Cuney's organizational backing, Rosenthal won even though he had opposition from many whites of the party.[20]

Except for Cuney, in a pattern that would be followed throughout the period from 1875 to 1900, blacks were victorious in securing positions in the temporary organization of the party, but were usually defeated in their quest for the permanent spots. For example, C. M. Ferguson became temporary chairman and A. White, was chosen as temporary secretary at the 1886 convention. By the same token, Samuel Austin, H. T. Richardson and W. A. Hill were all defeated in their bid for permanent secretaries. They were made assistants instead. On the Platform and Resolutions Committee, there were only two blacks out of a total of eleven members, W. H. Blount and N. W. Cuney. The Credential Committee had a lone black member, Walter Burton.[21] Still, whites expressed fear and dissatisfaction over what they regarded as "black domination" of the party. This emotion was expressed amidst the fact that the convention nominated all white men to the ticket and made no reference to blacks in the party platform. Instead of the above fear dissipating, it widened in 1888. It grew in large part because blacks would not back down in their demands for their fair share in the coalition. Thus, when the convention met in Fort Worth on April 24–25, 1888, blacks were again able to secure nine out of twenty-six delegates to attend the Republican National Convention. The district delegates were M. A. Baker, Joshua Houston, Alexander Asberry, H. C. Ferguson, A. J. Johnson, M. M. Rogers and W. H. Blount; N. W. Cuney and C. M. Ferguson were chosen as at-large delegates. Again in this convention, Cuney's delegation was seated over Mallory's. But following the same pattern as before, permanent positions went to whites, while temporary ones went to blacks. The only difference was that this time, only one black W. A. Pete, was elected to a temporary post.[22]

When the Republicans met again in convention September 20, 1888, to discuss the issue of a state ticket, Jacob DeGress, Chairman of the State Executive Committee, wanted a straight-out ticket, but was overruled by Cuney, Texas National Committeeman, who expressed a desire to support an independent candidate, Marion Martin.[23] The ticket faction of the party, then, accused the non-ticket faction of introducing fradulent voters and proxies to gain control of the convention. But this was not the case. Clearly, Cuney had the votes on his side. More than this, whites had not yet come to the realization that blacks were willing and ready to follow a black leader. Losing the Texas National Committeeman position to Cuney was bad enough, But losing on the ticket issue was a pain in the neck, because the latter defeat placed whites in a precarious position. They could not afford to bolt the convention because such action would have meant alienation from federal patronage. Thus, they were forced to take whichever candidate Cuney had to offer them or split into their own party.

If the state convention in September prepared the way for a split within the rank and file of the Republican party, the presidential election of 1888 brought matters to a climax. This occurred when President Benjamin Harrison appointed Cuney as Collector of Customs of Galveston, one of the most powerful positions in the South. Whites, fearful of Cuney's power and jealous of his possible role in the distribution of future patronage, broke rank to organize a white man's Republican party in Houston, November 30, 1889.[24] This was the beginning of what Cuney called the "Lily White" movement in Texas. To some extent, the fear of the Lily Whites was not justified, because while Cuney was in control of Customs appointments, white minority leaders were in charge of the Justice and Internal Revenue appointments of the state. It may be surmised from their actions that the Lily Whites wanted all or nothing.

Meanwhile, the Lily Whites attended the Regular Republican party convention held on September 3–5, 1890 at San Antonio. The purpose of their presence was to wrest control of this organization. But the black majority at the convention showed the Lily Whites that like "a tree planted by the waters, they would not be moved." Consequently, all of the positions at the convention were filled by Cuney's men, while none of the Lily Whites contesting delegations from Harris, Bexar, and Dallas counties were seated.[25] Failing to be recognized, the leader of the Harris County delegation, Dr. Max Urwitz, walked out of the convention and accused Cuney of running the party for federal officeholders.[26] In order to bring the party together, Cuney made some concessions that would later come back to haunt him. First, he gave his blessing to Sam J. Wright, a former Lily White, to be elected permanent chairman. Secondly, he shied away from some racial issues which would have benefited blacks. For example, when blacks made an attempt to get the convention to declare itself against the demands of Democrats for separate railroad coaches for the races, this resolution was rebuffed by Cuney who felt that it would be unwise to further agitate the race question at that time. Similarly when an effort was made by some blacks to nominate a black Superintendent of Public Instruction, it failed because leaders of the party felt that the Lily Whites would probably not bolt if they had an all-white ticket.[27] In making these concessions the black leadership misconstrued the motives of the Lily Whites. What concerned these whites was not the civil rights of blacks, but what they called "black domination" of the party. Moreover, it seems unlikely that black leaders would make concessions on their civil rights when blacks outnumbered whites three to one at this convention. The flaw in their leadership was not that they made concessions, but that they did not receive nor were they promised anything in return.

At the state convention March 8, 1892, which met to select delegates to the Republican National Convention, blacks remained in complete control. Even though the Lily whites had called a separate reform convention for April, they were in attendance at this regular convention.[28] Lily Whites came because they realized that any movement that they might undertake was contingent upon the approval of the National Executive Committee. If they were to have any claims of recognition on the national level, then it was necessary for them to go to the convention and try to have their delegation seated. But if they had any hopes of securing recognition at this convention, they were sadly mistaken. Not only were blacks in the majority, but they were instructed by county conventions to vote for black men as delegates to the national convention. Since counties were allowed to send delegates in proportion to the number of votes cast for the Republican ticket in the previous presidential election, the counties in the Black Belt area had a preponderance of influence. Thus, four of the eight at-large delegates were black: They were N. W. Cuney, Alexander Asberry, Charles M. Ferguson, and C. F. Choce. Reminiscent of a statement made by an elated black in regard to their victory in the last convention that "we got them white folks where the hair is short," [29] another black of this convention quipped: "The boys had a great success at Austin and re-elected Alex Asberry to the national convention." [30] So well were Cuney forces organized that none of the contesting delegations were seated, not even the one led by a black, Charles Ferguson of Fort Bend County.

At this point whites realized that the only way for them to take over the party was to divide the colored voters. Hence, they sought to do this by supporting Charles M. Ferguson in his bid for temporary chairmanship of the convention against Norris Wright Cuney. But the efforts of Ferguson were soundly curtailed as Cuney won handily.[31] Having lost on all issues, the Lily Whites decided to go ahead with their reform convention on April 12, 1892 and to elect delegates to be sent to the national convention. At the national meeting, the regular Texas delegates easily defeated the Lily Whites for the right to represent the state.[32] Coupled with this victory, Cuney won reelection as National Committeeman for another four years.

When Republicans met in Fort Worth, in the fall of 1892, to discuss the ticket issue, Cuney was at the peak of his power. But when he announced that he would support conservative Democrat, George Clark, his power and influence began to dissipate even among his black supporters. While the majority of blacks went along with Cuney in not putting a ticket in the field, they could not understand why Cuney would not support the more progressive Democrat, James S. Hogg. Neither Clark nor Hogg expressed great concern for blacks, but Hogg had at least made gestures toward eliminating lynching from the state. So, to many blacks, he was the lesser of two evils. Apparently, Cuney misread or miscalculated the events of the time. For in the fall of 1892, he backed two losers, George Clark and President Benjamin Harrison. Harrison's defeat cost Cuney the control of Texas patronage. This setback, coupled with the animosity of the Lily Whites toward him, and blacks' discontent with his leadership, meant that Cuney would soon be eliminated as a force in Texas politics.

Under the disguise of reconciliation, Lily Whites of the party seized upon the division among the rank and file of Cuney's organization and called for a meeting of all Republican factions on June 12–13, 1894. With both Regular and Lily White Republicans in attendance, it was not long before this meeting came to naught. It failed because Lily Whites refused to seat interracial delegations and insisted on a census plan of representation that would create a majority of white delegates. This plan called for two delegates at-large, one white and one black from each county with a Republican organization, plus one additional delegate from 250 or a fraction of votes over 100 cast for President Harrison in 1892, to be divided between whites and blacks in proportion to the white and black population of the county.[33] Such a plan was naturally unacceptable to blacks who made up the majority of the votes in the Republican party.

Unable to reach an agreement, both factions proceeded with plans to hold separate state conventions. The Lily Whites group met on August 6, 1894, in Dallas with about 150 delegates in attendance. Interestingly, one of the first actions taken by this group was to change its name from Lily White to the Republican party of Texas. Before adjourning, they nominated a full slate of candidates for State office and adopted a platform, which among other things advocated the setting up of an independent black Republic. Twenty-two days later, the Regular Republicans also convened in Dallas. At this gathering, Cuney was still very much in control. If he had lost some support among the rank and file due to his endorsement of the candidacy of George Clark, the census plan of the Lily Whites served as a stimulant in placing him at the forefront of the Republican party when it convened August 28–29, 1894.

That Cuney was in charge became clear when he ran against J. B. Moore for the chairmanship of the State Executive Committee. Moore had been elected to that post two years earlier over Cuney's protest, because he was able to secure the help of C. M. Ferguson and his followers. This time, when Moore decided to seek reelection, he wrote a letter to the Lily Whites and invited them to come to the convention to help him oust Cuney. Somehow Cuney got a copy of this letter and when he arrived in Dallas, he told reporters that he was going to work against the reelection of Moore. Realizing Cuney's control over blacks and knowing that unless he could win some blacks over to his side that he would be defeated, Moore made a bid for the colored votes by announcing in his opening speech that he was in favor of a black man as president of the convention. Next, he made an attempt to stack the Credentials Committee with his friends in order to ensure his reelection. In an effort to counter Moore's last move, Cuney came up with his own candidate, John Grant of Denton, Texas. Afterwards, Cuney called his followers of seven to eight hundred blacks together and denounced the tactics used by Moore to stack the committee. When the election was held, Grant received 368 votes to 247 for Moore. More than that, a full slate ticket was nominated with the blessing of Cuney and his lieutenants.[34]

Despite their numerical strength, blacks made very few attempts to nominate other blacks at the convention of 1894. Except for H. M. Broiles who was nominated for Superintendent of Public Instructions, but withdrew in favor of another black, A. H. Colwell, and C. P. Williams, who was mentioned for Attorney General, but declined, all the other nominees were white — most of whom were nominated by blacks. In accordance with black appointments in past years, only three blacks were named to the State Executive Committee, William M. McDonald, John Caine, and Henry Ferguson. The lone black on the Platform Committee was Charles Ferguson. In this convention, blacks won some battles, lost some and blundered through others. They were successful in persuading the convention to pass a resolution condemning the law passed by previous Democratic legislatures which prevented blacks from becoming school trustees. Likewise, a resolution calling for the creation of the color branch university was accepted. To the contrary, the convention was not so receptive to a resolution condemning separate railway coaches. On the other hand, even though the black leadership did not and could not visualize it at the time, Cuney blundered when he chose John Grant as chairman of the State Executive Committee, because Grant would later challenge Cuney's legitimacy in the party.[35]

That more blacks did not move quickly and precipitously to nominate and elect more blacks to major offices in this convention, as well as in previous ones where they had the numerical strength to do so, probably reflects the extent to which they were themselves divided by suspicion of each other that sometimes rivaled those which they harbored about their white colleagues. These occasional failures may reflect a deeper problem than a mere lack of aggressiveness. Nowhere was this better evidenced than in the next Republican convention.

When the convention of Regular Republicans met on March 24, 1896, it turned out to be one of conflict between the Cuney and anti-Cuney forces. The upcoming presidential campaign between William McKinley and William B. Allison which started in 1895, played a large role in this fight. In that year Marc Hanna, William McKinley's campaign manager, sought unsuccessfully for the support of the Texas Republican organization via Norris Cuney. Cuney turned a deaf ear to Hanna because he had promised to support his friend and old acquaintance, William Allison.[36] In part because of Cuney's choice of candidate, many of his black and white supporters began to desert him. For instance, James Flanagan and John Grant joined the McKinley forces. At the Seventh Congressional District Convention, blacks argued over whether or not to support McKinley or to side with Cuney in favor of Allison. While Cuney thought that he had control of the majority of black voters in the First Congressional District, the election returns showed that the counties of Bee, Bastrop, and Washington gave their support to McKinley.[37]

Feeling somewhat uneasy because of what had occurred in the county conventions prior to March 24, 1896, Cuney called his men together two days before the Republican state convention assembled, and mapped out a strategy of how he was going to control the convention. This discipline of his organization paid off when the State Executive Committee recommended Cuney for temporary chairman and Cuney beat A. J. Rosenthal by a 573 to 205 vote. It is well to remember that Cuney won not by black votes alone. He was also elevated to that post with the support of Thomas B. Reed, Speaker of the United State House Representative and William B. Allison, a presidential candidate. The Reed and Allison men joined forces against the McKinley men to achieve this desired result. Before the above vote was taken, however, a bargain was made by Cuney to put Reed men as chairmen of a number of important committees in return for their support of him as temporary chairman. This deal was implemented by William McDonald, a supporter of Reed. Consequently, the following Reed men received chairmanships: R. B. Hawley, Resolution Committee; W. M. McDonald, Credential Committee; and J. P. Elliott, Permanent Organization. In the end, this coalition proved beneficial to Cuney because the Credential Committee unseated all contesting Lily White or anti-Cuney delegations. Later, the temporary officers were made permanent, a move which put Cuney in full control of the convention.[38]

Because of both Cuney's and Credential Committee's actions, McKinley delegates openly denounced the proceedings of the convention. They also protested because Cuney ruled against the pro-McKinley minority report on the grounds that it had been written after the convention had adjourned and, therefore, was invalid. They were further angered when one of Cuney's men, E. Henry Terrell of San Antonio, handed another of his supporters, Eugene Marshall, a list of at-large and alternate delegates to the national convention. Cuney quickly recognized Marshall who read the following names on the back of the envelope. The at-large delegates were N. W. Cuney, W. K. Makemson, E. H. Terrell, and H. C. Ferguson. The alternates were C. D. Keyes, F. W. Gross, B. F. Caine, and W. F. Smith. Cuney hurriedly pushed through a motion for approval and declared the slate elected.[39] When that happened, all hell broke loose. A group of about one hundred McKinley supporters squeezed around Cuney in an attempt to take over the convention. It was a free-for-all brawl. Some men beat Cuney with their fists; others beat Webster Flanagan. One black man held a gun on another black who had been beating Cuney with his cane. At this moment, the police stepped in and rescued Cuney. Cuney, then, made a short speech and adjourned the convention by a voice vote.[40]

Immediately after Cuney and his supporters left, Dr. John Grant, whom Cuney had elevated to state chairmanship in 1894, called the

McKinley supporters together in another convention. Richard Allen was elected chairman of the new convention. The proceedings of this convention were very short in that they simply allowed for election of a slate of delegates and instructed then to vote for William McKinley. Robert L. Smith, a black representative, was placed on the Platform and Resolutions Committee and was chosen as a delegate to the national convention. Another black receiving honors at this convention was the first black Presidential elector, A. H. Colwell.[41] A few days later, the Lily Whites held their own convention and nominated their delegates to the national convention. Thus, Texas sent three delegations to the national convention: those of Cuney, McKinley, and the Lily Whites. Grant did not represent the Regular Republicans, but still his delegation was chosen over the others.[42] This action was taken because Mark Hanna was Chairman of the Credentials Committee and had not forgiven Cuney for his refusal to support McKinley. At this point, it became obvious that Cuney had lost his grip on the party. To add insult to injury, Dr. John Grant was appointed Texas National Committeeman for the next four years.

To be sure, this was the beginning of the end for Cuney and he knew it. Before the convention assembled for its state gathering to discuss the ticket issue in the fall of 1896, Cuney made a valiant attempt to regain control of the party by openly supporting McKinley's candidacy. But his plea for harmony came too late. Whites had already gathered their forces against him and had done equally well in promoting opposition of Cuney among blacks. Thus, when the nomination for temporary chairman was made, whites pitted Henry C. Ferguson against Cuney. There was nothing wrong in Ferguson aspiring for this position, but it seemed that he was doing so only to appease Lily Whites who had manipulated him. When he arrived at the convention, Ferguson told reporters that: "It is time for Cuney and Bill McDonald to step down and I have come to help that downfall." It was not surprising, then, that with the backing of whites and some blacks, when the votes were taken, Cuney went down in defeat. Ferguson won by a vote of 373 (and one-third) to 205 (and one-half).[43]

For those who believed that Cuney's overthrow would mean a change in the status of blacks within the party, they were sadly mistaken. Those who rose to the helm of leadership did not do any more for blacks in terms of electing and nominating blacks to office than had been the case when Cuney was in power. As usual, the number of blacks elected to significant positions was small. For example, while four blacks, R. L. Smith, W. Easton, M. W. Lawson, and J. T. Harrison, were nominated as secretaries to the Executive Committee, none were elected. Since the decision was left up to the committee, it chose only one black as secretary, William McDonald.⁴⁴ Likewise, no attempts were made either by Ferguson or other blacks in positions of power to push through resolutions or planks that could be incorporated into the platform which would affect the civil rights of blacks. In part because of the lack of black assertiveness in this regard, the only plank in the platform which dealt with the interest of Afro-Americans was one which said: "We insist that laws should be specifically enacted, extending to our colored youths the opportunities of a university education." ⁴⁵ Apparently, this was simply a gesture made by the party to get black votes.

Without a doubt, Cuney had been defeated in the 1896 convention, but still his influence was not dead. Consequently, Cuney and McDonald forces combined with E. H. R. Green's money and elected the latter chairman of the State Executive Committee in the fall of 1896. This victory was short-lived because when the ticket issue came up, Cuney and McDonald lost to the fusion faction. It was alleged by some newspapers that the reason the Republican party did not want a ticket in the field that year was because blacks wanted important places on the ticket. Whether or not this was true is uncertain. What was true was that in the absence of Green, Cuney, and McDonald, a plenary committee voted five to four for fusion with the Populist ticket. In light of the action taken, McDonald refused to accept the fusion agreement and resigned from the Executive Committee. Hurt, humiliated and defeated, Cuney died one year later. Cuney's biographer alleges that the Republican National Party played a large role in this state convention of Texas, by making compromises to give the Lily Whites more votes in the party and keeping the black boss, Cuney, down.⁴⁶ There may have been some validity to this assertion. When Republicans assembled in Austin in 1898, this convention was not only marked by a majority of white delegates for the first time in thirty-one years, but also by a reunion of Lily Whites and regular Republicans. Moreover, in 1897, H. F. McGregor had written James Newcomb that the course of the Lily Whites would depend on whether Cuney lived or died; that if Cuney died, blacks would no longer be a controlling factor in the party.⁴⁷ As McGregor wrote this letter, Cuney was dying, but he made his adversaries wait until March 4, 1898.

Prior to the convention of 1898, McDonald had sent out a circular letter suggesting the reelection of Green as chairman of the State Executive Committee and calling for better treatment of blacks within the party. After reading this letter, Lily Whites and former Lily Whites quickly came to the conclusion that McDonald only wanted to take the place of Cuney.⁴⁸ Thus, they not only rejected the content of the letter, but they used it as a unifying factor. Because of this letter, R. B. Hawley and John Grant put aside their differences and worked to defeat the Green–McDonald faction for the control of the convention. This same Hawley–Grant faction had pitted Charles M. Ferguson against William McDonald for temporary chairman. Then, in an ironic twist of events, Hawley turned around and supported Green's reelection as chairman of the Executive Committee. Neither Hawley nor many other whites saw Hawley's support of Green as a contradiction. To them, this action was only in keeping with the objective of the party, to turn over, if not complete control, then, certainly the major offices, to whites.[49]

Feeling somewhat secure that within a short period of time they would be in total control of the party, many Lily Whites now said that they were willing to forget the color line. On the other hand, most blacks felt insulted and saddened that their status as copartners, which they had fought so hard to establish, was being eroded before their very eyes. More painfully, they experienced bitterness as a divisive element — the McDonald–Ferguson controversy — ripped through their majority within the party which had allowed them to assume control and leadership for thirteen years. In an attempt to do something about the untenable position of blacks, Dr. A. G. Mosley of Dallas organized the Republican Protective League: the purpose of which was to find out why, since Cuney's departure, not a single black held a top flight position in the party.[50] Not only were the efforts of Mosley aborted in this attempt, but Ferguson aided and abetted the cause of the Lily Whites by boasting of his minor and temporary position, saying, "I don't understand any color in my profession." [51] By contrast A. J. McCauley, a black supporter of McDonald, argued that the greatest enemy of the black was not the Democrats, but those whites who had withdrawn to form the Lily White party and those blacks who indirectly joined forces with them.[52] A white Democrat, Louis J. Worthman, shared the same view when he wrote that: "It is true that a Negro was made temporary chairman, [but this was solidified by R. B. Hawley]. Had it not been for the fact that the defeat of a colored delegate from Hawley's District [would] imperil his chances for returning to Congress, Ferguson would have been put to sleep by Judge Ogden." [53] A. J. McCauley, probably summed up the situation best when he argued, with much logic, that the same force that had supported Ferguson in his ousting of McDonald would come back to conquer him.[54]

In sum, it can be said that if the death of Cuney marked the onset of a decline in the influence of blacks in the Republican party, the McDonald–Ferguson quarrel signaled an acceleration of the process. So blacks went into the twentieth century with a shattered leadership, with their status as equal partners in the coalition in jeopardy, and with a sense that they were not the manipulators but the manipulated. At a time during which disfranchisement of blacks became legal and division among blacks in the Republican party became acute, blacks were easily manipulated by the very force which had opposed them all along — a force that sought to make the Republican party more respectable, but at the same time more white — Lily White.

[7]

Fusion or Fission

Depending upon the forces and circumstances, fusion politics can take on several meanings. For Texas Republicans in the last quarter of the nineteenth century, it was a strategy employed to regain control of the state. After being reduced to minority status in 1874, leaders of the Grand Old Party turned to the game of practical politics by fusing with various third parties or supporting Independent candidates to overthrow the Bourbon Regime. For some blacks, fusion politics, based upon the arithmetic of political bargaining, was another way of getting elected to state office. To wit, they availed themselves of the first opportunity which presented itself, that is, the Greenback party. The Greenback party, which drew most of its strength from discontented farmers and advocates of soft money, was first established in Texas in 1878. This party was especially attractive to blacks because it advocated improved schools, suffrage rights, and the protection of every citizen irrespective of race, color or creed. Moreover, in an attempt to gain black votes, the Greenbackers made concessions to blacks by nominating and placing them on their state ticket. The result was that five of the eight blacks who won seats to the House in the Sixteenth Legislature were elected on the Greenback ticket.

Because the Greenback party consisted of many diverse elements (tenants farmers, disgruntled Democrats, and soft money men), the election of 1878 was probably the best time during post-Reconstruction for blacks to capitalize on the split in the white vote. But not all blacks took advantage of this opportunity. By 1878, the black leadership was completely divided between Greenbackers, Republicans, and Democrats. For example, while Shack Roberts came out openly for the Democratic gubernatorial candidate, Richard Coke, and Richard Allen embraced the Straight-Out Republicans, Walter Burton, Jacob Freeman, and Jeremiah J. Hamilton followed the mandate of Edmund J. Davis in supporting a Greenback candidate for governor.[1] Friction between black leaders during this election was probably best exemplified when a fight erupted at a political rally in Hearne, Texas, between Richard Allen and Hal Geiger. Allen, who had accepted the second spot on the Straight-Out Republican ticket, was addressing a mixed audience of Greenbackers and Republicans when Geiger stood up and told his followers to take Allen out and "Hang [the SOB] if he attempts to speak again." The candidate for Lieutenant Governor, then took shelter in the arms of the city officials, Mayor A. Bailey and Marshall E. Bishop. Authorities were later called in, at which time Geiger was arrested and charged with bulldozing and striking Allen. He was later tried before a Greenback judge and was aquitted for a lack of evidence.[2]

Not only was the black leadership split over fusion, but the followers were split as well. In Harrison County, black voters were split between Republicans and Greenbackers. At Liberty Baptist Church, five miles south of Marshall, Texas a joint meeting was held on November 2, 1878, between the two contending groups in an attempt to reconcile their differences, but nothing was accomplished. The meeting broke up with Republicans and Greenbackers accusing each other of being uncooperative.[3] In Robertson County, a similar situation existed. Blacks were split straight down the middle in their support of the Greenback and Republican parties. The contest between the two was further complicated when Robertson County sent sixty black delegates to the Dallas convention which nominated a Straight-Out Republican state ticket in opposition to the Regular Republicans who fused with Greenbackers.[4]

It must be emphasized that more often than not, whenever a black politician of influence canvassed the field in support of a particular party in 1878, that party usually was victorious. For example, in Brazos County, where Elias Mayes campaigned and was elected on the Greenback ticket, not one vote was cast for the Republican party. Similarly, Andrew Sledge and A. B. Guy joined the Greenback bandwagon in Washington County and won as a result of a split in the white votes. The campaign efforts of Hal Geiger and R. J. Evans also resulted in a

Greenback victory for themselves as well as other blacks in Robertson and Grimes counties. Moreover the Greenback candidate for governor carried Republican Bastrop County largely due to the efforts of Robert A. Kerr, who was secretary of the Greenback club in that county. On the other hand, in Fort Bend County where Walter Burton was recognized as one of the prominent black leaders, the Regular Republicans carried that county and B. F. Williams was elected to the House. A similar situation existed in Harris County, the home of Richard Allen. There, Greenbackers did not receive any votes.[5]

Even though the Greenbackers made a good showing in terms of electing blacks to office in 1878, they did not win the race for governor. Consequently the leadership of the Republican party decided not to fuse with the Greenbackers in 1880, but rather placed a ticket in the field. The result of which was that most of the black leaders who had canvassed the field for the Greenback party would now return to the Republican camp. Among the few blacks who remained visible in the Greenback fold were Hal Geiger and R. A. Kerr. When the Greenback party met in June 1880, to nominate a state ticket, Kerr's name was placed on the ticket as representative from Bastrop. Geiger, on the other hand, had a little more politicking to do before his name could be placed on the ballot. Thus, when the Greenback state convention reconvened in September 1880, Geiger seized the opportunity for which he had been looking. After the first session of the General Assembly, Geiger took blacks to a nearby church and solicited their support for his reelection. This strategy apparently worked. Before the convention adjourned, Geiger was nominated for a seat in the House.[6]

During the campaign of 1880, Norris W. Cuney urged blacks not to follow Hal Geiger because, as he put it: "Geiger was the cause of dissension among blacks who would otherwise probably follow the lead of Davis and vote the Republican party." In Cuney's opinion, Geiger seems to have been making the contest one between Greenbackers and Republicans.[7] This statement was creditable enough to cause Geiger to lose in the general election, but in truth, the Greenback party offered little or no competition for the Republicans. Not only did black leaders' support for the Greenback party begin to wane in 1880, but also, so did that of the masses of blacks. Whereas in 1878, the Greenbackers captured nearly half of the black votes, the Greenback candidates for governor in 1880 carried only three predominately black counties, Walker, Montgomery, and San Jacinto. The Greenbackers elected one senator and three representatives, only one of whom was black — R. A. Kerr.[8]

Even though Republicans elected two senators and eight representatives in 1880, they still lost the gubernatorial race. With this defeat, the grounds for fusion were laid for the next election. Yet many blacks had mixed reaction about fusion. Some blacks opposed fusion on the grounds that the instruction to fuse Texas Republicans with independent candidates came from the national office in Washington. Other blacks argued that if the Republican state ticket would include independent candidates, then, a Republican ticket should be placed at the county level. Still others opposed fusion because they realized that white independents would not vote for blacks even if they ran on the same ticket.[9] Opposition aside, the Republican leadership decided to support George W. Jones, an Independent, as their candidate for governor in 1882. While Jones received an almost solid backing from blacks, blacks did not receive support from the Independents. This became apparent when only two blacks — R. J. Moore and George Wyatt — won state offices and two others — R. J. Evans and R. A. Kerr — ran on the Republican ticket for reelection in a losing cause.[10]

Inspired by Jones's campaign in 1882, Greenback and Republican leaders discussed the possibility of solidifying their loose coalition into a new party for the next election. But about the only thing that came out of this effort was that Republican delegates, by a vote of 308 to 80, decided to support the candidacy of Jones again in 1884. As in previous years, the black leaders were again split over fusion. Shack Roberts, R. J. Evans, Richard Allen, and Walter Burton were opposed to it, while Robert A. Kerr, James Washington, and William H. Holland were in favor of it.[11] Many blacks, including some of their leaders, had not yet come to the realization that supporting an independent candidate was not helping their cause. At the same time, there were some blacks, as well as some disgruntled whites who had begun to question the feasibility and the viability, as well as the chances of success of an independent party.

By the time the election of 1886 rolled around, most disgruntled Democrats had returned to their party in hope that a stronger Democratic party could and would achieve the same goals that they were seeking in a third party. Meanwhile, blacks who were still disillusioned with the Republican party and who could no longer depend upon the Greenback party, or other third parties, defected to the Democratic camp. One such example of this defection was a group of Bastrop County blacks who organized themselves into a Democratic club before the election of 1886. A similar movement had begun in Washington County in August 1884. White Democrats of that county established the People's party and invited all citizens to join "irrespective of politics." This fusionist party proposed to replace dishonest "Radical Rule" with a people's administration that would be responsive to the needs of all its citizens. The People's party ticket strengthened its position when its leaders decided in 1886 to support R. J. Moore, a black incumbent, for reelection to the state legislature. This maneuver not only made the plea for a people's administration appear genuine, but more importantly it enabled the party to gain a few black converts, but no members of any significance. Thus, R. J. Moore, the people's candidate, was pitted against W. H. Blount, a black Republican.[12] Moore, who was running for the third time, had fallen out of favor with the Republicans and saw the Democratic People's party as a way of remaining in politics. It should be noted at this point that his flirtation with Democrats did not do anything positive for blacks. Moore won not because he ran on the People's ticket, but because blacks voted for him. Had not Moore run for reelection, Blount would have easily won, thus giving Washington County its black representative anyway. Moreover, Moore's election did not prevent the Twentieth Legislature from being all white, because H. A. P. Bassett, a black candidate, was elected from Grimes County that same year.

Notwithstanding the fact that black flirtation with the Democratic and Greenback parties was short-lived, interest in independent candidates among the black Republican leadership continued through the 1890s. Yet while Republicans used a number of tactics and strategies to overthrow the Bourbon regime, no real threat came to that hegemony until 1890. In that year, James S. Hogg, former Attorney General, was nominated for Governor by the Democratic party and subsequently won election against Republican Webster Flanagan. If Hogg's election, as well as his philosophy, created unrest within his party, his establishment of a Railroad Commission in 1891, caused a three-way split within the Democratic party. The first faction consisted of the Bourbons. Led by George Clark, they sought to regain control of the leadership of the party by opposing the commission. The Farmer Alliance, the second faction, was opposed to the commission of the grounds that it was appointive rather than elective. The third faction was regarded as the progressive wing of the party. It consisted of businessmen and young professional politicians who believed that Hogg's policy regarding the commission best represented their views. To be sure, democracy had begun to divide. So when the election of 1892 came up, Norris W. Cuney, leader of the Republicans, had good reason to believe that fusion would work.

However, by 1892, the whole idea of fusion had taken on a different meaning. It could no longer be used as it had been used in the past, that is as a strategy to overthrow the Bourbon regime. Because this tactic became a *fait accompli* with the election of Hogg. If on the other hand, fusion meant allying with a white independent who had denounced his party and was willing to support Republicans — black or white — for office, then perhaps it was worth the effort. As the undisputed leader of the party, Cuney failed to differentiate between the various meanings of fusion and in so doing produced dissension among his protagonists, as well as antagonists. It is safe to say that when Cuney chose not to put a ticket in the field in 1892, most blacks did not object to fusion per se. What they disagreed with was his choice of candidate, a Bourbon Democrat, George Clark. Cuney's endorsement of Clark caused such a furor within the Republican party (especially among blacks) that the Republicans did not support another independent candidate until past the midpoint of the twentieth century. Many blacks believed, as did David Abner Jr., son of former black legislator, David Abner Sr., that Cuney's support of Clark was prearranged. There seems to have been some validity to this statement. As early as February 1892, Cuney had called for fusion between Republicans and anti-Hogg forces. In an interview regarding the Democratic convention, Cuney said: "If the opponents of Governor Hogg have the courage to go to this convention and if they are not afraid of the old slogan of 'Democracy, Edmund J. Davis and Negro domination,' there will be a bolt." When asked what would be the position of the Republicans if this should happen, Cuney replied: "In the event of a bolt, I shall in the interest of my state, use my influence to have my party abstain to secure the election of the candidate." [13] The following day, George Clark announced his candidacy for the Democratic nomination. Furthermore, when the Republicans met in convention in March 1892, to select delegates to the national convention, no date was set by Cuney to reconvene Republicans in order to discuss a state ticket. This dilatory tactic was employed by Cuney so as to allow the Democrats enough time to call their convention and to nominate a candidate. As Cuney would have it, Hogg was renominated and the convention was bolted by some of its members. Thus, Cuney moved ahead with fusion by supporting Clark.

To many blacks who had worked long and hard to overthrow the Bourbon regime, Clark was a hard pill to swallow. They could not support Clark even though there were allegations that Hogg, during his campaign, had made derogatory remarks about blacks.[14] Although they were asked to vote for Clark, a large number of blacks defied the advice of their leaders and offered their service as organizers, speakers, and supporters of Hogg. For example, David Abner Jr., President of Guadalupe College at Seguin, offered to aid the Hogg campaign via his position and his three newspapers. Hence, Hogg clubs, established, sponsored, and run by blacks, sprang up throughout the state.[15] More interestingly, these supporters of Hogg did not fail to capitalize on the Governor's record on race relation. They pointed out that the Governor, on numerous occasions, had offered rewards for the apprehension of perpetrators of mob violence and lynching. His pardon of black offenders was also brought into focus. Such gestures and posture on the part of the Governor caused Walter Burton, former state senator, to jump on

Hogg's bandwagon. As such, Burton wrote the Governor, not only endorsing him, but also telling him of how impressed he was with his stance on lynching. Cognizant of the fact that the black vote would be split between Hogg and Clark, but feeling assured that the incumbent would emerge victorious, one of Hogg's black supporters wrote: "Cuney can sell us but he can't deliver us." [16]

Still Cuney, along with Jacob Freeman, was able to deliver the bulk of black votes to Clark. Even though he lost the election, Clark carried seven of the sixteen counties with a majority black population and fourteen others with a black population of twenty percent to forty percent. While Cuney was able to persuade the majority of the blacks (who voted) to cast their ballot for Clark, this number was much smaller than the ones he had delivered in previous election years. This was due to two reasons: (1) Cuney miscalculated black dissatisfaction with Clark, as well as black support for Hogg; (2) Cuney misread the events of the time, that is, that the newly-formed Populist party was waiting in the wings to accept anyone who was disgruntled with the two traditional parties.

The Populist party was established in Texas in 1892. It evolved from the agrarian revolt which first touched the South in 1874. Although conservative, southern leaders talked about a "New South" after the Civil War and pointed with pride to the growth of business and industry in their section of the county, still, most whites and blacks earned their living by farming. As a matter of fact, the farms of Texas, the earth of which was never hard hit by the ravages of the Civil War, began to produce bigger and better after 1870. Yet, bigger crops did not bring prosperity to farmers. Instead, this increased farm output created a larger crop surplus and drove farm prices down. Falling prices, in time, brought financial hardship throughout the country. Thus, as more and more farmers faced the loss of their farms, they turned to the government for relief. Farmers blamed their plight on "big business" and on government policies which favored manufacturing and railroad interests at the expense of the farmers. So, in 1877, the Southern Farmer's Alliance was established to act as a lobby group to push for government policies which would benefit farmers. It should be noted that the Southern Farmer's Alliance denied black membership, but did encourage blacks to set up a parallel organization of their own. Thus, the Colored Farmer Alliance was established in Houston, Texas, in December 1886. From this time, both black and white organizations grew very rapidly throughout the South, Midwest, and West. In 1890, whites and blacks held separate conventions to discuss common grievances of farmers. In 1891, these conventions came together and established the Populist party, or the People's party, as it was sometimes called.[17]

Once the People's party was established, farmers and Bourbon Democrats soon became embroiled with each other over the fundamental issue of economics and political supremacy. Notwithstanding the great faith placed in the native white citizens by the People's party, the leaders of that party soon realized that support from this group was not enough to sustain their party in power. Ergo, blacks became an object of solicitude. Needless to say, black disgruntlement with the Republican party made the task of the People's party leaders much easier. Thus, when the Populists held their first state convention in Dallas, Texas, in 1891, one black delegate reported that "the colored people are coming into the new party in squads and companies." [18] Another black delegate, Henry Jennings, stated that he "had organized many people's party colored clubs in Texas and had branded them." Fearing that whites might be overwhelmed by the large numbers of blacks coming into the party, a white delegate offered a resolution to deny black representation on party committees. No sooner was the resolution presented, than did a black delegate from Fort Worth rise to the occasion. He said that "the vote will be the balancing vote in Texas . . . If you are going to win, you will have to take the Negro with you." He continued, "You must appoint us at convention and make us feel that we are men." The remarks of this black delegate were reinforced by the white president of the convention when he said: "I am in favor of giving the colored man full representation . . . he is a citizen just as much as we are and the party that acts on this fact will gain the colored vote of the south." [19] The president's views were applauded and upheld as two blacks were elected members of the State Executive Committee.

Alienated by the Cuney fusion agreement in 1892, many blacks turned to the Populist party. Likewise, Populists made an extra effort to convert blacks to their cause. This crusade to win black votes included newspaper campaigns, the formation of black clubs, concessions made toward black civil rights and the use of "fluence men." The People's party wanted black votes, the methods used to secure them notwithstanding. Thus, as soon as they found a press responsive to their request, they published letters, articles and other information which not only urged blacks to support the Populist crusade, but they also published propaganda which was damaging to the Republicans and Democrats alike. Partly as a result of this newspaper effort, Populist clubs were formed throughout the state. These clubs were very active and strong at the local level. For example, one-third of the membership of the Gonzales club was black. Similarly in Colorado County, membership of blacks was equal to whites. In other counties black representation was large enough to warrant black county and precinct chairmen. Extensive efforts and energies were expended in Fort Bend, Waller,

Brazoria, Robertson, Wharton and Matagorda to achieve the desired results — black votes.[20]

In the above areas, "fluence men" played an important role. One such individual was J. B. Rayner. Born to a white father and a slave mother in Tarboro, North Carolina in 1850, Rayner came to Robertson County in 1881. Prior to coming to the Lone Star State, Rayner attended Shaw University and St. Augustine's Collegiate Institute. After his college days, he served as a constable, magistrate, and deputy sheriff in his hometown of Tarboro. Upon leaving North Carolina, Rayner settled in Calvert, Texas. There he taught school, pastored a church and worked with the United Brothers of Friendship before he became involved in politics. In 1892, Rayner became disgruntled with the Republican party and turned to the People's party. An advocate of Populism, Rayner went up and down the state encouraging blacks to join this third party. Rayner spoke to both white and black groups wherever Populist sympathizers could be found. He spoke on Populism in cities and dreary isolated sections of Texas. It was largely due to Rayner's effort that the Populists carried his home county, Robertson, in the elections of 1894 and 1896.[21]

In order to entice blacks to the party, populist leaders also sponsored picnics, barbecues and dinners for them. In addition to these trite rewards, blacks were summoned to jury duty in Nacogdoches county and colored days were designated at camp meetings just before election. Such actions on the part of white Populists led one Republican to fear as early as 1892 that "most of the colored farming population [would] vote the People's party in the next election and neither Cuney nor anyone else [could] stop them from it." [22] To a certain degree this gentleman was right. Between 1892 and 1894 the People's party experienced an increase in membership as was evident in the number of votes cast for its gubernatorial candidate in 1894. The Populist party's candidate received 50,000 votes more than he had received in 1892. He carried three of the sixteen counties with black majorities of fifty percent or more and twenty-four of fifty-four counties with a black population over twenty percent in East and South Central Texas. The result of which was that the Populist candidate ran well ahead of both the Regular and Lily White Republicans candidates. Even though Cuney had been an avid supporter of fusion, his aversion to, and misunderstanding of, Populism, caused him to push for a Republican ticket in 1894, a year during which his party was torn with internal strife between the Lily White and Regular Republicans.

The first serious attempt at fusion between Republicans and Populists came in 1896, after Cuney had been dethroned from the Republican leadership. The bitter factional dispute between the Regular Republicans and the Lily Whites to rid Cuney of his powers resulted in a loss of prestige for the party among blacks. For the above reason, many blacks turned to the Populist party and by the same token many blacks who did not join, became more susceptible to fusion between Republicans and Populists. So, in order to win over the dissatisfied element of the Republican party, Populist leaders took to the campaign trail again. One in particular — J. B. Rayner — made speeches in seventeen counties between April 30, and May 25, 1896. In addition, he wrote two lengthy articles in the *Farmer's Alliance Weekly Newspaper* entitled "Political Imbroglio in Texas" and Modern Political Method." In the latter, he told his fellow Populists: "We must manuever to get our recruit from the Negro and how we do this should tax our power of research and ingenuity." [23] Heeding the advice of Rayner, Populists made a concerted effort to get more black votes in the election of 1896 than they had in previous ones. Not only did they get black votes, but they were also able to persuade leaders of the Republican party to fuse with them; leaders who had once accused Cuney of stifling the party by not putting a ticket in the field.

An interesting scenario took place in this election. In 1896, the Populist party was placed in the same predicament as that of the Republicans — they were not in agreement on whether they should place a straight-out ticket in the field or fuse with one of the two major parties. When the Populists met in the state convention in 1896 J. B. Rayner called a separate caucus of blacks to decide whether they should support a "Gold" Democrat, if such became the choice of the General Assembly. After some discussion, blacks decided that they would support McKinley unless a Populist was placed at the head of their ticket.[24] When the General Assembly convened at the second session, white Populist delegates joined blacks in opposing fusion with the Democrats. Instead they decided to fuse with the Republicans in delivering the electoral vote of Texas for William McKinley. In return, the Republicans promised to give their support to the candidacy of Jerome C. Kearby for Governor. Again, as in the past, fusion did not result in victory. The Democratic candidate David B. Culberson won by a vote of 298, 528 to 238, 692 for Kearby.

Despite the fact that Kearby polled the largest number of votes ever cast for a Texas Populist and carried eight of sixteen counties with black majorities, black Populism was a failure in Texas. It failed for several reasons. First, none of the former black legislators or influential black leaders embraced Populism. As a matter of fact, Elias Mayes spoke out openly against it. He told fellow Republicans "to stick with the Grand Old Party and not be led off by new ideas set up by the People's party." [25] Secondly, except for J. B. Rayner, most of the black leaders of the Populist party lacked both reputation and experience in politics. The most noted blacks of that party were R. H. Hayes of Fort Worth, Henry J. Jennings of McKinney, Melvin Wade of Dallas, and C. M. Ferguson of Houston. The latter two seem to have been trying to serve two masters, the Populist and Republican parties. When they became angry or dissatisfied with the Republicans, they would go over to the Populists. Melvin Wade's chief contribution to the People's party was that he canvassed Dallas, Waxahachie, Ennis, and North Texas, before the election of 1896. Aside from this, he expended his energy working within the Republican party. As for Ferguson, he was never serious about Populism. What he was serious about was power, and he would go anywhere possible to seize it. He flirted with Populism in 1892, and 1896, but never really left the Republican party. After 1896, he became a Republican par excellence. Too, black Populism did not succeed because most blacks who came into the party, joined for nebulous reasons which ranged from dislike of Cuney, disgruntlement with the Republican party to hatred of the Democratic party. One black man said: "I join because I don't like the Democratic party. The People's Party say they are against the Democratic party, therefore, I am going with the People's party." [26] Moreover, the history of black Populism in Texas reveals that a very few of the black Populists of Texas understood the philosophy underlying agrarian discontent. To be sure, most black citizens of Texas were subjected to the abuses of capitalism and were victims of the economic depression of the nineties. Yet, few black Texans interpreted the organization of the People's party as a political expression of low income working groups for change and progress.[27] Finally, black Populism failed because most blacks remained loyal to the Republican party. The bond — material or idealogical — that welded them to the party could only be broken by a program that would appeal to the masses with concrete promises and gains. Outside of being summoned to jury duty, and winning a few local and insignificant offices, blacks made no substantial gains in this party. Moreover, despite the organization of the Colored Farmers' Alliance, most black farmers retained their ties with the Grand Old Party.

In sum, it can be argued that fusion with independent movements or third parties was not advantageous for blacks. They simply kept alive dissenting views and opposition of organizations which eventually merged to gradually eliminate blacks from the political arena. For example, black Populism helped to build the image of "Negro Domination" through the balance of power concept, which eventually led to the formation of the White Democratic Primary. Yet, in reality, most of the public offices held by blacks were neither significantly important nor numerous enough to warrant the Democratic cry of "Negro Domination." Fusion movement in most cases was no more than an exercise in frustration because it united every possible group and individual hostile to the Democratic party — farmers, soft money men, disgruntled Democrats and Republicans — only to have them refuse to support black candidates. Given the declining status of blacks in the Republican party between 1874 and 1900, it appears that blacks were caught between a rock and a hard place as they fought for their political lives. So, it was not uncommon nor unwarranted that they employed fusion as a game of practical politics. What does seem ironic is that blacks continued to use fusion in cases where it was obvious that they were not going to win. Still the record does not show that black elected state officials, former or at that time, came together with Cuney in an effort to try to persuade him to change his mind when it became clear after 1884, that fusion was not working. After that date, the only thing that fusion did was cause confusion. For one thing, blacks spent too much time squabbling among themselves over the idea of supporting a white candidate rather than spending more time in county conventions nominating blacks and canvassing the field to get more blacks elected to state office from those predominantly black counties. In other words, fusion gave rise to fission. Unlike some other Southern states where fusion effectively challenged Bourbon rule, in Texas, fusion candidates did not pose any real threat to the political hegemony of the Bourbon Democrats even with the support of blacks. In the words of Lawrence Rice, fusion for black Texans was an "unholy coalition." [28]

Part Three
The Danger:

Methods Of Removal

[8]

Rejection, Reduction, Retrenchment:

"The Election is now going on. Sambo and the white man voting together but Texas will yet be a white man's state." So wrote W. H. C. Davenport December 2, 1869. "[I would] rather be chairman of a white league, Capt[ain] of a rifle club or Mayor of Marshall [because] We make congressmen," wrote Amory R. Starr April 20, 1882.

To many white Democrats who had fought for the Confederacy, the election of blacks to state and local offices was painful. In order to alleviate the pain, immediately after the election of 1869, white Conservatives set out to redeem the state. That blacks continued to be elected to state and local offices after the state was redeemed, was all the more galling to these whites. So, in order to fulfill the above prophecy that "Texas [would] yet be white man's," it became necessary for whites to eliminate both black voters and black political leaders. Thus, in the conservative campaign to uproot black power, the three Rs strategy was employed: rejection through violence and intimidation; reduction through violence and disfranchisement, and retrenchment through demographic patterns and constitutional restraints. Once these acts were consummated, black legislators, as well as local black politicians, were effectively removed from the political arena, but not without a fight.

Violence, the tactic that was most frequently used and supported by native whites, was not only widespread but in some areas, all-encompassing. It is well to remember that individual and mob violence had been endemic in the Lone Star State for many years.[1] This lawlessness was due in part to the frontier condition of the state, but it was also due to racial and political reasons. Without a doubt, white violence in general, and organized violence of the Ku Klux Klan in particular, had the effect of reducing the political activities of blacks. It should be noted that while all of the violence committed during Reconstruction was not that of the Ku Klux Klan, as Allen Trelease puts it: "The Klan institutionalized a white vigilantism which long preceded and followed it."[2] Throughout the period of 1868 to 1900, blacks in Texas were forcibly removed from their offices, as well as their homes, because of what some whites, particularly klansmen, called their "obnoxious conduct" — too much interest in politics.

How many blacks were beaten, flogged and murdered for either voting or attempting to vote for Republican candidates, may never be known. In order to get a picture of the dangers that blacks encountered because of their political activities, one has but to look at the affidavits by scores of freedmen during Reconstruction. A black man from Red River County testified that he was stopped en route to his home by four white men after registering to vote. He was shown a heavy rope and told that it would be used to hang him if he failed to vote the Democratic ticket in the 1869 election.[3] Another black testified that blacks in Rusk County had ceased voting because "they were being watched by white men of the Democratic party . . . and were afraid of being hurt."[4] In many other instances, physical violence was not only a threat, it was for real. In accordance with this, James Taylor swore that because of his political activities, he was taken about three miles from his home by a party of white men who "tied him hand and foot and hit him three hundred lashes with a leather strap . . ."[5] These affidavits are only examples of mild cases of violence; black victims of the most violent crimes left no affidavits, only homicide statistics.

In addition to the physical forms of violence, economic coercion frequently was used to influence black voters. The absence of any governmental land reform program in the state during Reconstruction virtually assured the financial dependency of many freedmen on the conservative landowning class. Coupled with the above negative factors, black Texans entered the postwar period with no capital, little property, and simple skills which were largely agricultural. By the 1870s, black tenancy was widespread, and many black agricultural workers simply "lived on the place" where they worked. Given this situation, one can argue that the threat of eviction was probably the most effective of all the means of intimidation used by the Democrats. According to the affidavit of E. M. Mitchell of Shelby County, "the colored men were threatened that if they voted the Republican ticket they would be driven from their homes."[6] Another freedman, Matthew Polk, said that he and other blacks of Rusk County were threatened with "higher rent" for their land if they voted Republican.[7] Needless to say, former masters of freedmen made skillful use of such economic pressures.

If violence was perpetrated against black voters, it certainly did not escape black legislators. When Stephen Curtis attended the first Republican convention in 1867, he was armed because of a threat against his life.[8] In 1871, Matt Gaines wrote Governor Davis to ask his advice about the Klan. "Write me," said Gaines, "as soon as you can let me know what to do. Some of the white people of this county [Washington] have said that I will not get back to Austin again. They say that before . . . I . . . get back [to Austin], they will see me in hell."[9] The Klan was a bit more serious about Goldstein Dupree. He was killed by them in 1873, while campaigning for Davis's reelection.[10]

In part because of such intimidation and harassment, the election of 1872 saw not only a decline in the number of black legislators, but a decline in the number of territories represented by them. As shown on the roster of black legislators, eleven districts were represented by blacks in 1870, as compared to six in 1872. The six that were represented were the Seventh, Twelfth, Thirteenth, Fourteenth, Fifteenth, and the Sixteenth. There were no blacks elected from the Eighteenth and Twenty-fifty Districts which had more than a fifty percent-plus black population. Similarly, there were no blacks elected from the Seventeenth, Nineteenth, and Twenty-seventh Districts, which had a black population of a little less than fifty percent, but which had been represented by blacks in the previous legislature.[11]

The Democratic victory in the gubernatorial election of 1873, firmly established the white Redeemer's regime. Not only did this victory write the end of Reconstruction government in Texas after thirty-four months, but it signaled a systematic pattern of reduction of black elected officials. The drafting of the Constitution of 1876 was a case in point. In order to make redemption a *fait accompli*, the Democrats felt that it was necessary to rewrite the laws. Thus, one of the first tasks that the delegates of this constitutional convention undertook was to reapportion congressional, representative, and senatorial districts.[12]

When Texas was readmitted to the Union in 1870, it was comprised of four congressional districts. Of those four, the Third District had the largest number of blacks, that is, forty-four percent of the population. This district was the only one where blacks could possibly have elected a United States Congressman, that is if the white votes were split. Yet, while it was possible to elect a black representative between

Table I
SENATORIAL DISTRICTS 1881

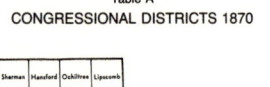

Table A
CONGRESSIONAL DISTRICTS 1870

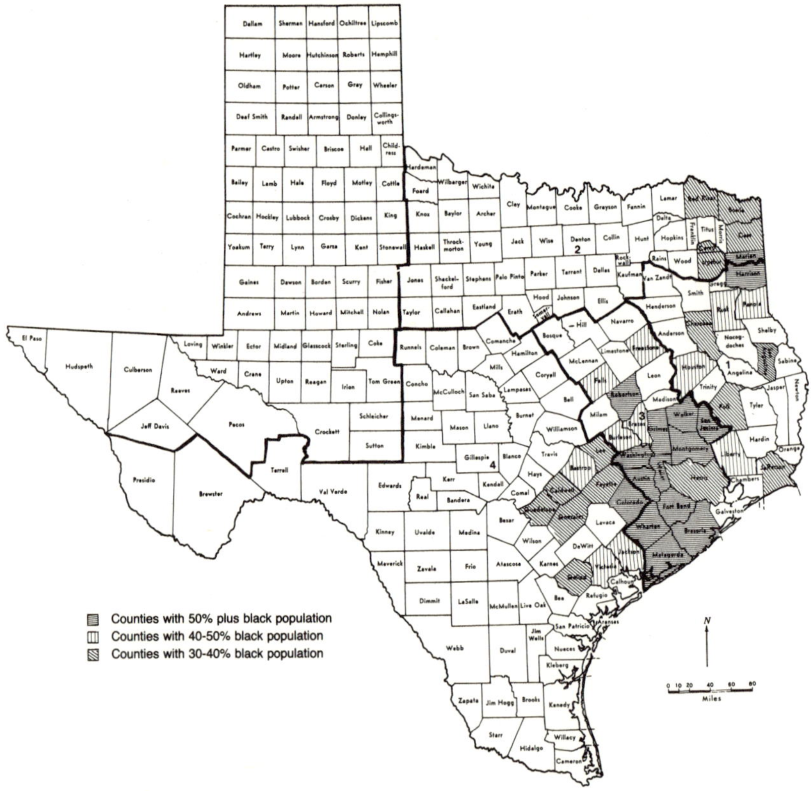

▤ Counties with 50% plus black population
▥ Counties with 40-50% black population
▧ Counties with 30-40% black population

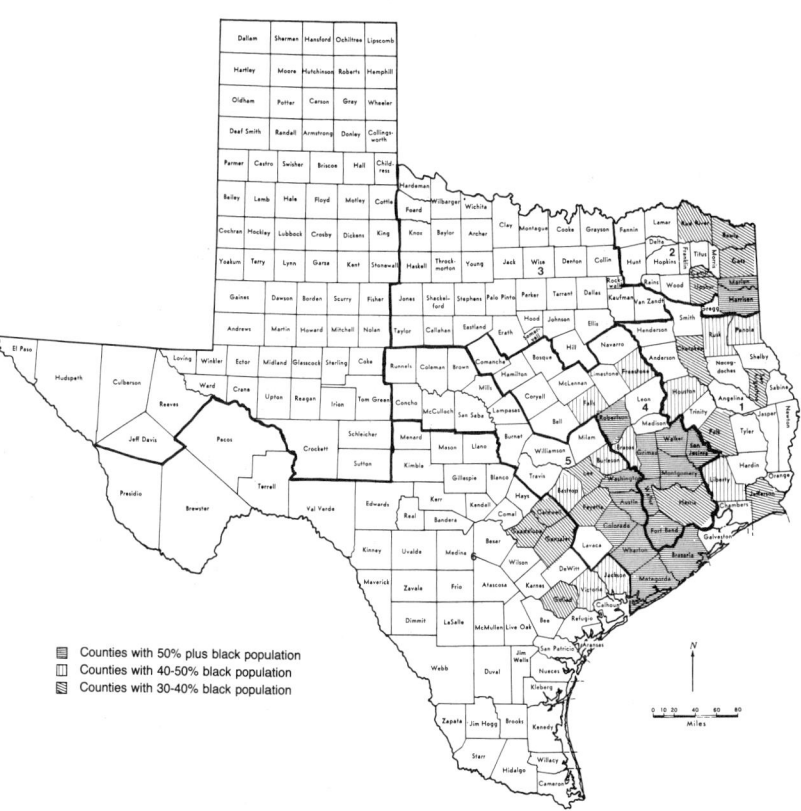

Table B
CONGRESSIONAL DISTRICTS 1876

Table C
CONGRESSIONAL DISTRICTS 1881

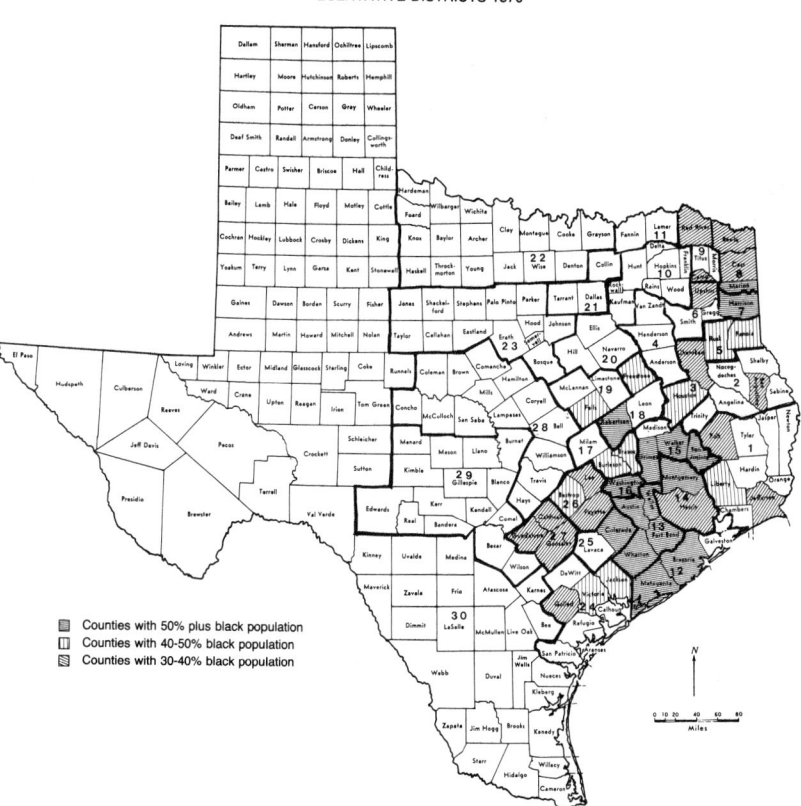

Table D
REPRESENTATIVE DISTRICTS 1870

138 THROUGH MANY DANGERS, TOILS, AND SNARES

Table E
REPRESENTATIVE DISTRICTS 1876

Flotorial Districts

9th—Panola, Shelby, Rusk
16th—Smith and Gregg
20th—Lamar, Fannin and Delta
30th—Grimes and Madison
34th—Harris and Montgomery
36th—Matagorda, Brazoria and Galveston
49th—Grayson and Collin
63rd—Fayette and Lee
66th—Travis and Blanco
67th—Williamson and Lampasas
72nd—Bexar and Comal
79th—Cherokee, Rusk, Panola, Shelby and Harrison

Rejection, Reduction, Retrenchment

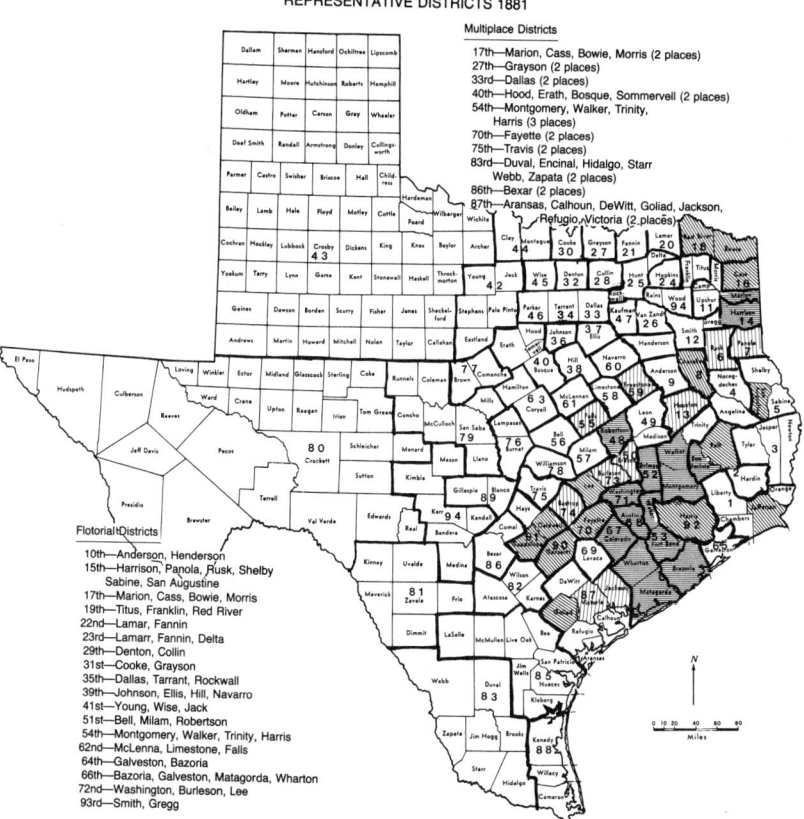

Table F
REPRESENTATIVE DISTRICTS 1881

Multiplace Districts
17th—Marion, Cass, Bowie, Morris (2 places)
27th—Grayson (2 places)
33rd—Dallas (2 places)
40th—Hood, Erath, Bosque, Sommervell (2 places)
54th—Montgomery, Walker, Trinity, Harris (3 places)
70th—Fayette (2 places)
75th—Travis (2 places)
83rd—Duval, Encinal, Hidalgo, Starr Webb, Zapata (2 places)
86th—Bexar (2 places)
87th—Aransas, Calhoun, DeWitt, Goliad, Jackson, Refugio, Victoria (2 places)

Flotorial Districts
10th—Anderson, Henderson
15th—Harrison, Panola, Rusk, Shelby Sabine, San Augustine
17th—Marion, Cass, Bowie, Morris
19th—Titus, Franklin, Red River
22nd—Lamar, Fannin
23rd—Lamarr, Fannin, Delta
29th—Denton, Collin
31st—Cooke, Grayson
35th—Dallas, Tarrant, Rockwall
39th—Johnson, Ellis, Hill, Navarro
41st—Young, Wise, Jack
51st—Bell, Milam, Robertson
54th—Montgomery, Walker, Trinity, Harris
62nd—McLenna, Limestone, Falls
64th—Galveston, Bazoria
66th—Bazoria, Galveston, Matagorda, Wharton
72nd—Washington, Burleson, Lee
93rd—Smith, Gregg

Table G
SENATORIAL DISTRICTS 1870

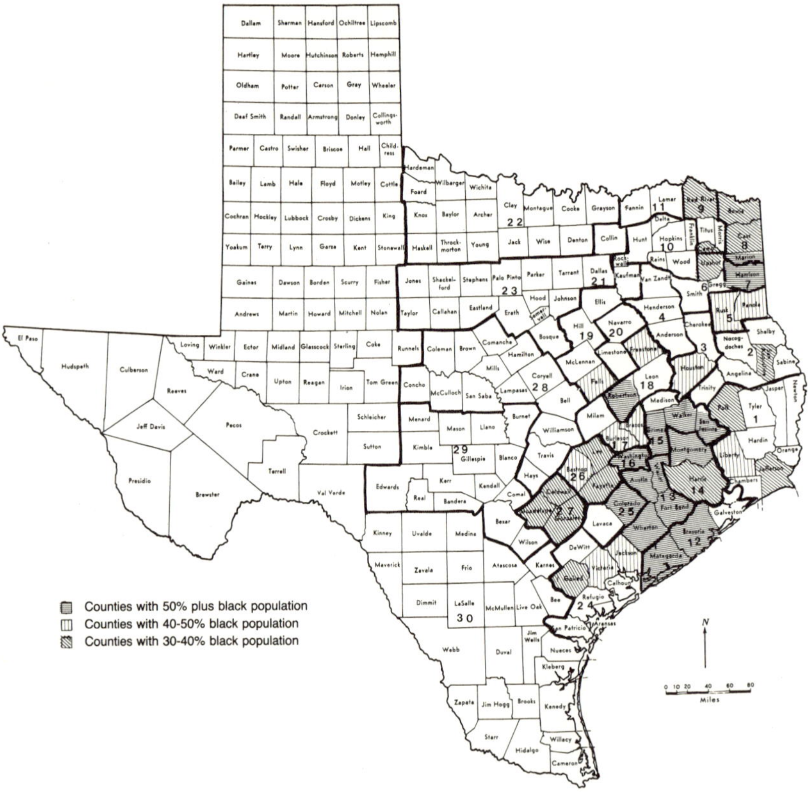

Table H
SENATORIAL DISTRICTS 1876

1871–1875, it was highly improbable by 1876. For in that year, Texas was divided into six congressional districts and black political strength was further diluted.[13]

The senatorial districts were apportioned not according to population, but rather according to the "number of qualified electors." To be sure, such a method worked to the disadvantage of blacks, because there were a number of men of color who, for one reason or another, were not classified as "qualified electors." Moreover, in many cases a large number of blacks were not included in the census report, much less on the voter registration list.[14]

Redistricting of representative districts was even more ridiculous. It was done in three ways: (1) by a single district based on population, (2) by a flotorial district, and (3) by a multiplace district. The flotorial district, more than any other, worked to the disadvantage of blacks. A floater district was established whenever a populous county would elect one or more representatives on its own and then join forces with a less populous neighboring county(ies) to elect another representative. In cases where a predominately black county was lumped together with surrounding white county(ies), the representative elected from the floater district was always white. The reason for this was simple. There were enough whites in the combined counties to overshadow the black plurality. As shown on the Map of Representative Districts. District 15 was a floater district which consisted of Harrison, Panola, Rusk, Shelby, San Augustine, and Sabine. Harrison alone had a total of 17,196 blacks, but whites in the combined counties totaled 24,206.

A careful examination of Map F reveals that with few exceptions, a flotorial district had only one representative and was usually located in the Black Belt area. Because of the structural design of the flotorial districts, all blacks who ran in such districts met with defeat — Norris Cuney in 1876, Shack Roberts in 1880, Jacob Freeman, J. Polk, and Ed Patton in 1890. On the other hand, a multiplace district which worked more to the advantage of whites than to the disadvantage of blacks usually could be found outside the area of heavy black concentration.[15] A multiplace district either consisted of one county or a combination of counties. The number of representatives from such a district was always two or more. As confusing as it may sound, it was possible for a district to be classified as both flotorial and multiplace. Probably an article in the *Panola Watchman* expressed best the intent of these white legislators when it reported that "districts were Gerrymandered, the purpose being in these elections and properly enough to disfranchise the blacks by indirection. In achieving this end, districts were elongated most absurdly . . ."[16] Had those districts not been gerrymandered in such a fashion, blacks would have had more representatives at the state level. So, it can be argued that for various reasons, equality of representation in the legislature simply did not exist.

Closely akin to reapportionment in the reduction of black elected officials were demographic patterns. Texas was the fastest growing state in the Union during Reconstruction. From 1860 to 1870, the population rose by one-third, while that of the nation increased by one-fourth. Needless to say, the demographic patterns which occurred adversely affected blacks. To begin with, blacks were in the minority. Furthermore, the black population declined from thirty-one percent in 1870 to twenty-five percent of the total population in 1880. Numerically, the black population increased from 253,475 to 397,304 in the same ten-year span. But by the same token, the white population grew from 564,700 to 1,197,237 in that same period.[17] While the black population increased in every Black Belt county save Austin[18] between 1870 and 1880, the white increase was enough by 1900, to reduce the number of Black Belt counties with a fifty percent-plus population from fifteen to twelve.[19] This does not mean that blacks were leaving those areas in large numbers. As a matter of fact, next to Florida, Texas had the smallest percentage of native blacks living outside the state.[20] What was happening was that whites were moving into the state en masse, but not necessarily in the Black Belt counties. It is well to remember that those whites who came to Texas were, for the most part, farmers who came mostly from older southern states, looking for land and economic opportunities. These individuals soon joined forces with the Democratic party, which had the support of the state's white protestant and white catholic majority. The Democratic party was able to attract such followers because it identified itself with state's rights and the white supremacy tradition. To be sure, this influx of strangers (rich and poor, protestants and non-protestants) lessened black political potency. As such, in 1874, blacks represented only four districts, the Seventh, Thirteenth, Fifteenth, and Seventeenth, all of which had a fifty percent-plus black population.

Without a doubt, after 1875 reapportionment and demographic patterns took a toll on black elected state officials, as well as the territories they represented. As shown on the Map of Representative Districts, except for the year of 1878, when ten blacks represented nine counties in the Sixteenth Legislature, black representation never exceeded six in number during the post-Reconstruction. In the Seventeenth Legislature, six blacks represented seven counties. Two blacks were selected from three counties in the Eighteenth Legislature. The Nineteenth Legislature consisted of three blacks representing three counties, while the Twentieth had two blacks who were responsible for two counties. The Twenty-first Legislature saw an additional member and county. The same combination existed in the Twenty-first Legislature. In the Twenty-second and Twenty-third Legislatures, one black represented two counties. In 1893, two blacks were chosen from three counties. In the Twenty-fifty Legislature, one black was selected to represent one county. At no time after reapportionment did blacks represent an entire district alone. It was only in the Fourteenth Legislature in 1875 that an entire district was represented by blacks — the Seventh District which consisted of Harrison County.

As has been stated in previous chapters, blacks did not fail to react to the idea of dismembering their counties or districts especially if it meant a dilution of black votes. Concomitant with this stance to retain their political strength, in 1880, R. J. Evans offered an amendment to House Bill 49 to make Grimes County the returning county of the Thirtieth District.[21] This was a very important amendment because the returning county was responsible for counting the votes of the district. Since the Thirtieth District consisted of Grimes and Madison counties, and inasmuch as Grimes had a black majority of over fifty percent of the population, while Madison had a black population of less that fifty percent, it seemed only fair that Grimes would be the returning county. Needless to say, this amendment died before reaching committee. In keeping with their determination to prevent the dilution of black votes, all blacks of the Seventeenth Legislature, Beck, Evans, Gieger, and Kerr voted against a bill that would have added Waller and Fort Bend to the Fifty-fourth Flotorial District.[22] Moreover, when the question of dividing predominately black Brazoria County (in order to form a new county) came up in 1894, Nathan Haller opposed it because he felt that division was not in the best interest of his people. When asked if he had received threatening letters because of the position that he had taken, he replied "yes," and "they were signed [from] Brazoria and Matagorda counties." [23]

If blacks were determined not to have their voting strength diluted, whites were equally determined to make them less politically potent. Nowhere was there better evidence of this than in the organization called the White Man's Party. This was one of the most effective means of eliminating blacks from the franchise. Such an organization was established to "assure that white supremacy must obtain" and to bar blacks from participation in politics. Hence, the first white man's union of Texas was formed in Harrison County in 1878, where the black population was seventy percent of the total. Two years prior, the Democrats had organized a Citizen's party in that county and had stipulated ". . . that no colored voters be allowed to vote in the primary election, unless the judge had positive information that the applicant had heretofore voted the Democratic ticket." [24] Such primary stipulation did not affect blacks, since most were Republicans and were allowed to participate in the general election. Neither did the threat of violence prior to the election of 1876, prevent blacks from voting Republicans into office. As a matter of fact, the fourth and last black senator, Walter Ripetoe, was elected from Harrison County in that year.

The election of 1878 was an entirely different story. The Citizen's party, which later took the name of the White Man's Party, won control of the local government in October. In the words of R. L. Jennings, the editor of the *Marshall Star*, "by stuffing boxes, playing tricks on blacks and particially by force, the county radical wing was overthrown." [25] One of the tricks the Citizen party employed to gain control of the government of Harrison County was by use of the same color ballot as that used by the Republicans.[26] Republicans used blue-backed ballots so that illiterate blacks would be able to identify the ballots of the Grand Old Party by color. Thus, because the Citizen party's tickets were the same color as those of the Republicans, many blacks unknowingly voted for the Citizen party's nominee. The above law was employed in Harrison County before it became a state law in 1879, and is probably one of the reasons why a black man, Patrick Dennis, lost in a contested election for a seat in the House in 1878.[27]

It is interesting to note that after the term of Shack Roberts expired in 1878, no blacks were ever elected to represent Harrison County in the legislature. Blacks were allowed to vote after 1878, but so much fraud was committed that many stopped on their own, saying "their votes in state and national matters were never counted." [28] Because of the controversy which surrounded the ballot in Harrison County, the legislature passed a new election law in 1879. This election law, which worked to the disadvantage of blacks, required that all ballots be printed on white paper with the party's name at the top. In order to strengthen this law, the whites of Harrison County amended it with a resolution in 1888, which allowed only white men to vote in the Democratic primaries of Harrison County. This action, in turn, gave rise to the White Man's Party. Such a document led a white conservative, Amory Starr, to comment that instead of running for Congress he would "rather be chairman of a white league, Capt of a rifle club or Mayor or Marshall [because] we make congressmen." [29]

Following the lead of Harrison County, many other counties attempted to establish a White Man's Party. For example, the White Man's Party of Montgomery County was successful in ousting local blacks from office in 1878. In that same year, Grimes County whites tried to duplicate what had happened in Harrison and Montgomery, but were unsuccessful. Subsequently, Grimes's blacks were able to elect H. A. P. Bassett to the legislature in 1887. But if Grimes's White

Man's Association was a failure, that of Fort Bend gained recognition as the most effective means of excluding blacks from public office. From 1870 to 1885, blacks, who made up eighty percent of the population, controlled the politics in Fort Bend County. They sent a black representative to the House consecutively from 1872 to 1885, and had a black senator for six consecutive years. In addition to being politically active, blacks of Fort Bend also proved to be economically and educationally as capable as some of their white counterparts. Because of their visibility in politics at the county level, whites, such as Colonel P. E. Pearson and a number of other Democrats, spent much time and gave much thought to ousting these "undesirable" blacks from office. The opportunity that Pearson was waiting for came in 1884, when Grover Cleveland was elected as President of the United States, the first Democratic victory since the Civil War. The next year, Pearson organized the Rosebud Club, which was later called the Young Men's Democratic Club. The purpose of this club was to establish a "white man's government" and to put black Republican politicians out of office.[30]

In 1887, Republicans (mostly blacks) nominated an all white "Woodpecker" slate, that is, white Republicans who cooperated with blacks. Despite the fact that for the first time in thirteen years no blacks were on the ticket, Democrats still wanted them removed from office, as well as from the franchise; and thus, they did whatever was necessary to have them removed. There were two incidents that occurred in Fort Bend which led to the immediate ouster of black politicians. The first incident was the assassination of J. M. Shamblin, a white Democrat and member of the Young Men's Democratic Club, on August 1, 1888. The second incident was the assassination of Henry Frost, a white businessman and also a member of the Young Men's Democratic Club, on September 3, 1888.[31] The Democrats thought that it was northern white Republicans who had urged blacks to kill these influential whites. Believing this notion to be true, white Democrats met in front of the Fort Bend County courthouse September 5, 1888, two days after Frost was killed, and passed a resolution which required that the following black politicians leave the county within ten hours: C. M. Ferguson, H. G. Lucas, Peter Warren, Tom Taylor, J. D. Davis, Jack Taylor, and C. M. Williams. To make certain that this resolution was carried out, about one hundred white men armed with shotguns, rode up on each black politician's house and read the resolution. The blacks named immediately fled and found residence in other counties.[32]

It is interesting to note that none of the former legislators from Fort Bend — Henry Phelps, Jacob Freeman, W. H. Holland, B. F. Williams, Doc Lewis, Walter Burton, or George Wyatt — were included on this list. Extant data prevents one from being able to pinpoint the exact reason for their exclusion; however, one might speculate. Except for B. F. Williams, all other legislators appeared to have been conservative — the type that did not rock the boat. By 1885, B. F. Williams had become mellow to the extent that he was probably more concerned with land speculation than he was with politics. Another black, who was not a legislator, but who was very active in politics, and whose name was not included on that list was Henry C. Ferguson, brother of Charles Ferguson. The reason why his name was not included probably had something to do with the fact that whites knew that they could manipulate him. Thus, when Henry Ferguson left town shortly after his brother, he was encouraged by whites to return to the county to ask blacks to either vote the Democratic ticket or not to vote against it. Because he was so accommodating, whites promised Ferguson that blacks would be allowed to vote for a member of their race for the legislature in November.[33] So, on September 16, 1888, Henry Ferguson returned to Richmond and made a short speech in which he told a small group of blacks to stay out of politics, be thrifty and to seek advancement in industry. He asserted that he had left Fort Bend because he did not want to live where law-abiding men, such as Shamblin and Frost, were assassinated, and that many of his friends were Democrats.[34]

Despite Ferguson's apology for the Democrats, the Woodpeckers, with the support of blacks, carried the county in the November election of 1888. But this was only the calm before the storm. The Democrats were determined that "white supremacy must obtain" and on August 16, 1889, they attacked the Woodpeckers in the courthouse of Fort Bend. In this mêlée, the sheriff and four justices of the peace were shot. By the time that Governor Lawrence S. Ross sent in the militia, it was too late. Many officers had died and others had vacated their posts. In September, the last judge resigned and thus allowed the Democrats to take complete control. On October 3, 1889, they organized themselves into the Jaybird Democratic Organization, which was in fact the White Man's party. Once established, only whites were eligible for membership and no member could become a candidate for office without the endorsement of the party's membership or serve as a security of bond or endorse a nonmember. With such stipulations, the association wrote the end to blacks in Fort Bend County politics and gave a death blow to the Republican party in that county.[35]

In November 1888, Wharton County followed the lead of her neighbor in establishing a White Man's party. Matagorda and Brazoria Counties did likewise in 1894, after Nathan Haller announced his candidacy for reelection. Patterning themselves after other "senegambia counties" the white taxpaying citizens of Brazoria County formed a Tax Payer's Union after Nathan Haller unseated a white Democrat in a contested election and won a seat in the Texas House for a second time. So upset were whites over this election that they not only posted notices that blacks elected to local offices could not assume their duties, but even went so far as to throw armed guards around the courthouse to enforce their edict.[36] It is important to note that once a White Man's party was established in a county, no blacks were ever elected to office.

As has already been pointed out, the White Man's party sometimes went hand in hand with violence. In 1882, in Waller County, masked men disrupted the election in which George W. Wyatt was a candidate for the state legislature by carrying away the ballot box before the votes were counted.[37] In Washington County, a coffin carrying the names of four black leaders was put on display in 1879. In the same county in Chapel Hill in 1884, masked men entered the polling place while the ballots were being counted and began shooting. They severely wounded three blacks, H. H. Knoxson, candidate for county commissioner who later died of his wounds; Allen W. Wilder, attorney-at-law and former member of the legislature, and Lewis Maxes, an election judge. The white citizens severely condemned the masked villians who attacked the ballot boxes at Chapel Hill, but indignation quickly dissolved when it was discovered that the Democrats, who under the disguise of the Citizen's party, had won all but one of the county offices. After the votes were counted, whites celebrated the victory by saying: "It is gratifying to realize that the grand old county of Washington, so long bound to the shackles of Republican black rule, has at least risen in her might and unfurled to the breeze of the Democratic banner. Long may it wave!" [38]

While Democrats were elated over their victory in 1884, they still were not in total control of the county. Hence, in 1886, they would make an appeal for black support since people of color held the balance of power in Washington County. When this appeal to blacks did not work, they tried to divide black votes by supporting R. J. Moore's candidacy for reelection to the legislature. Having failed to win the masses of black votes even though many blacks voted for Moore, Democrats then resorted to intimidation in efforts to take over the county. Recalling the shooting at Chapel Hill in 1884, some Democrats spread the rumor that if the polls opened again "there would be some dead niggers that night." [39] On election day, November 5, 1886, the fear of a recurrence of violence prevented the election judge from opening the polls at Chapel Hill. In all other precincts, Democrats closely watched the polls. When it appeared that the election was going against the Citizen's ticket, the county judge, Lafayette Kirk, sent a telegram to D. D. Bolton, white candidate for county commissioner, advising him that "things here look doubtful. Do your work." Shortly thereafter, masked men attacked the polls at Gragall and destroyed the ballot boxes. At Flewellys, however, the blacks were prepared for possible trouble. When three masked men armed with drawn pistols entered this polling place and demanded that the ballot box be handed over, one of the blacks, Polk Hill, reached for his shotgun and fired twice. He wounded one of the men and killed another. After the shooting, everyone scattered and left the ballots uncounted. In the next few days the sheriff arrested Polk Hill and eight other blacks, several of whom had not even witnessed the shooting. On the day following the election, one hundred of the "best" citizens met in Brenham and appointed a committee to investigate the outrages on November 5, 1886. This committee announced the findings which condemned Republicans and congratulated "the good people of Washington County for the election of the Citizen's party." [40]

On the night of December 1, 1886, three of the eight blacks arrested were taken from their jail cell at Brenham and lynched. Within days of the lynching, several white Republicans received notices demanding they immediately leave the county. These individuals later presented a petition to the United State Senate complaining of political oppression. On January 27, 1887, the Senate responded by authorizing the Committee on Privileges and Election to investigate the "alleged election outrages in Washington County, Texas." In conjunction with the Senate investigation, the government filed a federal suit against Lafayette Kirk and others for "unlawfully interfering with officers of an election, especially a representative in the Congress of the United States." [41] In spite of all the publicity that surrounded this investigation, nothing came of it. It simply ended in a hung jury and gave power indirectly to the Democrats.

One final act of violence which occurred in 1888, placed the Democrats of Washington County squarely in power. With black Republicans suppressed and most white Republicans driven from the county, the party leadership fell to Joseph Hoffman, the only white Republican who consistently won county office despite the efforts of the Democrats to destroy his political appeal. During the summer of 1888, Hoffman organized a Republican dominated fusionist ticket with Independent Democrats and challenged the Democratically controlled Citizen party. His challenge, however, ended in tragedy. On the night of September 6, 1888, he and his Democratic supporter were killed.[42] With Hoffman out of the way and blacks eliminated from power, Democrats now ruled supremely. So, what the White Man's party had done in other Black Belt counties, physical force accomplished in Washington County.

Violence, whether threatened or actual, had the desired effect of reducing the political activities of blacks. In the northeast section of the state, by far the worst in the nation in the 1890s as far as violence against blacks was concerned, "white capping" activities frightened blacks into political inactivity. In Hearne, Robertson County, where blacks remained in office at the local level until 1896, violence was as Texan as armadillos and cowboy boots. It was not uncommon to find white horsemen breaking up elections in black precincts by riding into buildings or polling places and stampeding the crowd.[43] Such violence was aided and abetted by men in high places such as Judge O. D. Cannon, who was District Judge from 1890–1900. He killed one black legislator (Hal Geiger), and wounded another, (Alexander Asberry). Cannon was not very discriminatory in meting out violence, for he also killed three white men. In 1896, Cannon, as well as other Democrats, decided to put an end to black rule. So when the election of state and county officers took place in November, forty men armed with Winchesters were placed at the polling place in Franklin, Texas, to turn away blacks who came to vote. In order to make sure that blacks would not brave past these forty men, O. D. Cannon stood at the door of the election booth room with his six-shooter in his hand. At another precinct, blacks were marched four abreast out of the polling place and told not to stop. In order to enforce this edict, two of Cannon's deputies stood at the election room door, one with a gun and the other with a baseball bat. This election, not only wrote the end to "black rule" in Robertson County, but also signaled the end of the election of blacks to the state legislature in the post-Reconstruction era.[44]

Given white animosity toward blacks as well as the frontier condition of the state, it is not surprising that such violence was perpetrated against black legislators and that their days, as well as their number, in the Texas Legislature were somewhat predetermined. The question that naturally comes to mind is why black leaders did not make more vigorous and aggressive efforts to resist violence and intimidation meted out to blacks. As has already been pointed out in chapter two, black leaders consistently and repeatedly urged the creation of a state militia which became law in 1870. But the Davis administration could not and did not eliminate lawlessness from Texas. State police activities and infrequent declarations of martial law pacified part of the state, but suppression of black and white Republicans continued in other areas. On the other hand, black leaders never came together in an organized fashion to discuss violence or stage a protest against it. Throughout the period from 1868 through 1900, black leaders denounced white violence in strong terms, but except for Matt Gaines, the idea of resistance by force received little endorsement from them. The reason for this was twofold: (1) given their minority status, blacks feared that armed confrontation would be calamitous to the black community; and (2) many of the black legislators had been made examples of violence — two had met with violent deaths; one was wounded and many were threatened.

It can be argued that while some of the violence perpetrated against blacks during Reconstruction and post-Reconstruction was personal and indiscriminate, much of it was directed against the black leadership at the grassroots level. These obscure men, lost to history, represented what whites feared greatly — the growth of a local leadership based on farmers, laborers, and sharecroppers in rural Texas. White violence was especially aimed at those men who instructed other blacks of their political rights. How much of the killing off of this local leadership contributed to black state legislators' passivity remains to be studied.

If restriction of black office holding reflected, in part, white's desire to monopolize public office, the determination of the black voters to brave the bullet for the ballot, and the doggedness of the black legislators to fight for black rights, caused whites to resort to any means necessary to eliminate them from the political arena. Still, despite the many obstacles they faced, forty-one blacks participated in Texas politics at the state level at a time during which doing so was dangerous for a white Republican, and was almost impossible for a black one. Yet there might have been more blacks in the Texas legislature had they not been tracked down by the Three R(s) syndrome. That is, they were summarily rejected, reduced, and then removed.

Part Four
The Personalities:

Neither All Good Nor All Bad Men

A Preview

From the time that Union General Gordon Granger proclaimed on June 19, 1865 that black Texans were free, until 1898 when the last black left the Texas Legislature, myriad crosscurrents swept black social thought, ranging from militancy to accommodation. Such diverse proposals as integration, separation, terror, self-help and black–white unity have at one time or another been advanced by various black leaders. While there were no simple patterns to the thinking of these individuals, their basic aim was the achievement of social, political, and economic equality for black people. Still the intricacies of adjustment and compromise often diverted many from their ultimate goal. The student of leadership in black life must take the above points into consideration if he or she is to get an accurate picture of the cadre. Thus the purpose of this section is to show how the various personalities of these legislators were shaped during the period under study.

The individuals chosen best represent the types of personalities which were common among many of these politicians. Admittedly, one must make a distinction between a climber of sorts and an opportunist. To be sure, there is a thin line between the two, but there is a difference. While the climber of sorts seizes every opportunity to get what he wants, he can not work with others except on his own terms. On the other hand, while the opportunist seizes every opportune moment to get what he wants, he does not have any problem making compromises and he does not mind being cast into a peripheral role as long as he is in the limelight.

[9]

Matthew Gaines: The Militant

It is often argued that great crises produce great men and women, and conversely, great men and women bring about great crises. It goes without saying that it is difficult to establish the truth of either of these propositions to the exclusion of the other, inasmuch as the forces that operate and cooperate in each are factors of a common product. Matthew Gaines fits well into this category. Daring, keen of mind, courageous and firm in the principle of equality for all men without regard to race or color, Gaines was an outstanding leader of Reconstruction and stood out among his white colleagues like a sore thumb. He was by far the most vigilant guardian of black rights to sit in the Texas Legislature. A bitter critic of Southern conservatism and Northern hypocrisy, Gaines's critical attitude and independent action as a senator aroused the ire of Democrats and Radicals alike. Gaines's speeches made white Radicals shudder and caused moderate Republicans to reject their own party. When he went to the legislature, he was considered "dull, plodding and an ignorant ass." [1] By the time he left office he was regarded as a troublemaker, a rabble-rouser and a militant.

Born a slave near Alexendria, Louisiana, Gaines learned to read by candlelight in the evening from books smuggled to him by a little white boy who lived on the same plantation. It can be surmised that from this little white boy, Gaines also learned to speak French, as it was reported that he did speak a foreign language. While in bondage, Gaines escaped to freedom on two occasions, but each time he was caught and returned to servitude. His first escape came in 1850, after he was traded to a man from New Orleans, Louisiana, and was subsequently hired out as a laborer on a steamboat. Using a false pass, he made his way to Camden, Arkansas. For some unknown reason, Gaines left Arkansas six months afterward and returned to New Orleans, whereupon he was caught and brought back to his master. Nine years later, Gaines was sold to a Texas planter from Robertson County, and in 1863, he made another attempt to escape. Gaines's destination was Mexico, but he made it only as far as Fort McKavett in Menard County before being caught by the Texas Rangers. He was taken back to Fredericksburg, Texas, and remained in that area until the Civil War ended. During his tenure as a slave in Fredericksburg, Gaines worked as a blacksmith and a sheepherder. When emancipation came, Gaines moved to the Brazos River area and settled in Burton, Washington County.[2]

In the small community of Burton, Gaines soon established himself as a leader of the black community. The fact that he was a preacher, made it easier for him to function in a leadership capacity. In the words of Ann Malone: "Perhaps it was because of the oratorical skills that he gained as a slave preacher and the prestige which the black community customarily accorded lay ministers that Gaines was able to quickly build up a following in Washington County." [3] No doubt his prewar ministerial experience paid off. Four years after being set free, Gaines ran for and won a seat in the Senate over Benjamin O. Watrous, a well known and respected black who had represented Washington County as a delegate to the Constitutional Convention of 1868–1869.

When Matt Gaines entered the Senate chamber standing five feet and weighing 125 pounds, and Ferdinand Flake described him as "very black and African in feature," and said that "he has neither [the] culture nor shrewdness of Ruby, but has more hard stupid sense." [4] If "hard stupid sense" meant that Gaines would not compromise on racial equality, then he was stupid; if it meant that he would challenge conservative Democrats and moderate Republicans, then he was brave; if it meant that he was not afraid of speaking out against his allies in the Radical camp, then he was courageous. Gaines's posture as a militant was solidified when in one of his first speeches on the floor of the Senate, he said: "I am not afraid to speak a single word on this floor, the consequence of which I ever afterward shall shrink from." [5] Gaines's audacity, braveness and courage were demonstrated on such issues as the militia, immigration, and education bills, as well as on the right of blacks to hold public offices.

In regard to protection from violence, Gaines did not equivocate. He stood tall in support of the militia bill. Pointing to Washington County where blacks were being killed at will, Gaines argued that a militia was needed in Texas because a state of insurrection existed in this area of the state. In a quaint style, he told his fellow senators, "I do not profess to say that I am well educated . . . but I have enough education to know the price of a man's life." [6] To the Democrats who said that if the militia bill passed, "the old dead Confederate spirit of Vicksburg would rise up again," Gaines responded that if this bill did not pass, "the dead spirit of those [blacks] who were massacred at Fort Pillow would also rise." [7]

Gaines's concern for a militia was not only centered around protection of lives and property, but also protection from voter intimidation. And at every opportunity, he spoke on this issue. A case in point was the contested election of Republican Davis M. Peterson and Democrat E. L. Dohoney. In 1870, Dohoney received a certificate of election from the Eleventh Senatorial District, but his seat was later contested by Peterson. Because of evidence of fraud, violence, and intimidation committed upon the voters of Lamar County, the Committee on Privileges and Election recommended that Dohoney vacate his seat. When a roll call vote was taken on this measure, Gaines stated that his reason for voting against Dohoney was due to the fact that he was thoroughly "convinced by affiliates that the poor colored men were kept from the polls by intimidation from the Klu Klux Klan, who threatened colored voters if they voted the Davis–Peterson ticket that they would be expelled from the county." In light of the evidence presented, Gaines could not understand why some Republicans would side with the Democratic senator. But for those who did, Gaines, who controlled a large number of black voters, warned his fellow Republicans: "I will remember you in days to come." [8]

On the issue of equal economic opportunity, Gaines was equally adamant. No where was this posture better evident than on his stance on immigration in the spring of 1871. As has been stated earlier, Gaines waged a relentless battle in the Senate to attach an amendment to the immigration bill which would allow agents to be sent to Africa to recruit workers. When his amendment died on the floor, Gaines returned to his district and called a meeting to explain the reason for action. He said:

> We the colored people of the state of Texas have the same right to send for friends in Africa to come to us as well as the white members of the

Legislature who take the money that comes from our hard labor and send away for [whites] of Germany, France and Great Britain to come and buy up all of the land of the state of Texas, filling up the state with white labor, thereby turning out all the poor colored people out of doors and depriving them and their children of a home.[9]

In a rather dramatic manner, Gaines explained that as both a representative of the poor people of the state and of the African race, he had offered the amendment as a way of extending the "right hand of fellowship" to his African brethren to "share in the blessing of the glorious land of freedom." To those individuals, such as Senators W. Parson and G. T. Ruby, who opposed Gaines's amendment and referred to him as a bum, Gaines responded that he was working for the right of all poor people — white and black; that if he had been willing for poor people to bear the burden of paying an agent thirty-five thousand dollars per year to go to foreign countries to recruit white labor, then they would have supported his amendment. Gaines ended his speech by urging his constituents to inform him of their position on the immigration bill via newspaper or by letter.[10] To the surprise of no one, the only support that Gaines received on this measure was the sarcastic backing of the *Galveston Daily News,* which stated that, "The Senator is right in his demand for an agent to Africa. If the black man is equal, if the black man is as fit as the white man for power, society and office, then the black man is as valuable as the white for recruitment." [11]

After his stance on immigration in 1871, Gaines became embroiled in controversy after controversy. This was due in part to the fact that he became more critical of the Republican party and also in part to the fact that he became a more popular and forceful black leader. Most of his controversies stemmed from the fact that Gaines was no longer only a critic in the Senate, but an initiator of action outside of that chamber. This was best exemplified by his position on the Free School Bill of 1871. The idea of integrated classrooms, as was being proposed in the Free School Bill, produced a heated debate in the Senate and even caused white Republicans to openly side with Democrats in opposition to this bill. Leading the fight against the Free School Bill were Democrat J. E. Dillard and Republican Webster Flanagan. After listening to Flanagan and Dillard speak on the evils of integrated classrooms, Gaines stood up and told these senators that if they were afraid for whites to sit next to blacks, "[they] should resign their post and go home, because [he] did not particularly care to fraternize with them either." [12] When the School Bill of 1871 passed devoid of an integration clause, Matt Gaines said, "If a white man has a right to crawl into a colored woman's cabin at night and have children by her, that child has a right to sit beside [his sister or brother]." [13] Gaines's argument was that no one could separate the races in school because this was a violation of both the state and national constitutions. Hence, he told a group of black parents not only to send their children to integrated schools, but "to go with them and see who will put their hands on them . . . educate your children and stand up for their rights." [14]

In addition to pushing for economic and educational rights of blacks, Gaines's hope was that blacks would achieve meaningful participation in the state's government by means of election or appointment to major offices. Yet, little progress was made in that direction by 1871. Not a single major state office or even a congressional post was held by blacks during Davis's administration, although many local offices were filled by men of color. Because the paucity of blacks in major offices was distressing to Gaines, he decided to launch a crusade for a black congressman. Realizing the potential of black strength in the Third Congressional District, Gaines toyed with the idea of a black congressman as early as June 1870. He made his position known when he indicated on the floor of the Senate, that he would probably run for Congress in the next election. Later, he changed his mind about seeking the position for himself, but he did not give up the idea of a black man vying for that post. As such, he made an appeal for a colored candidate in February 1871. To the charge that a black candidate would cause Republicans to lose the race, Gaines countered: "That is just as good as to say that they will not go with us. Let us try them and see what they will do. If they go back on us or not, now is the time to try their faith and see what they will do. I'm willing to take to the field for a colored man. My people say a colored man and so do I." [15] Addressing the Union League in April, Gaines repeated the same assertion: "The time has come for action on our part . . . we have got men at home who know better what we need in Texas, therefore we must do all we can to send one of our own men to [Congress]." [16]

When the nominating convention assembled in August 1871, Gaines had the intention of testing his white colleagues on the above issue, but his efforts were stymied when George T. Ruby, who was the presiding officer of the convention prevented the name of Gaines's candidate, Richard Nelson, from being placed in nomination. Gaines condemned the Radical hierarchy for turning away from potential black candidates, but all to no avail. However, the week following the convention, Gaines got another opportunity to express his desires and interest for a black candidate. This moment was seized when Republicans of Washington County arranged a ratification conference for the candidate-elect, William Clark, and invited several speakers — including Gaines — to endorse Clark. When Gaines arrived, he received a tumultuous reception by an estimated three thousand blacks. As a matter of fact, the voice of the presiding officer was completely drowned out when he tried to introduce Gaines. According to a *Brenham Banner* reporter, the presiding officer "yielded quietly to Gaines because he had enough sense to see that his skin was too white for that audience." [17] The audience, who had shown disinterest in the presiding officer's speech, now gave Gaines their undivided attention. Instead of endorsing Clark, Gaines delivered a militant and emotional speech, attacking both Democrats and Radicals as exploiters of black people. Gaines made it clear that the shadow of death was hanging over his head because he opposed Clark and the leadership of the party, but in a daring manner he told his audience:

> If I die I pray that you who are present today will take seven fold vengeances for me . . . If they want to fight the war [there is] no better time than now. We will arm old women with ax and hoes and our young men with double barrel guns and clean them up . . . We are willing to give the white officers in proportion to their votes . . . but so long as we cast 19 out of 20 votes, we can't let them have all of the paying offices. . . . I am opposed to Clark and Stevenson. I am in favor of bringing and putting up some new men that have never been talked of and there is time to do it. The job is worth $90,000 [and] a man of slavery deserves it.[18]

After leaving this meeting, Gaines told the press that he had no confidence in Clark, because Clark was no friend of blacks; that Clark's ulterior motive was to get black votes, but Clark would not aid or work for a black man to get an office that had money connected with it. Gaines argued that blacks could manage their own affairs and he also made it clear that he had a special dislike for white Republicans "who hardly spoke and won't shake hands. But just before election they will knock at your door before daylight to let you know that they are a candidate and will even eat with you out of your dirty skillets." [19]

The rebellious action of Gaines, his influence among black Texans, his growing militancy, but most of all his desire to see more blacks in office, caused his allies, the Radical Republicans, to feel threatened, and to make attempts to silence him. The efforts to shut Gaines's mouth came from charges in the *State Journal* in September 1871, that Gaines was simply talking about a black candidate so that he could cover up for his indictment for a rape charge. When Gaines read this article, he was up in arms. He quickly introduced a resolution in the Senate to clarify his position and to call attention to the fact that this charge of rape was fabricated by James G. Tracy, Chairman of the Republican Executive Committee. In this resolution, which also called for declaring the State Printer Office vacant, Gaines said:

> I am attacked openly and abused by one whom I and my race, the Negroes of Texas have made rich and this attack is made in order to . . . kill my influence with the people of my race. These attacks wound my feelings personally [and] the feelings of my family . . . But I wish to say that my skin is too black and my record as champion of my race too well established by the record of this senate to give them any good hopes of success. They charge me with having been confined and imprisoned for rape. It is well known that I was arrested and confined at the time and place stated as an escaped slave. Tracy knew it, and this attack is simply another proof of my assertion that he is [a] Klu Klux [Klan].[20]

Gaines argued that the attack on him was aided and abetted by Governor Davis and all those Republicans who wanted him to sing their praise by telling the blacks "that Clark is a good man." Because he refused, his character was defamed. Not ready to sit by passively, Gaines warned his fellow Radicals that he would carry this war to Africa:

> I [shall] appeal . . . to my people — mine by color. . . . I . . . shall tell [them] . . . that these men [Davis, Tracy, and Quick] are their foes; . . . that these men use them, . . . as tools to elevate themselves to positions of honor and profit. . . . then the sight of a skin as black as mine awakens no feeling of gratitude in their heartless bosoms . . . They may kill me — they must, or loose the vote of the blackman . . . enter this fight, and shall die under this banner.[21]

Gaines's resolution was lost by a tie vote of eleven-to-eleven. The only Radical Republican who had the courage enough to speak out in favor of Gaines was Senator J. B. Pridgen, who said "I deeply sympathize with Senator Gaines in seeking publicly to repeal the foul assertion cast upon him. I vote aye because I feel it is the duty of the Senate to assist Gaines in breaking the yoke placed around his neck." [22] Upon leaving the Senate chamber, Gaines told the press that the Radical elites were as "dishonest as they were powerful; that they use their official positions to enslave the black through their ignorance of politics and their faith in the Republican party." He went on to say that Davis and his "corrupt ring had set themselves up as the 'Big God of the Negroes'; that they expected worship, offices, money and power . . . and deep in their heart . . . they despise blacks." [23]

Needless to say, after this critical attack upon the Radical hierarchy, Gaines became *persona non grata* with his party. But while his isolation by party Radicals did not dampen his spirit, he faced another road block in his political career when on December 9, 1871, he was indicted on a charge of bigamy by a Grand Jury in LaGrange, Texas.[24] He was later released on one thousand dollars bail and his trial was set for the following May. This trial, however, did not take place as scheduled because Gaines was able to postpone it by filing repeated petitions to have his case transferred to a federal court.[25] Meanwhile, though still under indictment, he continued his activities in the Senate in the Twelfth and Thirteenth Legislatures.

After the District Court denied Gaines's petition to transfer his case to Federal Court in 1873, he was brought to trial on July 15th of that year.[26] Gaines's conviction stemmed from the fact that in 1867, Matt C. Despallier (as Gaines had been known) had married Fanny Sutton. Later, Gaines was told by the minister who had performed the ceremony that it had been illegally performed. So in 1870, he married Elizabeth Harrison: thus, making him a man with two wives. Based on this evidence, the jury found Gaines guilty as charged and he was sentenced to one year in prison. Gaines appealed the case,[27] but while waiting for the outcome of the appeal, he was held in the Fayette County jail from July 15 to November 24, 1873. It should be noted however, that Gaines's stay in jail did not diminish his support among blacks. As a matter of fact, it increased it. The *Austin Statesman* reported that as early as July 19, 1873, many blacks were considering Matt Gaines as a candidate for governor.[28] But while Matt Gaines's gubernatorial candidacy never got off the ground, that of his senatorialship received wide support from the masses of blacks. Thus, four weeks after the Texas Supreme Court reversed the findings of the District Court, Gaines was set free,[29] and was reelected to the Senate of the Fourteenth Legislature over a white Democratic candidate, Seth Sheppard. Gaines's seat was immediately challenged by Sheppard on the ground that Gaines was a convicted felon and upon the recommendation of the Committee on Election and Privileges, Gaines was removed from office March 25, 1874.[30]

After Gaines left office, only sparing accounts can be found about him. Apparently local newspapers did not feel it necessary to carry many accounts, if any, of his activities. To be sure, the press did not silence Gaines, because Gaines would not be silenced. In 1875, Gaines was arrested for making civil rights speeches in Giddings, Texas. The *Brenham Banner* reported that "Matt's little black hide is stretched right over a bundle of nefarious meanness and will not fail to avail himself to such splendid opportunity as the Civil Rights bill offers for getting his black brothers into trouble."[31] The editor of this paper went on to say that Gaines was organizing blacks into secret societies to fight against white people. If such a thought frightened this editor, Gaines's assertion at the Republican convention of 1878, that blacks should not concern themselves with choosing between Greenbackers or Republicans, but should support only black candidates,[32] caused him to stop carrying the activities of Gaines completely. The last mention of Gaines by a newspaper came in 1884, from the *Galveston Daily News*, when it reported that Gaines was nominated at the Republican state convention for delegate at-large, but was subsequently defeated.³³ It is worth remembering that even though Gaines's political career was short-lived, his advocation of the inalienable rights of blacks did not die. Even as he returned to obscurity with his black Baptist congregation, he held strong to his ideals of civil and equal rights of blacks. According to recorded oral history, at the annual Juneteenth celebration, Gaines usually spoke for hours on political, as well as religious themes, and admonished his audience that in the eyes of God, blacks were as good as whites; that they should have pride and hold their heads up even in troubled times.³⁴

In sum, it can be said that throughout his politically active years, Gaines thought of himself, not only as representing black people, but as being black himself. He was not ashamed of his race and never lost an opportunity to remind whites of this fact. Gaines was essentially an ethnic leader with firm roots in his community, as was shown at the Clark ratification meeting, the Union League gatherings and the annual Juneteenth celebrations. It is probably safe to say that none of the lawmakers who sat in the legislature between 1870 and 1898 had the influence and authority among the black masses, as did Gaines. In a community that had no clearly defined upper or middle class, Gaines, together with a few other individuals, came to symbolize the aspirations of his constituents. He held enormous power within his community mainly because of his leadership qualities. Because of such qualities, as a senator, he was able to deliver the intangibles of racial unity and the tangibles of social reform in areas such as education, mental asylums, and prison construction.

Gaines did not publicly or privately regard political and civil rights as luxuries, but as fundamental and basic to all human beings. As such, he fought to support and protect these ideas. Using the advantage of hindsight, one knows that Gaines's hope for integration, equal opportunity, and first-class citizenship for black people proved unrealistic in the last half of the nineteenth century. Reality was, that in Texas at that time, integration was not a way of life, and equality of opportunity was embedded in such attitudes. But being the militant he was, Gaines fought for the civil rights of blacks because he knew all too well that "power concedes nothing without a demand."

[10]

George T. Ruby: The Party Loyalist

In a period during which black legislators were unmercifully scrutinized for shortcomings, George T. Ruby won the admiration of many of his party colleagues and even some Democrats. His personal qualities of tact and diplomacy, plus his education, tended to soften the reactions of his political opponents. Dapper in dress, Ruby made Conservatives uncomfortable when he took a white lady for his bride,[1] and refused to be passive in politics. On the other hand, Ruby flattered radical Republicans as he supported and spoke out in favor of their program. At the same time, he angered blacks as he catered more to his white constituents. Ruby's action in such cases had a great deal to do with his unquestionable loyalty to the Republican party.

Ruby, the most prominent black politician of Reconstruction, began his political career in Texas as an employee of the Freedmen's Bureau in September 1866. At a salary of one hundred dollars per month, he was employed as a schoolteacher at the Methodist Church of Galveston.[2] During his tenure in this post — from October 15, 1866, to May 3, 1867 — Ruby's school grew in such rapid numbers that at the time of his resignation, it was listed as one of the largest schools in the city.[3] Upon leaving this post, Ruby became a traveling agent for the Texas Freedmen's Bureau. As such, he visited Washington, Austin, Bastrop,

Columbus, Fort Bend, and a number of other counties in East and Central Texas for the purpose of establishing the Union League and organizing temperance societies. This position, as a traveling agent, was especially pleasing to Ruby, since it enabled him to evaluate the performance of the local Bureau agent and at the same time to influence the Bureau's policy toward blacks. But this job was a two-way street for Ruby. It also called for the Bureau to evaluate him. From Charles Griffin, Bureau Commissioner of Texas, Ruby received high ratings. Writing to the Freedmen's Bureau President, Oliver O. Howard, Griffin said: "[Ruby is] an energetic man" and "has great influence among his people." The head of the Texas Bureau particularly wanted Ruby as a traveling agent because as he put it: "In that capacity many freed people may be reached and much good accomplished." [4]

It was largely due to Ruby's influence that a league was established in Milam, Falls, Galveston, and Brazos counties. By traveling and establishing various leagues throughout the State, Ruby was able to get firsthand information concerning the political aspirations of blacks, as well as the obstacles that stood in their path to political progress. For instance, during the Millican riot, Ruby complained that violence was so rampant that the "Bureau agents dared not act as they should." Ruby went on to say that the area was "an exceedingly rough one and nearly as bad as in Robertson County." In his opinion, ". . . the white people of [that area] needed a little rough handling." [5] It is worth remembering that in the early stages of the development of the League, Ruby appeared much more militant on the issues of black rights than he would in later years — the time during which he would become a full-fledged Republican.

Ruby served in the capacity of a traveling agent until October 1867, at which time he was appointed Deputy Collector of Customs at Galveston.[6] Even though Ruby relinquished his former post, he still was affiliated with the League and consequently became President of that organization in 1868. It was the League more than anything else which enabled him to rise within the ranks of the Republican party; for through this organization, Ruby controlled the bulk of the votes of the party, that is, the black votes. Consequently, Ruby was elected as a delegate to the Republican National Convention in 1868, and was the first and only black in the Texas delegation. In that same year, he also became permanent chairman of the convention called by Morgan Hamilton. When the Hamilton convention merged with Tracy's, Ruby's name was placed in nomination for Lieutenant Governor, but it was subsequently withdrawn because he was only twenty-eight years of age. At Tracy's convention, Ruby served on the Platform and Resolution Committee and also won a term on the State Executive Committee. In the election of 1869, when many whites decided not to go to the polls, Ruby was elected to the Senate from the predominantly white Twelfth District. As Senator, he became one of the most influential and most powerful men of the Twelfth and Thirteenth Legislatures. The committees to which he was appointed, judiciary, militia, education, and state affairs, performed approximately seventy-five percent of the work in the Senate during the Twelfth Legislature.[7] Membership on those committees enabled Ruby to put his beliefs into practice, translate his political views into law and to show his loyalty to party and race. Thus, by the end of the first session of the Twelfth Legislature, Ruby was no longer only a senator from Galveston, but he was part of the inner circle of the ruling party. The question that naturally comes to mind is whether or not he was more of a party man than a race man.

To that end, Ruby's personal letters, his speeches in Senate debates and his editorials in the extant copies of the *Galveston Standard* and the *Freeman's Press,* makes one wonder to what extent he really did identify with blacks. While he spoke out for the civil rights of blacks, it seems that when his ideological commitments came in conflict with his Republicanism, he tended to choose the latter. This was evidenced by his behavior on several issues: (1) his support of the Union League being headed by a white man James P. Newcomb, as opposed to the one headed by a black, Johnson Reed; (2) his posture and voting record on racially sensitive issues; (3) his siding with the Clark faction over a black candidate for the congressional seat in the Third District; and (4) his close ties with well-to-do conservative white businessmen.

As has been pointed out in chapter five, Ruby controlled the Loyal League in 1868, but as Tracy and other white Republicans tried to play down the image of the Republican party as being that of a minority dominated party, they made changes in the League which removed the presidency from Ruby and placed it in the hands of a white, James P. Newcomb. Ruby did not protest this action, but rather continued to work as a good soldier in the organization. Moreover, when Tracy and others sought to break up the League in 1871, they used Ruby to pacify blacks by appointing him to a school directorship in Galveston, knowing quite well that the position was not viable. Ruby served in that capacity for only three months before being released. In August 1871, Jacob DeGress informed Ruby that "the governor deems [his] place as a school director incompatible with [his] official position as a state officer." Writing Newcomb, Ruby sadly lamented that "while in [Austin] the matter of [his] appointment as director was taken up with the Governor and Colonel DeGress, but at that time, there was no incompatibility with his present position."[8] Again, without protest, Ruby acquiesced to higher authorities. Rather than express anger, Ruby aided and abetted the breaking up of the local League in Galveston and named his protege, Norris W. Cuney, as president of the new chapter in that city.

Ruby's posture on racially sensitive issues such as immigration and the militia bill also left a lot to be desired. For example, Ruby sided with white Republicans and Democrats to defeat Gaines's amendment to the immigration bill which called for recruiting agents to be sent to Africa. Instead, Ruby preferred to get immigrants from the Western countries of France and Great Britain. The motive behind this bill was to get newcomers to help develop the unsettled land of Texas. The incentives offered immigrants, were the purchase of cheap land and the prospect of owning the best farm equipment. So concerned were white Texans in getting white immigrants to partake of this fertile cheap land in Texas, that they ran the following advertisement in several newspapers: "There is a large amount of the very best improved lands, with every necessary facility for farming or planting, also unimproved lands for sale, lease, rent on favorable terms. Half fare only will be charged on railroads from Harrisburg to Columbus." [9] Given the economic conditions of black Texans, it seems ironic that Ruby would not support Gaines's amendment, while at the same time he felt it necessary to extend the "right hand of fellowship" to men of the old western world.

But what one has to keep in mind is that even on issues where Ruby fared a little better in his identification with blacks, such as the militia issue, he did not appear to be as race conscious as the majority of his constitutents had hoped. A careful examination of the Senate debate on the militia bill reveals that when he spoke of the need for a militia, his emphasis was not upon the senseless killings of blacks, but upon the constitutional power of the governor.[10]

If Ruby's loyalty to his party has been in question up to this point, William T. Clark's nomination for congressman from the Third District should remove all doubts. While the majority of blacks either sided with Gaines in his support of a black candidate, or went along with a more liberal white (Louis Stevenson), Ruby supported conservative Clark. As previously mentioned in chapter five, Ruby almost singlehandedly controlled the convention for Clark by preventing any of Clark's opposition from entering the convention hall. The day after the convention, he wrote J. P. Newcomb: "Of course you are well informed that our Standard Bearer (Gen) Clark has been chosen. The action of the malcontent and bolters will only tend to strengthen us in that we are freed of the dead weight on the party." Ruby went on to suggest that these men should be replaced with "better and stronger Republicans." As he opined, [the Gaines and Stevenson] factions "would [only] lead to the destruction of the party." [11]

The week following Clark's nomination, Governor Davis made a trip to Galveston, Ruby's hometown. But according to newspaper accounts of the Galveston appearance, the Governor failed to salve the wound inflicted by Ruby and the others at the Clark nominating convention. Davis received a chilly reception from blacks of Galveston, and when he spoke of Clark as the legitimate Republican nominee, he was disrupted by loud cries of protest from blacks. Moreover, when he asked the body to vote for Clark, a black editor, Frank Webb, answered with a resounding *No*. Ruby, the only high-ranking government official to accompany Davis on this political canvass, ordered Webb's immediate arrest, but the governor, obviously shaken by the experience of being booed by his black constituents, told the police to leave the defiant blacks alone.[12]

In Galveston, Ruby was not the favorite of blacks and neither were blacks given special treatment by him. In June 1870, blacks accused Ruby of not wanting to see any blacks in office save himself. This allegation stemmed from Ruby's support of Thomas Ochiltree's city charter over that of a black man, John DeBruhl. Ochiltree's charter stated that in order to sit on the city council, one had to post a $5,000 bond; an amount which very few blacks could afford.[13] Also in the Island City, Ruby requested that Governor Davis replace as alderman, John Reed, black, with N. W. Cuney. Ruby told the Governor that this replacement would enable the city's already Republican government to prepare for the forthcoming election.[14] The implication was that Reed would not be loyal to the party. Davis, however, turned a deaf ear to that request.

It is interesting to note that whenever Ruby attended an all black gathering he usually "took" the Republican party with him. Two cases in point are the Colored Men's National Labor Convention of 1871, and the Colored Men Convention of 1873. In May 1870, Ruby, along with John DeBruhl and Richard Nelson, organized the Labor Union of Colored Men at Galveston. The idea of such an organization was the brainchild of national black leaders who organized the first Colored National Labor Convention in 1869. These individuals emphasized the need to improve the working conditions of blacks. Ruby pursued this idea, not only because he accepted the premise and *raison d'être* of the national organization, but because he saw black workers as a necessary element in establishing his urban power base. Prior to the Civil War, whites had dominated the work on the docks of Galveston, but after 1870, the situation changed. A large number of blacks began to move into longshoremen jobs despite the discrimination that was meted out to them. Thus, Ruby's organizational activities were welcomed by black workers on the dock. The philosophy of the local union movement, as well as

Ruby's fidelity to the Republican party, limited the effectiveness of this local colored union.[15]

Under Ruby's leadership the local Union became tied to the Republican hierarchy. Hence, when the annual labor convention was held in Houston, June 8, 1870, Ruby not only made sure that nothing unfavorable was said about the party, but also took advantage of the occasion by urging black workers to vote for William T. Clark, the party's nominee for the Third Congressional District. Ruby's posture became even clearer as he canvassed the convention floor daily with Clark by his side, trying all time to impress upon blacks that Clark supported their aspirations. Though the convention did not make a public endorsement, the implication was that it gave silent support to Clark's candidacy.[16]

As far as the Colored Men's Convention was concerned, Ruby stated that this conference was "something monumental in the life of blacks," but "shuddered at the thought that the motive might be misinterpreted." Even though he was one of the organizers of this convention, which was called to discuss the political, economic and social conditions of blacks, he did not address those issues when called upon to speak. Rather, he told his black brethren that "with little moderation [they] could become equal to whites." [17] He encouraged blacks to acquire land and homesteads as a means of securing complete freedom. And despite suggestion from the floor that blacks form a racial or independent party, Ruby was able to steer the delegation from this course of action. His efforts in this regard was best exemplified when whites and blacks met at the Republican convention in August 1873, and Ruby was able to persuade most blacks to give their support to Governor Davis.

In Texas, the political base of an emerging black politician was of prime importance. Whether rural or urban, the politician had to demonstrate to those he was serving, through policies and deeds, that he was alert to their interests and future needs. Ruby's power base was the urban, thriving metropolis of Galveston; a major seaport where nine-tenths of the state commerce passed through, making it one of the South's busiest ports even before the Civil War. During Reconstruction, most of the leading white citizens, such as W. Ballinger, Victor McMahan and William Sinclair had a vested interest in the city and were concerned with internal improvement, high tariffs and in developing Galveston into a port and transportation center second to none on the Gulf Coast. For this project, they would need the support of the senator, but likewise, he would need their support.[18] To be sure, Ruby met the qualification of the white Galvestonians. His dress, refined manner, intelligence and economic conservatism enabled him to meet the city's elite on common grounds.[19] Also, while Ruby was Deputy Collector of customs, he established contact with merchants, shippers and financiers. He was on a first name basis with such prominent white businessmen as C. B. Gardiner, President of the First National Bank; Victor McMahan of the Banking House of T. H. McMahan, principal backer of the city's railroads and one of the three directors of the Harbor Board. Ruby also had close contact with District Judge C. B. Sabin, and County Judge Samuel Dodge.[20]

In the interest of white Galveston businessmen, Ruby sponsored considerable legislation, such as a joint resolution instructing the congressional delegation to urge Congress to survey and construct a ship canal across Florida, a waterway that would bring Europe closer to Galveston.[21] He also presented a bill for the incorporation of such railroads as the Galveston and El Paso, and the Galveston, Houston and Tyler.[22] Similarly he pushed for the incorporation of the Harbor Trust Company,[23] as well as a number of insurance companies. During Ruby's four years in the Senate, Galveston businessmen had little to complain of as the value of their export rose from $14,869,601 in 1871 to $17,629,633 in 1875.[24] Ruby realized that black voters alone (with their minority status and lack of economic power) could not keep him in office; therefore, he would have to support the interest of whites. It was not so much that he used his influence within the Republican party to acquire material gains, as well as fringe benefits for his white constituents, but that he often catered to the needs of whites at the expense of blacks, who made up the bulk of his votes in his district. To be sure, whites outnumbered blacks two to one in Galveston, but the Island city was not responsible for Ruby's stay in power. Rather, Ruby's political strength came from Brazoria and Matagorda Counties.[25]

As stated earlier, Ruby was the chief patronage broker for Galveston, and as such displayed such partiality for his white well-to-do conservative friends in his choice for local and state offices that some of his more radical black constituents became restive. Having been disappointed in his search for a high position within the Galveston Customs House, Silas Blonover, a former black employee of the Freedmen's Bureau, complained bitterly to Governor Davis that "this George T. Ruby is not a favorite of the colored people of Galveston."[26] While Ruby appeared to have good relations with prominent white Galvestonians, he did not appear to have the same with blacks. Ruby seemed to have been at odds with most of the important blacks of the city, except for N. W. Cuney. Likewise, the record does not show that he pushed, recommended or encouraged any black to run for office.

In 1869, Ruby was known as "a militant nigger carpetbagger," the black who went to Washington to bar Texas entrance into the

Union, because he said that the state's constitution was "soft" on ex-Confederates. However, once Ruby became hitched in the Republican saddle, it appears that he, too, became "soft" on certain issues relative to blacks. Ferdinand Flake of *Flake's Daily Bulletin* bore out this point when he wrote: "Ruby has improved very much over the past year. He has abated and concealed his egotism that made him offensive in the constitutional convention. He is one of the most gentlemanly Senators on the floor." [27] To a certain extent this was true. While no one can deny that Ruby fought for the rights of blacks, it appears that at times he had problems identifying with them.

Ruby's failure to stay in office after 1873, stemmed not from the lack of personal skills and judgement, but from the difficulty of simultaneously serving the interest of both his black and white constituencies with their diverse and contradictory needs and wants. As Carl Moneyhon put it: "The interest of a landless agrarian and urban work force which comprise the bulk of Ruby's party were inimicable to the business interest of the planter and merchant group." [28] In the end, his support among blacks began to wane, while his former white supporters deserted him. Whites deserted him because of his stand on racial issues and because they could not out vote his black supporters. It should be noted that however much Ruby might have differed with black leaders of his district, it was not they, but white members of his own party who pressured him not to seek reelection in 1873, so that a white man could become the candidate. Because Ruby himself realized the unlikelihood of his reelection and thought that the German Republican Chauncey B. Sabin might have a chance, he refused to seek the office of Senator again. When the district convention met at Brazoria, blacks insisted that Ruby be nominated, but the faithful Republican refused to campaign against Sabin, and instead supported Sabin's candidacy. So, Ruby's fall from power came at the hands of his own party — the party to which he was totally committed, rather than from Democratic opposition.

[11]

Richard Allen: The Opportunist

It cannot be overemphasized that the prevailing vocalized expression of black thought in the postwar years was characterized by a broad program for the advancement of the race based upon an equalitarian approach. The franchise, education, civil rights legislation, the acquisition of property and wealth, and the cultivation of morality, were all elements that were designed to achieve integration into American society. In trying to accomplish these goals, it was not uncommon to find contradictions among black leaders that often bordered on opportunism. One such victim of this fate was Richard Allen. Allen used every possible means, individuals, organizations and issues to achieve his end. It is not so much that he used the Republican and Greenback parties, the Black Exodus or black Masons to accomplish his goal, but that he told each audience what it wished to hear, thereby throwing constraints of consistency and intellectual honesty to the wind. This ambivalence tended to undermine the credibility of his public record.

Richard Allen started his political career as a traveling agent for the Freedmen's Bureau in 1867.[1] After one year with this organization, he became affiliated with the Republican party and moved rapidly through the ranks. From 1869 to 1896 he was a delegate at every Republican state convention and also a delegate to the Republican National Convention on five occasions.[2] As he functioned within the Republican party, James G. Tracy became Allen's alter ego. Which ever way Tracy went, so did Allen. He followed Tracy through thick and thin, even though such a posture put him at odds with a number of his black colleagues. But associating with Tracy, however, Allen was assured that he would be elected delegate to state conventions — fairly or unfairly — especially since Tracy had a habit of manipulating local Republican conventions in Harris County. As early as 1869, Tracy and Allen were in control of the Houston Republican party.[3] As such, Allen won the nomination for Representative from the Fourteenth Senatorial District and subsequently the election.

Allen's association with Tracy paid off in more ways than one. By 1872, Allen, had enough influence in the city to get a contract to construct sidewalks. Because the chief concern of the Houston City Council was internal improvement that year, contracts for the construction of one hundred and forty blocks of sidewalks were awarded to Hitchcock and Company to do brick and asphalt paving and to Richard Allen to do Wooden sidewalks. (The Property owners were allowed to decide which type they would prefer). Needless to say, this contract only helped to affirm a closer relationship between Tracy and Allen.[4] On the surface, however, it appears that this contract placed Allen in a precarious position. Even though he was a great supporter of Tracy, in order to stay in power he had to rely on black votes, which necessitated his acting contrary to the wishes of Tracy many times. Thus, Allen allowed his name to be placed in nomination for the congressional seat held by William Clark in 1871, even though he was not serious about this post. At that time, Allen was making plans to seek reelection as representative from the Fourteenth Senatorial District.[5] And even if he had been interested in the congressional post, his association with Tracy would have prevented him from pursuing it, since Clark was a Tracy man.

When the Houston Republicans met on August 9, 1873, to select delegates to the state convention, the members were split over whether or not they should select Tracy as a delegate. Blacks in particular were opposed to him. They had not forgotten that it was Tracy who tried to break up the Loyal Union League. Before the vote was taken, Allen was able to persuade a large number of blacks to cast their ballots for Tracy. Of this incident, the *Houston Telegraph* noted that in this convention, "Negroes showed their power, yet they were not free from white control."[6] The next year, in part because of the rumor that Houston blacks would hold their own political caucus and bar all whites, Houston Republican leaders, mostly whites, decided to hold a secret meeting rather than a public one to select candidates for local offices. At this conference, all whites, including some Democrats, were nominated with the blessing of Allen.[7]

The paradoxical nature of Allen was further shown in his simultaneous opposition and support of Independent candidates and tickets. Even though Allen was bitterly opposed to independent candidates on the state ticket, he sided with local white Republicans in support of an Independent Democrat on many occasions.[8] Similarly, in 1878 when most blacks turned to the Greenback party, not only at the urging of former Governor Davis, but because it presented a good opportunity to win the election, Allen opposed the move. Instead, he supported the Straight-Out ticket on which he received the second post.[9] But while he opposed the Greenback party on the state level, he was endorsed by, and won a seat for Street Commissioner of Houston on an independent ticket in the same year.[10]

Not having been successful in a state race since 1869, Allen tried to capitalize on the feelings of disenchanted blacks in 1879 by encouraging them to join the mass exodus to Kansas. Because of this posture, on July 19, 1879, Allen was chosen as a delegate to represent black Texans at the Nashville Convention on the Exodus.[11] When blacks returned to the state, they called for a convention to be held in Houston, in order to discuss whether or not they should join the Kansas Fever. Despite the efforts of Henry Adams, organizer of the conference, to exclude politicians from the meeting, Allen did not stay away. He came and subsequently was elected as chairman of the conference. In his acceptance speech, Allen blasted the Southern press in general, and the *Houston Telegraph* in particular, for their attack on the Exodus. He then scolded those unfriendly whites who were making attempts to stop the Exodus. After warming up the audience with his fiery preliminary remarks, Allen then proceeded to point out how the actions and attitudes of whites offended blacks. He deplored the fact that blacks, especially black women, had to purchase first class tickets on railroad coaches, but were forced to accept second class accomodations. In addition to this, he said that blacks were not appointed to school boards, nor could they say anything about the morals of those who taught their children. Allen went on to say that it was humiliating to see the word Negro written without a capital "N". He concluded his speech by saying that "blacks had appealed to the white man for too long. The time had come for "colored people to take matters into their own hands and better theselves [by going to Kansas]." [12]

After a lengthy discussion, the majority of blacks at this conference decided that they should leave the state of Texas in order to ameliorate their conditions. Yet, they were undecided as to where they should go — whether to other states of this country or to Africa, preferably Liberia. Richard Allen proposed that they take refuge on a large area of land in northwest Texas; that this land be reserved exclusively for blacks; that it be operated on the same basis as that of the Indian reservation and that no whites would be allowed to intrude once it was established.[13] Allen's argument was weak even to the most cursory observer. He knew or should have known that the prevailing idea of the period held that the rights of an Indian reservation could not be permitted to stand in the path of the white man's progress. Given the status of the black in society, there was no noteworthy reason why a black "reservation" could expect to survive unmolested, if "progress" decreed that the white man come in. By 1879, Allen could be regarded as urbane and middle class. Still, he preached the Indian reservation concept to a group of poor, rural blacks, who, if they embarked upon his course, were doomed to failure.

Though Richard Allen is regarded as one the most vocal of the black leaders on the Exodus, his support of the movement appeared to have been motivated by his political ambition, rather than a real desire to promote the welfare of the impoverished blacks. Despite all of his rhetoric about leaving the state along with other blacks, Allen lost interest in the movement when his territorial plan for Northwest Texas failed. One year later, Allen resumed his active work within the system and was elected delegate-at-large to the Republican National Convention. His efforts to gain black votes through his flimsy support of the Exodus, substantiate — rather than refute — the criticism of one of his detractors who stated that "Dick Allen is ambitious and feels that he cannot satisfy that ambition [without leaving Texas]. He not only wants the praise of the Negro but also the white." [14] This criticism was further substantiated when in July 1881, Allen was elected secretary of the American Baptist Missionary Association. At that time, the Association adopted a resolution which said nothing about Exodus, but instead, urged black Texans to educate their children and to give hearty support to any movement or to any party which advocated extension of educational facilities and which told blacks to show themselves to their fellow whites as thrifty economists and honest citizens.[15] The blessing given to this resolution by Allen must have pleased a number of white Conservatives who were frightened that Allen's support of the Exodus might have caused them to lose cheap labor.

If white Conservatives had any reason to doubt Allen's militancy in the past, they could breathe a sigh of relief in and after 1884. In that year Allen, who after being elected as an at-large delegate to the national convention, bolted the regular Republican convention and joined the Straight-Out group. It must be noted that Allen did not join the Straight-Out convention without a reward. He was later appointed chairman of the Committee on Address. Moreover, Allen sided with the unsuccessful seating of the A. G. Mallory delegation over Cuney's all-black delegation. Likewise, Allen was elected chairman of the bolted convention called by John Grant in 1896, a group which split from Cuney and the Regular Republicans.[16]

In assessing Allen's political career one can argue in all fairness to him, that there were times when he did fight for the rights of blacks, such as, when he served in the legislature. By the same token, there were other times when his actions became very questionable; times when his words did not always coincide with his deeds. It can be argued that on some issues concerning blacks, Allen was outspoken; on others, he simply spoke loud, but usually carried a small stick!

[12]

Robert Lloyd Smith: The Accomodationist

When Robert Lloyd Smith came to Texas in 1885, the country and indeed the South was undergoing the transition from a broad egalitarian approach of the Reconstruction period to the more narrow emphasis upon wealth and frugal virtues. This was also a time during which the political outlook of blacks was changing and took a number of different forms. Many individuals argued that if the Republican party was indifferent to blacks, then blacks should support and form other parties. Some argued that if black political avenues were closed, then economic and social development would be pursued. Still others said that if whites believed blacks to be inferior, then blacks must prove themselves equal to whites. As a result of living in a southern environment, the two latter views helped to forge Smith's philosophy of economic self-sufficiency; that the highest moral traits attainable were thrift, industry, and economy. As a conservative orthodox Christian, Smith stressed the values of piety, abstinence and grace. Although he embraced the philosophy of Booker T. Washington, Smith went a step further than his mentor in that he combined politics with his philosophy of self-help and became a two-term legislator in the Texas House.

Smith was an anomaly among his fellow blacks when he arrived in Oakland, Texas. He was literate, educated, and had never been a slave.

He was born January 6, 1861, in Charleston, South Carolina, to free parents. Smith's first formal education came in the public schools of Charleston, South Carolina, where his mother was a teacher. Afterward, Smith continued his education at Avery Normal Institute, a black private secondary school. In the fall of 1875, he entered the University of South Carolina and majored in Mathematics and English. When the legislature closed the school to blacks in 1877, he transferred to Atlanta University where he was trained as a teacher by Horace Bumstead, and graduated in 1879. The acquisition of the bachelor degree was followed by five years of teaching in Georgia and South Carolina public schools. In 1885, Smith moved to Oakland, Texas, a cotton farming community.[1] According to a recorded interview with William McDonald, Smith left South Carolina because of social pressure placed upon him for marrying a dark complexioned lady.[2]

When Smith arrived in Oakland, he found that it was in many ways typical of small rural villages of Southeast Texas. Located on the western end of Colorado County, this agricultural town had fewer then 300 people, a few churches, a few businesses and a school for white children. Of the 300 inhabitants, there was a sizeable and segregated black population, most of whom were displaced ex-slaves. A few of the blacks owned their own homes, but most rented dilapidated houses from white landowners. What few municipal services Oakland offered its citizens did not extend to the black district.[3] At first glimpse, it seemed that blacks in this rural village were caught up in a cruel and impossible situation.

As Smith saw it, "the Negro problem [was] to teach him how to live and how to take hold of the things about him." [4] Having defined the problem within his mind, Smith began to seek a solution to the condition of Texas blacks after he had lived in Oakland several years. In 1889, he read an article entitled "Youth's Companion" in which the author spoke of how self-improvement society had changed the lives of New Englanders. So Smith reasoned that, if relatively prosperous white New Englanders felt the need for such an organization, "how much more necessary was something of the kind for a people who had just come out of the house of bondage," the background of whose lives was centuries of oppression.[5] Hence, Smith would apply the method of white New Englanders to the condition of black Texans. In keeping with this, Smith called a meeting of black Oaklanders and established the Village Improvement Society in December, 1889. A platform drafted and ratified by charter members stated the purpose of the organization as such:

> [To] stimulate our members who are homeless to purchase homes, and to

urge those already possessed of homes, to improve and beautify them; to
purchase those things that are absolutely necessary for the comfort of our
families; to set our faces against, and unite our forces in fighting those
evils which debase our character and destroy our homes, the principal of
which are gambling, intemperance and social impurity . . . to refrain
from spending our time and money upon foolish and harmful projects.[6]

Accepting the challenge of their platform, the members of the Village Improvement Society set out to beautify their homes and neighborhood. Thus, by the time that Smith was elected to the legislature in 1894, the black section of Oakland had been transformed. Leaking roofs were repaired, window panes replaced, houses painted, fences rebuilt, lawns planted and roads repaired. But more than this, with land donated by Smith and money given by blacks of the community, a school was established for black youths.

In large part because of Smith's philosophy of self-help and the leadership role that he played in Oakland, Smith did not have any problems in getting elected to the legislature from a predominantly white district. As a matter of fact, even conservative Democratic newspapers, such as the *Houston Post,* endorsed his candidacy. Speaking of Smith, the editor of the *Post* wrote:

It would be hard for colored people of Texas to find a member of their
race better qualified to influence legislation in their behalf than the present representative . . . At home, he has the confidence and respect of all
classes irrespective of race, being a man of broad liberal views and of great
self-respect. [In Oakland] he has completely transformed the character of
the Negro settlement. . . . Here are thrifty, enterprising, law abiding,
intelligent and moral blacks . . .[7]

Smith was complimented for his work by whites because his work was not threatening to them and also, because Smith's idea of morality, industry and thrift were in accord with the traditional Protestant work ethic. Smith went to the legislature in 1895 under the premise that the great majority of whites, desirous of preparing blacks for citizenry, were "perfectly willing to co-operate with any responsible individual . . . whose aim is to make the race better."[8] To be responsible in Smith's view was to accept white values, have a good character, work hard and accumulate wealth. In the legislature, Smith was surrounded by whites, some helpful, some malevolent, but most indifferent to the concerns of blacks. The political power of the House resided in those men and they controlled the limits to which Smith could effectively exercise his influence. Smith knew the realities of Southern race politics, as well as the boundary beyond which he would be considered dangerous, and thus Smith chose the accomodationist approach. It should come as no surprise, then, that most of Smith's work in the legislature came in the area of education and in business designed to aid small entrepreneurs.

In the field of education, Smith ranked high as legislator. One of his first bills was to place black trustees over black schools. After having been successful in this venture, he then moved to his first love, vocational education. As a result of his interest in that area, one would find him much more aggressive on the Prairie View issue than on the Colored Branch University affair. It was Smith who was partly responsible for the 1896 bill which brought with it a grant of fifty acres of land for Prairie View College.[9]

Smith's concern and effort in aiding Prairie View had a great deal to do with his faith in vocational education as a scheme for improving the economic condition of black Texas farmers. He had long believed that improved farming methods were essential to the betterment of black lives and only Prairie View could provide this sort of technical instruction for the race in Texas. So at every opportunity he got, he pushed for financial aid for Prairie View. It was Smith's hope that Prairie View would become a "beacon on the hill" for many black youths who wanted to pursue a degree in vocational education.

On the other hand, without denegating the importance of Prairie View, Smith reasoned that because of the limited college facilities, as well as its locality, many students were deprived of the opportunities which the college provided. Thus, before leaving the legislature in 1897, Smith proposed that his Village Improvement Society establish a private vocational school. Smith argued that in order to improve the black standard of living, a student needed to be exposed, from the first grade, to the correct morals, attitudes, and ideals of thrift, economy and industry and that such instruction should be continued through college. While pushing strongly for industrial education, Smith made it clear that his advocacy of private school was being made not to eliminate the existing public schools, but only to augment their curriculum with vocational agriculture and home economics.[10]

As has already been inferred, Smith was not opposed to a liberal arts education. After all, he himself had one. Furthermore, the Twenty-fifth Legislature's refusal to pass a law establishing a "Colored Branch University" did not prevent Smith from voting for appropriation for The University of Texas. When he was chided by a fellow white colleague for voting for appropriation to a university which denied admission to black students, Smith replied: "I know that I cannot enter The University of Texas as a student, but I would rather place the fate of my race in the hands of the educated, rather than to put it in the hands of the ignorant."[11] After making that statement, the President of the university asked Smith to make a speech on that subject, but he refused, preferring to use his influence indirectly to get the bill through the House.

Smith's concern for education was not only relegated to liberal arts and vocational, but also to other aspects. This became evident as he introduced a resolution "that the state of Texas recognize the Afro-American Fair and Interstate Exposition." The objective of the fair was to stimulate, encourage and expose the advancement made in arts, science and general husbandry by Afro-Americans residing in the United States. One can easily see how this resolution would pass, whereby the one sponsored by Smith to acknowledge the death of Frederick Douglass did not. A similar fate also came to a concurrent resolution sponsored by Smith to recognize Cuba in its struggle for independence from Spain.[12]

Although it appears that Smith devoted most of his time in the legislature to education, in all fairness to him, it should be pointed out that he did propose bills and fought for the civil right of blacks. He introduced legislation opposing lynching, election fraud, and the Landlord and Tenant Act. Needless to say, the above bills met with defeat and whether or not broken in spirit, Smith did not pursue any of them a second time. Not feeling comfortable to stage a protest or to rock the political boat on these issues while still a legislator, Smith waited until he left office. Upon vacating his post, he wrote Booker T. Washington and admitted that "Lynch laws, peonage, whitecapping and all kindred evil have their root in the rape of the ballot." [13]

Regardless of the setback that Smith might have met at the hands of his colleagues, being embedded with Christian virtue, he believed in playing the game of politics fairly. Thus, he supported a Democrat from Washington County over a Republican in a contested election even though the majority of the Republican House members voted for the man of their party. He did so because he said that the committee didn't have enough evidence to oust this gentleman. Moreover, Smith voted against the Conference Free Bill which purported to regulate the salary of county officers. He gave his reason as such: "Instead of limiting the fees of county officers in large counties, it reduces the salaries of county officers in small counties." Likewise, he protested the action of the House's attempt to shut off debate of the minority.[14]

One might argue that Smith believed in fairness in things that were purely political, but in things that were purely social, he steered a clear course. While Smith made a brilliant speech against the separate waiting rooms when he first arrived in Austin, he steadfastly refused to engage in the growing controversy over "social equality." This amorphous term was a lighted stick of dynamite. To whites, it meant the social mixing of the races. Whites presumed that if unleashed, the blacks would necessarily choose this course. The degree to which white legislators felt threatened is indicated in the Jim Crow laws that they passed before, during and after Smith left the legislature. Smith, the pragmatic and to some degree, the accommodationist, realized that a firm stand against social equality was essential to any success he might have in improving the economic condition of Texas blacks. More than this, he believed that social equality was wrong for both races. Illustrative of his belief was an episode that occurred while he was a freshman legislator, when Smith cosponsored a bill that consecrated the San Jacinto Battleground as a historic site. At the dedication ceremonies, the Daughters of the Republic of Texas honored with a reception those legislators who had supported the bill. Of this occasion Smith wrote:

> [When] the Sergeant-at-Arms called for the members of the legislature to form a line in order to be presented to this band of lovely patriotic women, I considered that this portion of the program partook of a social nature equality and I did not fall in line, not desiring in the least to let my position as a representative allow me to desire any social recognition of this kind.[15]

Smith eventually yielded to the pressure from his colleagues and joined the reception line. Torn between being a part of, and still outside of, the legislative circle, Smith would later write that he was accepted as a member of the legislature on the same terms as other whites. He added that "we worked for the common good and did everything possible to advance the best interest of all people regardless of color." [16] As one looks at the record of the Twenty-fourth and Twenty-fifty Legislatures on race relations, one can clearly state that the common good of all was not attended to. Smith's vision in this regard was probably blurred by his belief that race was not a problem; that "the only time [he] thought in racial terms and feelings was when some laws came up that singled the race out for special legislation, such as the waiting room."[17]

The above statement of Smith might account for the fact that he sided with the Lily Whites against Norris W. Cuney at the Republican state convention of 1896. Somehow Smith believed that such action would put him in the good graces of the better element of the party. Instead, this posture backfired upon him. When Smith left the legislature in 1898, he wanted to remain active in politics; therefore, he tried to procure, through Booker T. Washington, a post with the Internal Revenue.[18] But President Theodore Roosevelt, though he respected Booker T. Washington's opinion in the selection of blacks to federal posts, was unreceptive to Smith's application because of opposition to Smith among lily white Republicans who dominated the party in Texas in 1901. What really happened was that Lily Whites used Charles M. Ferguson to voice their opposition of Smith to Roosevelt. Ferguson had an audience with Roosevelt in 1901, and told him that Smith had campaigned against the only Republican candidate for Congress, H. B. Hawley; that he had refused to stop campaigning for the Democratic opponent unless he was paid or his brother-in-law was endorsed by Hawley for postmaster. So, when Roosevelt wrote Washington concerning Smith's appointment, he said: "Everyone seems to think that Mr. Smith has done well in education, but there is some strong feeling that he is not straight in political matters. By straight, I mean not merely in a party sense, but that he is not straight because he will not work unless there is something in it for him personally." [19] To the above, as well as similar allegations made earlier, Washington's response to Roosevelt was that "his [Smith's] political enemies have brought [these] charges against him, [and that] if he is not appointed, it will ruin his influence in educational and other works in Texas among our people and the whites." [20] In order to reinforce his endorsement of Smith, Washington enclosed a letter of recommendation from Robert Ward, a white Democrat who sat in the legislature with Smith. Of Smith, Ward said: "By reason of his individual merit and capacity he commended the friendship of each man of the House." [21] Writing to Smith on the same day, Ward said: "If all colored men in Texas were like you, the race problem would soon be settled." [22] Somewhat naive of the thinking and actions of most whites of that time, Smith wrote Washington about the situation: "I have gotten into people's minds that President Roosevelt pays no attention to machine charges . . . as I have proven the falsity of the charges made against me." [23]

A lack of available data prevents one from stating whether or not Smith exonerated himself of the above charges. What is clear, however, is that Smith used his political leverage as a legislator to help promote his ideas about vocational education and his program on economic self-sufficiency; the result of which was the establishment of The Farmers' Improvement Society. This organization, created in 1902, was designed to: (1) abolish the credit system, (2) produce better methods of farming, (3) create corporations to attend to the sick and dead, and (4) improve homes. Through this Society, Smith was able to establish a Society's school, a Society sick and burial insurance and an overall factory.[24] In part because of the contacts Smith made while in the legislature and the Republican party, he advanced from owning two acres of land in 1891, to sixty-one acres in 1896, and to one hundred and twenty-two acres in 1901.

Yet despite the economic and political progress that Smith made between 1890 to 1901, he did not receive the post that he was seeking with the Internal Revenue. Rather, he was appointed to the job of Deputy United States Marshall for the Northern District of Texas. This job, which carried a salary of $25,000 a year,[25] came mainly as an appeasement to Booker T. Washington. Yet, it brought Smith an added income and kept his hopes and activities in the Republican party alive. Constantly aware of his goal of economic self-help, and trying desperately to remain active in the Republican party, even though his influence was waning in that organization, Smith wrote Waller Burns in 1904, to ask his help in electing Smith as delegate at-large to the Republican convention.[26] Losing in this bid, Smith retired from politics and devoted his entire life to his Farmers' Improvement Society. It should be noted that even after he left the political arena, Smith continued, in an accomodating fashion, to speak out against political and economic indignities imposed upon blacks. A case in point was the showing of the movie, *Birth of a Nation,* at a theatre in Waco, Texas, on November 9, 1915. Smith wrote a letter which was carried in the *Waco News* with the following caption, NEGRO DENOUNCES BIRTH OF A NATION. R. L. SMITH, LOCAL BANKER, DECLARES BIG PHOTO PLAY SPECTACLE IS UNFAIR IN THAT IT PRESENTS COLORED PEOPLE IN IMPROPER LIGHT. An excerpt from Smith's article reads as follows:

> The old days of slavery are gone. Happily for us all, we are no longer master and slave, but . . . bound together by the ties of mutual interest, a part indissoluble, connected to a future which we must meet together . . . You [whites] are strong and great and powerful, we are weak, poor and unable to do more than make this plea to you. Give us the same chance to make something of ourselves that you would want if you were in our place.[27]

The Birth of a Nation was a motion picture produced and released by D. W. Griffith in 1915. The parts of the film that were offensive to many people (especially blacks) were the ones which distorted the story of black emancipation and enfranchisement. Offensive to both black and whites was that the film depicted the Ku Klux Klan in a favorable light. While one can applaud Smith for taking the above stance, one can argue that he was very accommodating in his approach, and persisted in that course until he died in 1942.

Some historians argue that the race philosophies of Booker T. Washington and Robert L. Smith were indistinguishable one from the other. Still there was a difference. While Washington acted covertly on political matters, as a legislator, Smith had no choice but to act overtly. But his overt acts were often marked by such conciliatory philosophy that it appeared at times that he confused his ends with his means. As a legislator, Smith sincerely believed that through cooperative spirit with his white colleagues and his philosophy of self-help, he could effectively change the lives of blacks. The only problem with that approach was that whites were anything but cooperative in the Lone Star State in the 1890s. Although he worked for full citizenship rights, economic equality and integration of blacks into the American society, Smith often masked these goals beneath an approach that satisfied influential elements which were often indifferent or hostile to the fulfillment of these goals.

[13]

Norris Wright Cuney: The Climber Of Sorts

Norris Wright Cuney, has been described by one writer as one of "the greatest political leaders of Texas." During his long and distinguished career, Cuney combined charismatic qualities with effective use of politicking to propel himself into the center of Texas Republican politics from 1870 to 1896. His rise through the party ranks was described best by his biographer when she wrote:

> In these early days, Cuney was a veritable "man on the make," a joiner, an organization man, shrewd enough to make useful political contacts. He was a climber of sorts, an energetic hustler selling himself and his capabilities to others. He had the "hail fellow-well met" qualities necessary for success in politics . . . Cuney fitted well into the fast moving atmosphere of crowded, noisy convention halls and the horse trading society of politicians . . . he appeared quite the suave politician.[1]

Though Cuney was never elected to the state legislature, a study of the black leadership would not be complete without an analysis of his role in this cadre.

Cuney was born in 1840, to white planter Colonel Phillip Cuney and a slave mother, Adelina Stuart, near Hempstead, in Waller County. In 1859, Cuney, along with his two brothers was sent by their father to George B. Bashon's Wyle Street Public School for Negroes in

Norris W. Cuney.
— Courtesy University of Texas Archives

Pittsburg, Pennsylvania. Upon completion of his studies at the above school, Cuney was supposed to have gone on to Oberlin College, but the Civil War brought an end to that dream. Cuney subsequently returned to the Lone Star State and settled in Galveston.[2] There, he began reading the law. At the end of the War, Cuney became acquainted with George T. Ruby, the man who would become his political mentor in years to come. It was Ruby who introduced Cuney to the "inner and higher" circles of the Republican party; and it was he who was responsible for Cuney's first political appointment — that of first assistant to the Sergeant-at-Arms of the Twelfth Legislature. Again, at the urging of Ruby, Cuney was appointed President of the Newcomb faction of the Galveston Loyal Union League on July 12, 1871.

It should be noted that in the early years of Reconstruction, Cuney was not concerned with state and county offices. Rather, his interest lay in serving in a federal post. As such, he was appointed night inspector of the Customs House of Galveston, on February 3, 1872. The following September, he resigned this job to accept the post of revenue inspector at Sabine Pass.[3] He stayed in this office only three months before asking to be reinstated in his original post. To this end, he wrote Governor Davis a letter stating how hard he had worked in Republican campaigns, including that of Davis.

Last December . . . Col. Patton promised to appoint me in the Customs House . . . In February one of the inspectors died . . . I understand that Clark interfered . . . and prevented the appointment. I resigned my position on the ticket as an elector and you know how hard I worked during that canvass. I spent my money and give my time [for the party] . . . I never held but one place since I have been in the party . . . How I want something to do . . . I am getting tired of the treatment I have been receiving at the hands of so-called Republicans. I can never learn how to support men who are constantly and openly ignoring and insulting me. If you have influence enough to enforce my appointment over C.'s opposition, it will be a great gratification to me.[4]

After writing the above letter, Cuney was again appointed Inspector of Customs at Galveston in August 1873. His term in this office lasted for only four years because when G. B. Shields became Collector of Customs in 1875, he made a concerted effort to achieve one of his major objectives, to rid the Customs House of all Davis's appointees.

Shields's action against Cuney was stimulated in part by a resolution which Cuney had sponsored at the Republican state convention of 1876. This resolution asked that all federal office holders be removed from the offices that they held within the party.[5] When Shields confronted Cuney on this subject, Cuney replied the he knew nothing about the matter. After Cuney refused to get Shields a copy of the resolution, and refused to sign a statement that he did not have anything to do with this document, Shields told him that he could expect to be removed.[6] Consequently, Shields wrote the Secretary of Treasury, asking that Cuney be replaced with "a more competent" William Evans.[7] But, instead of removing Cuney, the Secretary ordered that Cuney be restored. Shields insisted that Cuney had to go and subsequently, started looking for other evidence to have Cuney removed. Shields's search led to charges made against Cuney on February 21, 1875, concerning a Norwegian ship. On that date, Cuney allowed 800 bags of coffee to be lightered from a Norwegian ship that had not yet entered port. When this incident was reported to the Chief Inspector of Customs, for some unknown reasons, he chose not to get involved in this case; therefore, he deferred the decision to the Secretary of Treasury saying, "How far [this] was justified under all circumstance, is not for me to say." [8] Cuney was later called in to explain his action. He told his superior that he lightered the coffee only after the captain of the ship and superintendent of the lighter told him the ship could not go over the bar unless some of its weight was lightered. Furthermore, Cuney argued that he allowed the cargo to be taken ashore because the coffee bore no duty. After Cuney explained the reasons for his action, the District Attorney moved that Cuney had no intention to do wrong.[9] Shields, who especially resented Cuney's ambition and unscrupulous aspiration for office within the Republican party, still insisted that Cuney must go.

Cuney was as determined to remain in office as Shields was to remove him. After explaining his action about the Norwegian ship to the Secretary of Treasury, Cuney went over to Shields's office in order to talk over their differences. No sooner had Cuney arrived than an irrate Shields called him a nigger and asked him out of his office. Cuney left, but not before exchanging the same insult.[10] Cuney then wrote former Governor Davis to come to his rescue. Davis, in turn wrote J. P. Newcomb and told him that "Cuney {says} . . . that General Shields . . . is trying to put him out. See to that and put a stop to it." [11] The efforts of both Davis and Newcomb were to no avail. Cuney was removed at the request of Shields when the new Secretary of Treasury, John Sherman took office on July 25, 1877.

Cuney did not remain silent nor passive after his dismissal. Instead, he wrote a letter of protest to John Sherman stating that no black man in Texas had been appointed to a position of importance, although four-fifths of the Republican party in the state was black.[12] Former Governor Davis and Judge C. B. Sabin also wrote letters to the secretary in Cuney's behalf acknowledging his competence and fidelity to the party.[13] Despite the above support and protest, Cuney's dismissal remained in effect. Being the politician he was, Cuney did not take "no" for an answer. When Sherman left office in 1880, Cuney resubmitted his application and as a result was made Chief Inspector of Customs May 31, 1881, and Special Inspector January 20, 1882.[14] Cuney's last appointment was short-lived, for his election as alderman to Galveston City Council on March 4, 1883, disqualified him from holding a federal position. Cuney, then gave up a salary of $125 a month to become an alderman at eight dollars a month.[15] Seemingly, Cuney took a cut in salary, but it should be pointed out that when he became alderman, he also became a contracting stevedore and the titular head of the Republican party.

When N. W. Cuney became alderman from the Twelfth Ward to the Galveston City Council, he was the first black to serve in that position. Cuney made his first appearance in city politics when he unsuccessfully opposed Robert L. Fulton, a Democrat, in the mayoralty contest of Galveston on March 11, 1875. Notwithstanding his defeat, all was not lost for Cuney in this election, because it forged for him a friendship with Fulton that would serve as a basis for political alliance for years to come. One year later, Fulton had a falling out with his fellow Democrats and therefore, he went on to establish the People's party and to nominate a slate of candidates for city office. Cuney, a fusionist in principle, supported the people's ticket in the hope that dissident Democrats would support him in his bid for representative of the Thirty-sixth Floatorial District of which Galveston was a part in 1876. This idea turned out to be wishful thinking and ended up being a one-way street. Independent Democrats did not vote for Republicans, even though Cuney was able to influence a large number of Republicans to vote for independents.

Still, Cuney did not give up hope on the People's party. As a matter of fact, the year of 1877 found him campaigning very actively for the People's party organization. Moreover, in this election, Cuney was accused of repainting Republican posters and placing Demoratic candidates' names on them.[16] Some blacks went so far as to charge Cuney with actually sabotaging Republicans in order to elect Democrats in 1877. Another black asserted that Cuney "held Galveston Niggers in his hands and decided who the mayor and alderman would be."[17] Still others said that the merchants made use of Cuney so that they could succeed in local politics.[18] A lack of evidence prevented one from stating to what extent these allegations were true. What is clear, however, is that Cuney was a shrewd politician who used both whites and blacks to achieve his ends. Consequently, he was elected on the People's party ticket to Galveston City Council in 1883.

As alderman, Cuney did not fare any better nor worse than white city councilmen. However, he did work to support the interests of blacks. For example, when prominent businessmen George Ball gave a donation of two hundred thousand dollars to build a city public school, Cuney would accept this grant only if it meant that the school would be open to blacks and whites alike. The council had at first accepted Cuney's motion to that effect, but later rejected it, notwithstanding the protest of Cuney and his other black colleague, J. H. Washington. This issue was resolved only when Cuney threatened to take the case to the state legislature.[19]

It is worth noting that when Cuney served on the Galveston City Council in 1883, he was also a contracting stevedore. Yet his interest in the urban black worker started long before that date. It began in 1877, when a wildcat strike broke out among black railroad workers who claimed that they were not paid enough to support their families. Cuney played a key role in settling this strike. Contrary to white leaders who urged blacks to press the railroad company for damage and use violence if necessary to get what they wanted, Cuney took the non-violent approach. He told the crowd that violence would not help because the strike would easily be quelled by armed troops from Houston. He went on to say that blacks should go home and accept whatever price they could get the next day.[20] Although enraged, blacks dispersed peacefully. Two of several reasons can be cited for Cuney's action. Perhaps, as had been first alleged, he was working for white employers who wanted blacks to return to work. Secondly and more importantly, being a climber of sort, Cuney was trying to establish himself as a leader of these urban blacks.

The opportunity for Cuney to exert himself as a leader of black laborers really began in 1882, when trouble developed on the wharves of Galveston among white workers. Capitalizing on this instability which lasted into 1885, Cuney first organized black workers, purchased $2,500 worth of tools, established Texas's first black screwman organization and procured work for blacks on one of the major wharves, — Morgan's Wharf.[21] Cuney's next move was to get his men on the Mallory Wharf. The opportune moment for this endeavor came in October 1885, when white workers struck for higher wages.[22] White workers had threatened to strike in April, but an agreement had been reached in May at which time they agreed to accept a reduction in wages until September — a time during which business was expected to improve. The reduction in wages was from sixty to forty-cents an hour for all work for a four month period. When wages had not been restored by October, a committee of white longshoremen went before the Mallory company for an explanation. The company replied by firing all the members of the committee. Thus, a full-fledged strike developed. To add insult to injury, instead of trying to settle the strike, the captain of the Mallory Line, J. N. Sawyer, upon his return from an out-of-town trip, restored the old forty-cent pay scale permanently. So while white longshoremen struck, and were caught with their backs pressed against the wall, and with nowhere to go to redress their grievances, Sawyer used Cuney's men. Cuney agreed to let his men work on the Mallory Line if they would be retained on good behavior and have as equal a chance to work as white laborers.[23] Cuney permitted his men to work for lesser wages even though he earlier had said that he would accept the highest wages asked for by the white longshoremen. In response to Cuney's action, the Knights of Labor called for a general strike in sympathy with their affiliates in Galveston who were put out of work by blacks.[24]

After a few days of strike, a conference was held between the Knights of Labor, J. N. Sawyer, head of the Mallory Company, and Norris W. Cuney, who represented black workers. At this conference, Cuney emerged victorious. An agreement was made to divide the work equally between whites and blacks, working every other ship and alternating week of work.[25] Many white citizens of Galveston claimed that this agreement was a ploy by Cuney to use black workers to win the mayoralty election in the Island City. Others argued that this agreement was a plot between Cuney and Mallory to bring cheap labor to Galveston. Still others believed that this was a trick employed by Cuney to substitute colored labor for white labor on the wharves of Galveston. Cuney denied most of these charges.[26] While it is true that he permitted blacks to be used as scabs, by the same token, Cuney's role as a stevedore was important in improving the lot of urban black workers. Cuney's action allowed blacks to continue to work on both the Mallory and Morgan Wharves, but more importantly, it enabled each black to earn an average of about one thousand five hundred dollars a year. Cuney's role in this strike gained him influence among the businessmen and politicians of Galveston. His leadership role in this strike also provided him with an added income until he became Collector of Customs, July 1889. Moreover, it gave him more leverage as he maneuvered his way through Republican politics.

As previously stated, at about the time that Cuney became alderman, he also became head of the Republican party. If Cuney's rise to that position began when he was elected temporary chairman of the Republican state convention of 1882, it reached a new plateau in 1884, and reached its zenith in 1889. In 1884, Cuney showed what a shrewd politician he was when he was able to get himself elected as chairman of the party; to reorganize black and white Davisites, as well as federal officeholders to unseat a white delegation at the state nominating convention; and to win election as a delegate to the Republican national Convention. After arriving at the national convention, Cuney was given the honor of being elected vice-president of that body. Since Cuney went to Chicago as an uninstructed delegate, he cast his lot with James G. Blaine rather than the incumbent Chester Arthur. This was a smart move on Cuney's part, because Blaine received the party's nomination and by backing Blaine, Cuney ended up on the right side of the national Republican leaders. To be sure, he had won friends in high places and five years hence he would become the chief patronage broker of Galveston.[27]

So contrary to the statement in *Galveston Weekly News,* that "the day has not arrived when a black can be leader of even the decrepit Republican party of Texas," [28] not only had the time come, but it had come to one who was arrogant, obnoxious, and determined to be his own boss, for the good or for the bad; one who would not be deterred even by those whites who had helped him climb up the ladder. Nowhere was this more apparent than when Cuney became Collector of Customs in Galveston in 1889.[29] Unlike his mentor, George T. Ruby, who used J. P. Newcomb as his alter ego, Cuney made his own decisions. By the time he became Collector, he realized that Newcomb's racial view had changed and that Newcomb was now affiliated with the

Lily Whites. So, when Newcomb applied for postmastership at San Antonio, Cuney wrote the Secretary of Treasury telling him not to appoint Newcomb because "[Newcomb was] all things to all men and true to none." [30] Consequently, Newcomb did not get the job.

When Cuney was appointed to the Collectorship he became the undisputed boss of the Republican party. The Collectorship of Galveston was the most important government post given to a colored man in the South in grade and salary. For Texas Republicans, it meant that old white party veterans and dispensers of patronage such as James P. Newcomb, Jacob C. DeGress, Nathan Patton and A. J. Mallory, now had to submit to a black man, however grudgingly. But it should be noted that even though Cuney waged an unrelenting war against Lily Whites, he would not take this same posture toward other whites. For example, Cuney kept DeGress on as Postmaster despite demands to get rid of him. Likewise, he refused to remove Sam Houston's daughter as Postmistress in Austin even though she was leaning toward the Democratic camp. Similarly, his chief assistant was G. M. Patton, son of Nathan Patton, who was a former Collector of Customs at Galveston.[31] On the contrary, it should be noted at this point that there is nothing to indicate that Cuney's appointments of blacks were equal to that of whites. The only blacks who got a good paying salary were Samuel McCoy and Cuney's brother, Joseph.[32] This fact seemed a bit ironic since Cuney's tenure at the helm of the Republican party depended largely upon the masses of blacks.

As Cuney climbed the ladder of success and tried to hold on to power within the Republican party, how did he fare on other matters which affected blacks? On matters of race, Cuney said: "I abhor and detest . . . the question . . . of injustice . . . of color, religion, of nationality and it has been the labor of my public life for twenty years to eliminate these elements from our public policy." [33] Yet, outside of his protest about the exclusion of blacks from Ball High School in Galveston, and his demonstration against the separate railroad coach law, it appears that Cuney was too busy climbing to devote much of his attention to racial matters. He said nothing of Jim Crow law passed by the Texas Legislature in 1875, which required the state to take away the license of all hotel owners so as to prevent them from accommodating blacks as was prescribed by the Civil Rights Act of 1875. Aside from a plank to place blacks on juries, if Cuney made any attempts to include other civil rights planks in the Republican party platform during his tenure at the helm of the party, the record does not indicate such. Nor did he speak out against the smaller number of blacks elected to public office.

One could not expect Cuney to speak on all issues affecting blacks, but that he did not speak out on the above issue, makes one wonder to what extent he was concerned with the plight of his brothers. For it was Cuney who said that "the black [man] . . . is equally responsible for the good or evil which may flow from the performance of his public duties." [34] Cuney was no ordinary man. He was the only black leader who had a statewide following. To the black masses, his ability to stay on the top of the Republican hierarchy was an indication of strength and heroism. So, when he did not speak out on certain issues, the question that naturally comes to mind is how much did his ambition for office silence him?

On the subject of education, Cuney appeared to have been somewhat of a paradox. Even though both he and his daughter received a liberal arts education and even though he said that he was in favor of both industrial and liberal arts training, a careful analysis of Cuney's speeches and letters placed him squarely in the industrial education camp. On occasion he stressed solvency and inferred that blacks should become self-sufficient farmers who could raise crops for market. At other times, he told blacks not to pursue liberal fields just to imitate the white man.[35] Moreover, Cuney argued that literature was the last and highest expression of a people's development; something that blacks were not ready for at that time. As Cuney fought with Lily Whites for power within the Republican party, his above statements and postures must have comforted many of them in their beliefs about what blacks were good for and where they should be held on the occupational hierarchy.

As to violence, Cuney spoke out against the killing of blacks and the removal of other prominent blacks from Fort Bend County in 1888. However, as he continued to climb the political ladder of success, his vision became blurred as to what power the governor had and could exercise in the prevention of mob violence. A case in point centered around the mob violence in Lamar County during the election of 1892. Because Cuney was campaigning for George Clark and against James Stephen Hogg, who had said that if elected he would put an end to mob violence, Cuney argued that it was not within the governor's power to quell violence.

Cuney assumed the position of a black leader because he reached the black masses effectively through politics. Still, Cuney never could have monopolized so effectively this leadership role had not the masses of blacks remained in Texas during the Kansas Exodus. Thus, Cuney wanted no part of the Exodus and believed that the South provided the black man the best chance to improve his condition. In keeping with this posture Cuney said: "I am of the South. It is my home. It is the home of my race. There lies our interest [and] I can elevate my people down in the South." [36] Yet even though Cuney's rise and stay in power in the Republican party rested squarely in the hands of rural blacks, he did little to improve their lot.

As far as black legislators were concerned, it appears that Cuney did not have a close relation with any of them. As a matter of fact, he had open quarrels with Richard Allen and Robert Smith. Still, despite Cuney's shortcomings, he was a strong leader, one who commanded the respect of both whites and blacks. In the Black Belt counties, his name was not only synonymous with that of achievement, but also with that of a "tough black" who would stand up to whites. But as far as Cuney's role in the black leadership of Texas was concerned, Cuney can best be classified as a "climber of sorts."

Postscript

For over a century, the first black political leaders of Texas have been under a cloud. Today, research has revealed that despite their slave birth, their inexperience, their general lack of educational opportunities and white prejudice, they made a credible record. Black elected state officials were men of varying backgrounds, abilities, and attitudes. Some were remarkable natural leaders; others, diffident and inexperienced, were dull and uninspiring. Still, others initiated measures and debated actively and intelligently, showing themselves capable of defending themselves and their race against disparagement by white members.

On the basis of available research data, one can argue that the majority of these black politicians did not differ markedly from most of those they sought to lead. The average black lawmaker came from the ranks of slaves, not freedmen; he was of dark complexion not light. He was the son of an uprooted slave immigrant from another Southern state, not a descendant from a Texas family. He was more likely to have been a runaway slave than a soldier fighting beside his master in the Civil War. He was neither highly educated nor illiterate. Of the forty-one black legislators, at least one had completed a four-year college; six had attended or completed a (two-year) normal school (for teachers); three had completed elementary school; twenty-seven had a rudimentary education and only four were not educated.

On the subject of origin and social characteristics, it is clear that as a group, the political leaders of Texas could not be regarded as elite, but rather as lower middle class, who was far more fortunate in term of occupation and wealth than the overwhelming majority of freedmen. As to occupation, the majority came from the ranks of farmers, teachers, artisans, and ministers. Except for farmers, politicians of the above mentioned occupational groups were usually fortunate in massing a great deal of wealth during the period of their political careers. Some, in fact, demonstrated remarkable upward mobility. The entrepreneurial propensities were evident among such men as Richard Allen, B. F. Williams, David Abner, Walter Burton, and Robert L. Smith. It must be emphasized that while there was a distance in the social origin (in terms of occupation and wealth) between the black masses and their leaders, it was never as great as that which existed in Louisiana and South Carolina, where the leadership consisted of a disproportionately high number of mulatto and well-educated blacks with considerable property.

The routes by which these men achieved political prominence were varied. There were some who established themselves and developed a constituency through their work in black churches, in black schools (both those of the Freedmen's Bureau and the state supported) and in the Union League. Yet, it is difficult to establish whether and to what degree the black church was actually responsible for the political prominence these individuals achieved. As Thomas Holt observed in *Black Over White:* "It was less a matter of the churches themselves being a basis for organizing a constituency than simply the attractiveness of the church for black men of ambition and leadership potentials." The same held true for blacks who came to political prominence via the schools and/or Union League. Like the church, the school and the Union League were only avenues which were opened to men who were politically motivated. On the other hand, some blacks rose to prominence without a strong connection to the church or the school; such was the case of Jeremiah Hamilton. Still, other blacks were clearly economically and politically ambitious individuals who came to Texas because they saw the opportunity to acquire wealth and power and to establish themselves in politics. Such were the cases of William Reynolds, George T. Ruby, and Henry L. McCabe. It should be emphasized that the individuals who belonged to the latter group were in the minority. Unlike a pattern that was to be found in Mississippi, where black carpetbaggers moved into the area of the state that was characterized by a lack of trained, sophisticated, local blacks and went on to seek office at the local, state and national level, this was not the case in Texas. Most of the leadership came from the indigenous South.

Even though the findings of this study have shown blacks as being different from whites in terms of numbers, educational achievements and social class, this does not and should not foster nor enhance the myth that black lawmakers did not contribute anything constructive to the state and its people. Despite their dismally small number, blacks were not simply pliant tools of white Republicans. They did exert as much (however small) of an influence as they could. As members of the state legislatures and constitutional conventions, blacks helped to lay the foundation for the public school system of the state, to make reforms in mental asylums and correctional institutions, and to pass laws which granted universal suffrage and the protection of civil rights

It is an undeniable fact that while blacks worked for the good of both races, they were especially concerned with enhancing the welfare of their people. But there were, in effect, few precedents to help them in this endeavor and their challenge was made even more difficult by the lack of a clear ideological perspective on the part of the black leadership in which to judge and determine the state legislative program. On the other hand, if it appears that black legislators did not accomplish very much for their constituents, it was because direct black influence was minimal in Texas politics, largely because there was not much of it. Of the thirty-seven blacks who were in the Texas House, the highest number to sit at any one time was eleven. Moreover, seventy-five percent of those thirty-seven served only one term, or two years. So, the opportunity to learn on the job was abbreviated even during the "Radical Regime." Being both black and newcomers, seniority for them was always out of reach. In the Senate, blacks fared even worse. The highest number to serve in this chamber was four with only two serving at any given time. Also blacks left the Senate much sooner than they exited the House. The latter being in 1898 and the former in 1882. So, despite their status in the black community, black state politicians of Texas never possessed more than a semblance of power. Black political power was limited for a number of reasons: (1) it was limited within the Republican party; (2) it was curbed by differences shared among blacks themselves; (3) it was obstructed by active opposition of conservative whites and (4) it was hampered by the number of blacks living in Texas.

Within the Republican party, the role of the black man was circumscribed. Most whites supported "black power" because they had no alternative. Without it they could not be retained in office. This meant that concessions had to be made to black interests, but these leaders tried to confine these concessions to the minimum numbers necessary to keep blacks in line without alienating natives whites. Ergo, on occasion blacks were granted minor offices in the temporary organization of the Republican party, but rarely did they hold major offices in the permanent organization. Beyond minor offices, white Republicans were willing to go only as far as black pressure compelled them. It was because of this pressure that Norris W. Cuney was elected head of the party in 1884, and blacks received eight at-large delegates to the national convention in that same year. But the influence of that pressure was diluted by the fact that when strongly applied, it divided the party and gave rise to the Lily White faction. Hence, this influence weakened the only party on which black hopes rested.

Black influence was further diluted as black Republicans were divided among themselves. On many occasions, they were split over the ticket issue — whether to support a Straight-Out Republican or fuse with an independent candidate. This meant that blacks were not united within the party and as such their bargaining power was limited. In part because of this divisiveness, even though they had the majority of votes in the party, they were only able on one occasion to nominate a black to a cabinet level post to run on a bolted Republican state ticket. Still it should be noted that the differences among black leaders were never as sharp as were those between Republicans and Democrats, or even between white and black Republicans. Yet these differences were sufficient to restrain some of black bargaining power within the party. A case in point was the contest for Third Congressional District where blacks were divided as to whether they should support a black man for office or support the party's candidate, a white man. The result of which was that the white candidate was selected.

Black power was also limited because of the whites who joined the Republican party. These men, according to James Baggett in "The Origins of Early Texas Republican Party Leadership," were not good material for fashioning a Republican party in Texas. For the most part, "they were Southern white men with pre-Reconstruction backgrounds." They joined the party either out of desperation or the mistaken notion that they would be able to lead and control blacks or out of opposition to the Democratic party. Most of these whites were not only white supremacists, but were also self-seeking, avaricious and power hungry individuals who did not hold the interest of blacks at heart.

The attitudes and activities of conservative white Democrats also helped to diminish blacks influence and to prevent black legislators from accomplishing many things they had set out to do. Inasmuch as these whites resented the status and independent role of black politicians, coercion was used to eliminate them. Force or a show of force took the form of violence and economic sanctions. To be sure, there was nothing subtle or hidden about the imposition of coercion. Violence appeared when the first black was elected and lasted until the final one left office in 1898. Unlike Republicans who had relatively little success in converting native whites, Conservatives operated from a position of strength, a broad power base that ranged from planters and businessmen to poor whites. All of these individuals converged under the banner of white supremacy and under the slogan that "blacks must be removed from politics." Thus, the failure of black Texans to send another black to the legislature after 1898 had less to do with the differences among black politicians than with a crusade among whites to make sure that white supremacy must "obtain."

If for no other reason black power was limited in Texas because of the small number of blacks who resided in the state. Texas had the smallest population of blacks of all the Confederate states. This fact placed black leaders in a dilemma. This dilemma raised the fundamental question — to what extent can the political problem facing blacks be dealt with through participation in electoral politics? To answer this question, it may be useful to conceptualize representation in terms of two abstractions — fair representation and sufficient representation. The former involves a question of procedure, while the latter involves a matter of substance. Fair representation would be that which results from following equitable electoral rules enacted through democratic methods and impartially administered. Sufficient representation would occur in situations in which representation of a particular group would mean adequate voting power to insure that issues and party matters which the group deemed especially important to their survival or liberation as a people would and could be resolved only with their concurrence. Data collected from this study indicates that black representation on the state level in Texas was not fair, and equally it suggests even if representation had been fair, it would not have been sufficient.

Given that blacks were in the minority in the Lone Star State; that Texas was run by a frontier system of justice where lawlessness was a way of life; that the solidarity generated by blacks in the Black Belt counties to win office made whites all the more determined to nullify their gains; it appears that the novelty of those black politicians was not merely that they got elected to office, but that for nearly a quarter of a century they weathered the storm, or in the words of the song, *Through Many Dangers, Toils, and Snares, {They} Have Already Come!*

APPENDIX A

ROSTER OF BLACK LEGISLATORS OF TEXAS

Constitutional Convention of 1868–1869

Legislator	County
George T. Ruby	Galveston, Brazoria, Matagorda
Wiley W. Johnson	Harrison
James McWashington	Montgomery
Benjamin O. Watrous	Washington
Benjamin F. Williams	Colorado
Charles W. Bryant	Harris
Stephen Curtis	Brazos
Mitchel M. Kendall	Harrison
Ralph Long	Limestone
Sheppard Mullins	McLennan

Twelfth Legislature, 1870–1871
SENATE

Legislator	District	County
George T. Ruby	12	Galveston, Brazoria, Matagorda
Matthew Gaines	16	Washington

HOUSE

Legislator	District	County
Mitchell Kendall	7	Harrison
Henry Moore	7	Harrison
Richard Allen	14	Harris, Montgomery
Goldstein Dupree	14	Harris, Montgomery
John Mitchell	17	Burleson, Brazos, Milam
Silas Cotton	18	Robertson, Leon, Freestone
Sheppard Mullins	19	McLennan, Limestone, Falls
Benjamin F. Williams	25	Lavaca and Colorado
Jeremaih J. Hamilton	26	Fayette and Bastrop
Richard Williams	15	Madison, Grimes, Walker
David Medlock	19	Fall, Limestone, McLennan

Thirteenth Legislature, 1873
Senate

Legislator	District	County
George T. Ruby	12	Galveston, Brazoria, Matagorda
Matthew Gaines	16	Washington

House

Legislator	District	County
Henry Moore	7	Harrison
Shack Roberts	7	Harrison
Henry Phelps	13	Wharton, Fort Bend, Austin
James H. Washington	15	Madison, Grimes, Walker
Richard Williams	15	Madison, Grimes, Walker
Allen Wilder	16	Washington
Richard Allen	14	Harris, Montgomery
Edward Anderson	14	Harris, Montgomery

Fourteenth Legislature, 1874
Senate

Legislator	District	County
Walter M. Burton	13	Austin, Fort Bend, Wharton

House

Legislator	District	County
David Abner, Sr.	7	Harrison
Edward Brown	7	Harrison
Shack Roberts	7	Harrison
Thomas Beck	15	Walker, Madison, Grimes
Jacob Freeman	13	Austin, Fort Bend, Wharton
John Mitchell	17	Washington, Burleson

Constitutional Convention of 1875

Legislator	District	County
David Abner, Sr.	7	Harrison
Lloyd McCabe	13	Fort Bend, Austin, Wharton
William Reynolds	15	Walker, Madison, Grimes
John Mitchell	17	Washington, Burleson
B. B. Davis	13	Wharton, Fort Bend, Austin
Melvin Goddin	15	Waller, Madison, Grimes

Fifteenth Legislature, 1876
Senate

Legislator	District	County
Walter M. Burton	17	Fort Bend, Walker, Wharton

| Walter Ripetoe | 4 | Harrison |

HOUSE

Legislator	District	County
Shack Roberts	10	Harrison
Henry Sneed	37	Waller, Wharton, Fort Bend
William H. Holland	37	Waller, Wharton, Fort Bend
Allen Wilder	39	Washington

Sixteenth Legislature, 1879
SENATE

Legislator	District	County
Walter M. Burton	17	Fort Bend, Waller, Wharton
Walter Ripetoe	4	Harrison

HOUSE

Legislator	District	County
Thomas Beck	30	Grimes, Madison
R. J. Evans	29	Grimes
B. A. Guy	39	Washington
Harriel G. Geiger	27	Robertson
Elias Mayes	28	Brazos
Andrew Sledge	40	Washington
Benjamin F. Williams	37	Waller, Fort Bend, Wharton
Jacob Freeman	37	Waller, Fort Bend, Wharton

Seventeenth Legislature, 1881
SENATE

Legislator	District	County
Walter M. Burton	17	Fort Bend, Waller, Wharton

HOUSE

Legislator	District	County
Thomas Beck	30	Grimes, Madison
R. J. Evans	29	Grimes
Robert A. Kerr	42	Bastrop
Harriel G. Geiger	27	Robertson
Doc Lewis	37	Wharton, Fort Bend, Waller

Eighteenth Legislature, 1883
HOUSE

Legislator	District	County
R. J. Moore	71	Washington
George W. Wyatt	53	Waller, Fort Bend

Nineteenth Legislature, 1885
HOUSE

Legislator	District	County
James H. Steward	48	Robertson
Benjamin F. Williams	53	Waller, Fort Bend
R. J. Moore	71	Washington

Twentieth Legislature, 1887
HOUSE

Legislator	District	County
H. A. P. Bassett	52	Grimes
R. J. Moore	71	Washington

Twenty-first Legislature, 1889
HOUSE

Legislator	District	County
Elias Mayes	50	Brazos
Alexander Asberry	48	Robertson

Twenty-second Legislature, 1891
HOUSE

Legislator	District	County
Edward Patton	2	San Jacinto, Polk

Twenty-third Legislature, 1893
HOUSE

Legislator	District	County
Nathan H. Haller	64	Brazoria, Matagorda

Twenty-fourth Legislature, 1895
HOUSE

Legislator	District	County
Nathan H. Haller	64	Brazoria, Matagorda
Robert L. Smith	63	Colorado

Twenty-fifth Legislature, 1897
HOUSE

Legislator	District	County
Robert L. Smith	67	Colorado

APPENDIX B

ROSTER OF BLACK LEGISLATORS' COMMITTEE ASSIGNMENTS

Constitutional Convention of 1868–1869

Legislator	Committee
George T. Ruby	Political and Legislative
Wiley Johnson	Public Debt
James McWashington	Finance
Benjamin O. Watrous	State Affairs
Benjamin F. Williams	Executive
Charles W. Bryant	Apportionment
Shephard Curtis	Immigration
Mitchell Kendall	Public Land
Ralph Long	Public Land
Sheppard Mullins	Public Land, Commerce

Twelfth Legislature, 1870–1871

SENATE

Legislator	Committee
George T. Ruby	Judiciary, Militia, Public Land, Engrossed Bills
Matthews Gaines	Penitentiary, Privileges and Election, Counties and Boundaries, Indian Frontier Affairs

HOUSE

Legislator	Committee
Mitchell Kendall	Public Building and Grounds, Militia, Counties and Boundaries
Henry Moore	Commerce and Manufacturing, Militia, Public Land
Richard Allen	Finance, Road and Bridges, Commerce, and Manufacturing
Goldstein Dupree	State Affairs
John Mitchell	Penitentiary

Silas Cotton	Agriculture and Livestock
Sheppard Mullins	Election and Privileges, Federal Relations, State Affairs
Benjamin F. Williams	Printing and Contingent Expense
Jeremiah J. Hamilton	Engrossed Bills
Richard Williams	Engrossed Bills
David Medlock	None

Thirteenth Legislature, 1873
SENATE

Legislator	Committee
George T. Ruby	Engrossed Bills, Education, Contingent Expense
Matthew Gaines	Immigration, Printing and Contingent Expenses, Indian Frontier Affairs

HOUSE

Legislator	Committee
Henry Moore	Education
Shack Roberts	Private Claims, Immigration
Henry Phelps	Roads and Bridges
James H. Washington	Public Debt, Agriculture and Stock Raising
Richard Williams	Indian Affairs
Allen Wilder	Public Land and Land Office

Fourteenth Legislature, 1874
SENATE

Legislator	Committee
Walter M. Burton	None

HOUSE

Legislator	Committee
David Abner	Education
Edward Brown	Agriculture and Stock Raising
Shack Roberts	Claims and Account, Roads and Bridges, County and Boundaries
Thomas Beck	Agriculture and Livestock
Jacob Freeman	Privilege and Election, Penitentiary
John Mitchell	Public Land

Constitutional Convention of 1875

Legislator	Committee
David Abner	Bill of Rights, Crime and Punishment

Lloyd H. McCabe — Education
William Reynolds — Executive
John Mitchell — Public Land and Land Office
B. B. Davis — Immigration
M. H. Goddin — State Affairs

Fifteenth Legislature, 1876
SENATE

Legislator	Committee
Walter M. Burton	Agriculture Affairs
Walter Ripetoe	Agriculture Affairs, Education

HOUSE

Legislator	Committee
Shack Roberts	Commerce and Manufacturing
Henry Sneed	Agriculture and Livestock
William H. Holland	Education
Allen Wilder	Public Land and Finance

Sixteenth legislature, 1879
SENATE

Legislator	Committee
Walter M. Burton	Education, Roads and Bridges
Walter Ripeto	Penitentiary

HOUSE

Legislator	Committee
Thomas Beck	Roads, Bridges and Ferries, Federal Relations
R. J. Evans	Education
Harriel G. Geiger	Roads, Bridges and Ferries
B. A. Guy	Federal Relations
Elias Mayes	Counties and Boundaries, Federal Relations, Roads, Bridges and ferries
Andrew Sledge	Education
Benjamin F. Williams	Counties and Boundaries
Jacob Freeman	None

Seventeenth Legislature, 1881
SENATE

Legislator	Committee
Walter M. Burton	Roads and Bridges, Contingent Expense, Crimes and Boundaries, Agriculture and Judiciary

HOUSE

Legislator	Committees
Thomas Beck	Agriculture, Roads, Bridges and Ferries
R. J. Evans	Education, Federal Relations
Robert A. Kerr	Counties and Boundaries
Harriel G. Geiger	Roads, Bridges, Ferries and Agriculture
Doc. Lewis	Agriculture

Eighteenth Legislature, 1883
HOUSE

Legislator	Committee
R. J. Moore	Penitentiary, Roads, Bridges and Ferries
George W. Wyatt	Counties and Boundaries, Stock Raising

Nineteenth Legislature, 1885
HOUSE

Legislator	Committee
James H. Stewart	Education
Benjamin F. Williams	Finance
R. J. Moore	Penitentiary, Roads, Bridges and Ferries

Twentieth Legislature, 1887
HOUSE

Legislator	Committees
H. A. P. Bassett	Education, Stock Raising, Military Affairs
R. J. Moore	Education, Privileges and Election, Stock Raising

Twenty-first Legislature, 1889
HOUSE

Legislator	Committees
Elias Mayes	Penitentiary, Education
Alexander Asberry	County Government, County Finance, Mining and Minerals

Twenty-second Legislature, 1891
HOUSE

Legislator	Committees
Edward Patton	None

Twenty-third Legislature, 1893

House

Legislator	Committee
Nathan H. Haller	Penitentiary, Roads and Bridges

Twenty-fourth Legislature, 1895
House

Legislator	Committee
Nathan H. Haller	Labor, Federal Relations, Stock Raising, Counties and Boundaries
Robert L. Smith	Education

Twenty-fifth Legislature, 1897
House

Legislator	Committee
Robert L. Smith	Education

APPENDIX C

Black Legislators Who Were Delegates At Republican National Conventions

Year	At-Large Delegate(s)	District Delegate(s)	Alternate Delegate(s)
1868	George T. Ruby	None	None
1872	George T. Ruby	Richard Allen B. F. Williams	Robert Kerr (At-Large) W. M. Burton (District)
1876	None	Richard Allen	J. H. Washington (At-Large) J. J. Hamilton (At-Large) W. H. Holland (District)
1880	W. H. Holland	None	Richard Allen (At-Large)
1884	Richard Allen	R. J. Evans	None
1888	None	Alexander Asberry	None
1892	Alexander Asberry	None	Robert Kerr (At-Large)
1896	Richard Allen	None	Robert Smith (At-Large)

* The above list is restricted to black legislators, however, there were a number of other blacks who served as delegates. For more information on other black delegates see Casdorph, *The Republican Party in Texas 1865–1965*.

NOTES

Chapter 1 THE CONSTITUTIONAL CONVENTION OF 1868–1869

1. Randall Woods, "George T. Ruby: A Black Militant in the White Business Community," *Red River Valley Historical Review*, I (1974): 269–280; Barry Crouch, "Self Determination and Local Black Leaders in Texas," *Phylon*, XXXIX (December 1978): 344–355; J. Mason Brewer, *Negro Legislators of Texas and Their Descendants* (Dallas, 1935), pp. 20, 27, 47–48, 115, 125; See G. T. Ruby to Charles Garreston (Acting Adjutant General), September 14, October 17, 1867, Bureau of Refugees, Freedmen and Abandoned Lands, Record Group 105 (National Archives, Washington, D.C.); *Austin Daily State Journal*, October 13, 1870; *Austin Weekly Republican* August 29, 1868: July 18, 1869; James M. Smallwood, *Time of Hope, Time of Despair: Black Texans During Reconstruction* (Port Washington, New York: Kennikat Press, 1981) pp. 71, 91, 108, 138–141, 146–148.

2. Carl H. Moneyhon, *Republicanism in Reconstruction Texas*, (Austin: University of Texas Press, 1980) p. 242; *Austin Weekly Republican*, April 24, July 18, 1868; Harrell T. Budd, "The Negro in Politics in Texas 1867–1898," (M. A. Thesis, University of Texas at Austin, 1925), p. 18.

3. Brewer, *Negro Legislators of Texas*, pp. 20, 23–24, 28, 115, 125: *Houston Telegraph*, February 16, 17, 18, 1866; *Flake's Daily Buletin*, February 16, 17, 18, 1868; *U.S. Congress, Senate Document (40th) Congress*, (2nd) (Sess.) No. 53 (Serial 1317); Moneyhon, *Republicanism in Reconstruction Texas* p. 79.

4. Brewer, *Negro Legislators of Texas*, pp. 20, 24, 47, 49, 53; *Houston Union*, July 6, 1870; *Austin Daily State Journal*, August 17, October 13, 1870; Clarence Wharton, *History of Fort Bend County* (San Antonio; Naylor Co., 1939), p. 187; See also B. F. Williams, "Circular of the Union League," J. P. Newcomb Papers, Eugene Barker Texas Collection, The University of Texas at Austin); B. F. Williams to J. P. Newcomb, July 17, August 28, 1869, July 24, 1870, Newcomb Papers; *Texas Legislature, House Journal of the (12th) Legislature* (1st) (Sess.) (Austin, 1870): 1482.

5. Washington D.C. *New Era*, June 16, 1870; Central Texas Genealogical Society, McLennan County, Texas, Cemetery Records (2 Vols.; Waco, 1965), I, 87; Charles Edson to Shep Mullins, December 19, 1865, W. D. Chambers to Shepperd Mullins, January 1, 1866, S. P. Ross to Shep Mullins and Andy Nowlen February 21, 1866; T. H. Barron to Shep Mullins, December 28, 1867, L. S. Ross to Shep Mullins January 27, 1868, Fred Quarles to John Fuller and Shep Mullins, May 18, 1872, Deeds Records, McLennan County Courthouse, Waco Texas; Betty J. San-

dlin, "The Texas Reconstruction Convention 1868–1869," (Ph.D. Dissertation, Texas Teck University 1970), p.51; *Journal of the Reconstruction Convention of 1868–1869*, 2 Vols. (Austin, 1870), II. 535.

6. Budd, "The Negro in Politics in Texas," p. 18; The *Austin Weekly Republican*, April 29, July 18, 1868; Moneyhon, *Republicanism in Reconstruction Texas*, p. 246.

7. Sandlin, "The Texas Reconstruction Convention," p. 213; Moneyhon, *Republicanism in Reconstruction Texas* p. 241; *Austin Weekly Republican*, April 24, July 16, 1868.

8. Ray A. Walter, *History of Limestone County* (Austin: Von Boeckmann Jones, 1959,) pp. 56–58; Sandlin, "The Texas Reconstruction Convention," pp. 278; Moneyhon, *Republicanism in Reconstruction Texas*, p. 242; *Grosbeck New Era*, July 29, 1876.

9. Budd, "The Negro in Politics in Texas," p. 19; Moneyhon, *Republicanism in Reconstruction Texas*, p. 238; *Austin Weekly Republican*, April 29, June 18, 1868.

10. Budd, "The Negro in Politics in Texas," p. 19; Brewer, *Negro Legislators of Texas*, pp. 24, 125; Sandlin, "The Texas Reconstruction Convention," pp. 213; Moneyhon, *Republicanism in Reconstruction Texas*, p. 242.

11. *Journal of the Reconstruction Convention* I: 12–17, 235, 696–697; *Galveston Daily News*, April 26, September 8, December 21, 1867; June 16, August 22, 1868; *Flake's Evening Bulletin*, April 22, May 6, 14, July 5, December 22, 1867; *Weekly Freeman's Press*, July 20, 1868, clipping in the E. J. Davis Biographical file, Barker Texas Collection, University of Texas.

12. *Journal of Reconstruction Convention*, I:28, 75; Moneyhon, *Republicanism in Reconstruction Texas*, pp. 86–87.

13. *Ibid.*, I: 794, 797, 921–922.

14. *Journal of Reconstruction Convention*, I: 235, 696–698; See also Article III, Section 21 of The *Texas Constitution, of 1869*.

15. *Journal of Reconstruction Convention*, II: 510–511.

16. *Ibid.*, II: 308, 488; *Texas Constitution 1869*, Article I, Section 3.

17. *Ibid.*, II: 90.

18. *Ibid.*, 247; See also Article XII, Section 3 of *Texas Constitution of 1869*.

19. *Ibid.*, I: 267.

20. *Ibid.*, I: 416; See also Article XII, Section 27 *Texas Constitution of 1869*.

21. *Ibid.*, I: 456; See also Article XII, Section 14 *Texas Constitution of 1869*.

22. *Ibid.*, I: 251, 474; *Galveston Daily News*, July 10, 1869.

23. *Ibid.*, II: 318.

24. *Ibid.*, II: 117.

25. *Ibid.*, I: 248.

26. *Ibid.*, I: 304, 463.

27. Nathan H. Randlett to Charles A. Vernon (Acting Assistant Adjutant General) July 9, 1868, Assistant Commissioner or Box 18; July 23, 1868 AC, LR, R-178 Box 9, Bureau of Refugees, Freedmen and Abandoned Lands Record Group 105 National Archives; Report of Lieutenant N. H. Randlett in *Galveston Daily News* July 17, 18, 21, 1868: See also *Galveston Daily News*, August 12, 13,, 27, 1869.

28. *Ibid.*, See also Criminal Offenses Committed in the State of Texas, AC,

Austin, Vol. 13, p. 156, case numbers 1954–1961. George Brooks was a minister, an election registrar and a member of the Union League. He was also a paramedic who attended to the medical needs of both whites and blacks during the epidemic in 1867. For more on Brooks's work in this regard, see Barry Crouch and L. J. Schultz, "Crisis in Color: Racial Separation in Texas During Reconstruction," *Civil War History* XVI (March 1970): 9, 3, 49, 31.

29. See *Journal of the Reconstruction Convention* I: 481, 586–589.

30. *Ibid.*, I: 450.

31. *Austin Daily Republican,* August 29, 1868.

32. *Galveston Daily News,* August 7, 1868.

33. *Journal of Reconstruction Convention* I: 681–688; *Galveston Daily News,* August 7, September 18, 1868.

34. *Ibid.*, II: 445–446, 458–459; *Galveston Daily News,* February 6, 1869; *Austin Daily Republican,* February 3, 16, 1869; *State Gazette,* February 27, 1869.

35. *Tri Weekly State Gazette,* January 23, 1869; *Austin Daily Republican,* February 3, 16, 1869.

36. *Houston Telegraph,* December 16, 1869; *Austin Weekly Republican,* December 23, 1869.

37. *Journal of Reconstruction Convention,* II: 398–399.

38. *Ibid.*, I: 160–162, 174–175, 180, 190–191, 205, 407–411; II: 278–279, 302; Sandlin, "Texas Reconstruction Convention," pp. 119–131.

39. Ibid., II: 518–519; 527–529, *Galveston Daily News,* February 14, 1869, *Austin Daily Republican,* January 23, 1869.

40. *Journal of Reconstruction Convention,* II: 520.

41. Sandlin, "Texas Reconstruction Convention," p. 213. Bryant did not cast a vote on the constitution because he had been expelled. However, given his track record, it is logical to assume that had he remained in the convention, he might have sided with the "Radicals." Mullins, for some unknown reason, abstained from voting.

42. *Journal of Reconstruction Convention,* II: 520.

43. *Ibid.*

44. *Ibid.*

45. See *Texas Constitution of 1869.*

Chapter 2 THE RECONSTRUCTION LEGISLATURE

1. Sheppard Mullins died while serving in the Twelfth Legislature, but since his death came near the end of the second session, no one was appointed to take his place. See Tommy Yett et.al., *Members of the Texas Legislature 1864–1939* (Austin, 1939) p. 63–66; *Texas Almanac,* (1870), p. 197; For the condolence extended to the family of Mullins by the House of Representative, see *House Journal of the (12th) Legislature* (1871), (2nd) (Sess.) II.

There has been at least one source which has indicated that J. F. McKee was black, but further research reveals that McKee was indeed white. This being the case, there were only 13 blacks who sat in the 12th legislature rather than fourteen.

2. Brewer, *Negro Legislators of Texas,* pp. 47, 50–51, 51, 61, 75; Lawrence Rice, *The Negro in Texas 1870–1900* (Baton Rouge: Louisiana State University

Press, 1971); pp. 58, 102, 104-hereafter cited as *The Negro in Texas;* John P. Carrier, "A Political History of Texas During Reconstruction 1865–1874 (Ph.D. Dissertation, Vanderbilt University, 1971); Ann P. Malone, "Matthew Gaines: Reconstruction Politics," in Alwyn Barr and Robert Calvert (ed.) *Black Leaders: Texans For Their Time* (Austin: Texas Historical Association, 1981), pp. 48–81.

3. Brewer, *Negro Legislators of Texas,* pp. 47, 49, 53, 125; Paul Casdorph, *Republican Party in Texas, 1865–1965* (Austin; Pemberton Press, 1965), p. 39; Rice, *Negro in Texas,* pp. 38, 49, 57, 64; *Dallas Herald,* February 8, 15, 1868; *Houston Union,* July 6, 1870; See Thomas H. Stubling, "To Whom It May Concern," April 18, 1867 — A letter authorizing Allen to establish a charter of the Union League of America throughout Texas, Newcomb Papers.

4. U.S. Twelfth Census, 1900 Population, Travis County, Texas Austin, Seventh Ward; *Washington, D.C. New Era,* June 16, 1870 C.V. Schafer to J. J. Hamilton, December 13, 1869. Deed Records, Bastrop County, Bastrop, Vol. 0. pp. 146, 454–455.

5. Narrative of Jerry Moore, son of former slaves Amy Van Zandt Moore and Henry Moore (Harrison County) WPA Slave Narrative of Texas. The University of Texas at Austin; Budd, "The Negro in Politics in Texas," p. 45.

6. *Austin Daily Republican,* January 21, 1878; Budd, "The Negro in Politics in Texas," p. 45; Rice, *The Negro in Texas,* p. 57; *Legislative Manual* (Austin, 1871) p. 5.

7. Brewer, *Negro Legislators of Texas,* pp. 59–60, 77; J. W. Baker, *A History of Robertson County* (Robertson County Historical Committee, 1970) pp. 162–163; Walter F. Cotton, *History of Negroes of Limestone County from 1860–1939* (Mexia, 1939), p. 25.

8. *Galveston Daily News,* March 12, 1873; *Legislative Manual* (1873), Budd, "The Negro in Politics of Texas," p. 46; William H. Gandy, "A History of Montgomery County Texas," (M.A. Thesis, University of Houston, 1950) pp. 171–172; See *Contested Election in the 14th District of 13th Legislature, State of Texas* (Austin: John Cardwell Printer 1873): 68, 249.

9. Secretary of State File on Bonds and Oath of Elected and Appointed Officials, *Oath File* 2–9/907 RG 307 (Archives Division of the Texas State Library — Austin); *Texas Almanac* (1870) p. 197; *Austin Daily Statesman,* March 19, 23, 1873; E. L. Blair, *Early History of Grimes County,* (Trinity, Texas, 1930), p. 206.

10. Secretary of State File on Bonds and Oath of Elected and Appointed Officials — *Oath File* 2–9/858; *Flake's Daily Bulletin,* January 19, 1891; Cotton, *History of Negroes in Limestone County* p. 25; *Texas Almanac* (1870) p. 197.

11. *Tri Weekly State Gazette,* May 16, 23, 25, 27, June 1, 3, 10, 13, 1870.

12. *State Journal Appendix Containing Official Reports of the Debates and Proceedings of the Twelfth Legislature of the State of Texas* (Austin: Tracy Siemering and Co., 1870) pp. 13, 82, 89, 91; Hereafter cited as *Debates of the 12th Legislature.*

13. John M. Brockman, "Railroad, Radicals and the Militia Bill: A New Interpretation of the Quorum Breaking Incident of 1871," *Southwestern Historical Quarterly* LXXXIII (October, 1979): 111–112; Ann Patton Baenziger "The Texas State Police During Reconstruction," *Southwestern Historical Quarterly,* LXXII (April, 1969): 470–474, 490–491; Otis T. Singletary, *Negro Militia and Recon-*

struction (Austin: University of Texas Press, 1951) pp. 4–5; *Galveston Daily News,* June 22, 24, 1870.

14. *Debates of (12th) Legislature,* pp. 87–91.
15. *Ibid.,* p. 13.
16. *Ibid.*
17. *Ibid.,* p. 82.
18. *Ibid.*
19. Brockman, "Railroad, Radicals and the Militia Bill," 112–113; *Tri Weekly State Gazette,* May 16, 23, 25, 27, June 1, 3, 8, 10, 1870.
20. See *Constitution of the Radical Republican Association,* June 4, 1870 and *Minutes of the Radical Republican Association* July 25, 30, 1870, Box 2F 108, Newcomb Papers; *Galveston Weekly News,* November 17, 1873. There were thirty-one Radical Republicans when the (12th) Legislature began and twenty-five when it closed. Of the six Republicans who switched from Radical to Moderate, two were black, Henry Moore and Mitchell Kendall.
21. On October 20, 1870 James H. Washington wrote the following letter to Frederick Douglas, editor of the *New National Era:* "The Republicans [here] are in a majority and we have a noble Governor, but our Legislature at its last session failed to meet the expectation of the people . . . Our leading men in the Legislature proved themselves corrupt . . . They were all, with a few exceptions crazy on railroads. I wish you would look at the Central Pacific Railroad bill and see who voted against the Governor's veto." *New National Era,* October 20, 1870, cited in Dorothy Sterling (ed.) *The Trouble They've Seen: Black People Tell The Story of Reconstruction* (New York: Doubleday, 1976) p. 414.
22. *Texas Legislature, Senate Journal of the (12th) Legislature,* second Session (Austin, 1871): 272–277.
23. *Ibid.,* First Session: 286.
24. *Ibid.:* 369.
25. *Ibid.:* 353, 354.
26. *House Journal of the (12th) Legislature,* Second Session: 303.
27. *Senate Journal, of the Twelfth Legislature* Second Session: 425, 835.
28. *Ibid.*
29. *Ibid.:* First Session: 58, 76.
30. *House Journal of the Twelfth Legislature* Second Session: 58–59, 635, 637.
31. *Ibid.:* second Session: 77.
32. *Senate Journal of the Twelfth Legislature* First Session: 785–786: second Session: 451.
33. *Ibid.,* Second Session: 725.
34. *Galveston Daily News,* February 14, 1871; *Flake's Daily Bulletin,* February 24, 1871; *San Antonio Express,* April 21, 1871.
35. *Senate Journal of the Twelfth Legislature* Second Session: 967, 1080.
36. *Debates of the (12th) Legislature:* 39, 45.
37. *House Journal of the Twelfth Legislature* First Session: 67.
38. *Ibid.,* 485.
39. *Ibid.,* 317, 803; Second Session: 82.
40. *Ibid.*
41. *Senate Journal of the Twelfth Legislature* Second Session: 500–501, 524–

525; See H. P. N. Gammel, *The Laws of Texas 1822–1897* VI (10 vols., Austin, 1898), pp. 50–60.
    42. *Galveston Daily News,* April 7, 1871.
    43. *House Journal of the Twelfth Legislature* First Session: 428, 865. Gammel, *The Laws of Texas* VI, pp. 323–324. See Ira Bryant *The Development of Houston Negro Schools* (Houston, 1928), p. 10. Allen was a charter member of the Gregory Institute.
    44. *Texas Superintendent of Public Instruction First Annual Report 1871* (Austin, 1872), pp. 88–100; Mary A. Lavender, "Social Conditions in Houston and Harris County 1868–1872," (M.A. Thesis, Rice Institute 1950), pp. 157–158.
    45. *House Journal of the Twelfth Legislature* Second Session: 18, Gammel, *Laws of Texas* VI, pp. 153–154.
    46. *Senate Journal of the Twelfth Legislature* First Session: 132, 154.
    47. *Ibid.*, Second Session: 111.
    48. *Democratic Statesman,* September 16, 1871.
    49. *Senate Journal of the Twelfth Legislature* First Session: 188; *Ibid.*, 1871, 2nd Sess: 343; Arthur Z. Brown, "The Participation of Negroes in the Reconstruction Legislature of Texas," *Negro History Bulletin,* XX (1959): 87.
    50. *Ibid.*
    51. *House Journal of the Twelfth Legislature* First Session: 384.
    52. *Bill Passed by Twelfth Legislature,* p. 182, (Austin: Texas State Archives, 1871).
    53. *House Journal of the Twelfth Legislature* first Session: 644, 664, 824; second Session: 439, 549, 801. *Senate Journal of the Twelfth Legislature* First Session: 76.
    54. *House Journal of the Twelfth Legislature* First Session: 824; *Flake's Daily Bulletin,* February 28, 1871.
    55. *Ibid.*, 474.
    56. *Senate Journal of the Twelfth Legislature* First Session: 79.
    57. *House Journal of the Twelfth Legislature* First Session: 859.
    58. *Ibid.*, 379.
    59. *Ibid.*, 553, 996.
    60. *Senate Journal of the Twelfth Legislature* First Session: 92.
    61. *Ibid.*: See also *Bills Passed by the Twelfth Legislature.*
    62. G. T. Ruby to E. J. Davis, December 14, 1871, E. J. Davis Papers (Austin, State Archives).
    63. Goldstein Dupree and Matt Gaines to E. J. Davis February 16, 1873, *Ibid.*
    64. N. Haller to E. J. Davis, February 16, 1873; Walter Burton et al to Davis August 19, 1872, *Ibid.*
    65. S. Mullins et al to E. J. Davis, February 6, 1871, *Ibid.*
    66. Matt Gaines and J. R. Moore, to E. J. Davis, June 16, 1871. See also R. Allen to E. J. Davis, April 6, 1871; John Mitchell et al to E. J. Davis, February 8, 1871; N. W. Cuney to E. J. Davis, undated; Henry Moore to E. J. Davis, January 9, 1871; W. R. Moore to E. J. Davis, October 23, 1871; James McWashington to E. J. Davis, March 12, 1871, *Ibid.*

Chapter 3 BLACKS AT THE CROSSROAD 1872–1875

1. Doyal T. Loyd, *A History of Upshur County* (Gilmer, Texas: Texian Press, 1966), pp. 114–115; J. H. Bealde, *Western Wilds and The Men Who Redeem Them* (Chicago: James Brother and Company, 1879), pp. 417–418; Brewer, *Negro Legislators of Texas*, pp. 65-68; Rice *Negro in Texas*. pp. 103–104; Sallie M. Lentz, "Highlights of Early Harrison County," *Southwestern Historical Quarterly*, LXI (October, 1957); 240–256; *Bastrop Advertiser*, March 22, 1879; *Marshall Tri Weekly Herald*, March 6, 1874.

2. Brewer, *Negro Legislators of Texas*, p. 64: J. H. Washington to J. P. Newcomb, August 24, 1871, Newcomb Papers; *Galveston Daily News*, July 17, 1871, July 26, 1871: *Legislative Manual of 13th Legislature* (Austin, State Archives, 1873).

3. Henry Phelps to J. P. Newcomb, June 30, 1871, Newcomb Papers; Clarence Wharton, *A History of Fort Bend County*, p. 179; See *Voter Registration List of Fort Bend County*, 1869 (Austin: State Archives); *Fort Bend County Return of an Election, February 15, 1876*, p. 17 (Clerk of Court Office, Richmond, Texas); *Legislative Manual* (Austin, State Archives 1873).

4. Rice, *The Negro in Texas*, p. 102; *Austin Daily Statesman*, March 20, 24, 1874, May 18, 1876; *Galveston Daily News*, January 4, 1876.

5. *Galveston Daily News*, March 11, 1873; William Hardy Gandy, "A History of Montgomery County, Texas," pp. 171–172; See *Contested Election in the 14th Senatorial District, Thirteenth Legislature*, pp. 68, 249. See also, *Texas House Journal of the (13th) Legislature*, (Reg.) (Sess): 605.

6. *Austin Daily Statesman*, March 19, 1873, *House Journal 13th Legislature*, Reg. Sess.: 60.

7. *Galveston Daily News*, February 13, 14, 1873.

8. *Ibid.*, March 12, 1873; See *Contested Election in the 14th Senatorial District of the 13th Legislature:* 68, 249.

9. Letter by M. D. Moore, a descendant of David Abner Sr., March 1970, Abner Family File, Harrison County Historical Museum; Interview with Abram Tompkins, great grandson of David Abner, February 21, 1982; Brewer, *Negro Legislators of Texas*, p. 69; see also *The Black Citizens in American Democracy: Past, Present and Future* (Marshall, Texas: Texas committee for the Humanities, 1976), pp. 1–9; *Marshall Tri-Weekly Herald*, March 30, 1876; *Legislative Manual* (Austin, 1874) p. 4; Melvin Bank, "Bishop College History," *Bishop College Herald*, November 1, 1975, Fall 1978; Randolph Campbell, *A Southern Community in Crisis* (Austin; Texas, 1983, State Historical Association), p. 266.

10. When Bethesda Baptist Church was organized in 1867, it was called the Baptist Colored Church. Among its first two deacons were David Abner and Patrick Dennis. This Church took the leading role in establishing the Texas–Louisiana Association, an organization which advocated the establishment of a black college in 1869. In a resolution, the leaders of this organization stated that: "Our people are perishing because of a lack of trained leadership in every walk of life." *Bishop College Herald*, Fall 1978; "History of the Bethesda Baptist Church," cited in the "Bethesda Baptist Church Anniversary Program 1982."

There had been a tendency for many authors to get David Abner, Jr., confused with David Abner, Sr. It was David Abner, Jr., who was the first President of Guadalupe College at Seguin, Texas and third President of Conroe Industrial College For Negroes. David Abner, Jr., like his father, became involved in politics, but not until the 1890s.

11. *Texas Legislative Manual of the Thirteenth Legislature,* (Austin 1873), p. 5.
12. *Ibid.*
13. *Ibid.*
14. Wharton, *History of Fort Bend,* pp. 178–179; Brewer, *Negro Legislators of Texas,* PP. 74–76, 81, 86–87; Burton to J. P. Newcomb July 15, 1871, Newcomb Papers; *Legislative Manual of the 14th Legislature;* Norman G. Kittrell, *Governors Who Have Been and Other Public Men of Texas,* (Houston: Dealy — Adeq Elia Co., 1921) pp. 97–98; For Burton's land see Thomas H. Burton Deed to W. M. Burton, Book J. 8357 p. 532 (Fort Bend County Commissioner's *Record of Deeds,* 1872).
15. Wharton, *History of Fort Bend,* pp. 178–178; J. G. Tracy to J. P. Newcomb, October 8, 1872; R. Burns to J. P. Newcomb, September 18, 1872, Newcomb Papers.
16. *Texas Legislature, Senate Journal of the Thirteenth Legislature,* first Session, (Austin; 1873): 50, 255–259, 243, 293, 567; See *Galveston Daily News,* February 23, 1874. Contrary to J. M. Brewer, Burton was elected to only two consecutive terms in the Senate. Because of the calling of the Constitutional Convention, he served a total of only seven years (1874–1875 and 1876–1882). Still, this tenure was longer than that of Ruby who left office in 1873; Matt Gaines who departed in 1874 and Walter Ripetoe, who exited in 1880.
17. Brewer, *Negro Legislators of Texas,* p. 86.
18. "Memorial of Seth Shepard" in *Texas Legislature, Senate Journal of the Fourteenth Legislature,* First Session (Austin, 1874): 568–570; *State v. Gaines,* Criminal Docket of District Court, 1872, Fayette County, Texas; *State v. Gaines,* Indictment, November 1872 p. 1, District Court, Fayette County; *State v. Gaines,* Order of the Court July 15, July 23, 1873; *Gaines v. State* (606) Supreme Court M6816 (1873); *Galveston Daily News,* March 22, 1874. See also *Breham Banner* March 7, 1874, quoted in *Galveston Daily News,* March 8, 1874.

Gaines was elected to a six-year term, but according to Article III, Section 3 of the 1869 Constitution, the senators who were elected after the drafting of this constitution were divided into three classes. The seats of those of the first class were to be vacated at the expiration of the first two years; the second class at the end of four years; the third class at the end of six years. Gaines belonged to the second class.

19. *House Journal, Thirteenth Legislature,* Regular Session: 132.
20. *Senate Journal, Thirteenth Legislature,* Regular Session: 500.
21. *Ibid.*: 532; Gammel, *Laws of Texas* VII p. 615.
22. *House Journal of the Thirteenth Legislature,* Regular Session: 437, 1010.
23. *Ibid.,* pp. 371, 650; *Senate Journal of Thirteenth Legislature,* Regular Session: 72.
24. *House Journal of the thirteenth Legislature,* Regular Session: 172, 420–421, 898.
25. *Senate Journal of thirteenth Legislature,* Regular Session: 127, 129, 371: 951, 102, 1, 1035, 1161.

26. *Ibid.*: 827, 828; Gaines was also successful in presenting "an act to establish a manual poor house and a convict labor system in each county of the State . . ."
27. *House Journal of the Thirteenth Legislature,* Second Session: 142.
28. Governor's Message [ed] Richard Coke, Fourteenth Legislature, March 16, 1874, (Austin: State Archives).
29. Texas Legislature, *House Journal of the Fourteenth Legislature,* first Session: (Austin, 1874): 184.
30. Gammel, *Laws of Texas,* VII, pp. 55–59.
31. *Galveston Daily news,* February 16, 1874.
32. *House Journal of the Fourteenth Legislature,* Second Session: 142.
33. *Galveston Daily News,* February 8, 1875.
34. *Ibid.*
35. N. Q. Henderson *Directory of Officers and Members of the Constitutional Convention* (Austin, 1875); J. E. Ericson, "The Delegates to the Convention of 1875: A Reappraisal," *Southwestern Historical Quarterly,* LXVIII (July, 1963): 22–29.
36. Wharton, *History of Fort Bend County,* p. 180; Brewer, *Negro Legislators of Texas,* pp. 71–72; *Galveston Daily News,* September 16, 1875.
37. *Journal of the Constitutional Convention of 1875,* (Galveston: *Galveston Daily News* Office, 1875), p. 821; *Panola Watchman,* December 15, 1875; Wharton *History of Fort Bend County,* pp. 182–183; Brewer, *Negro Legislators of Texas,* pp. 69, 126.
38. *Journal of the Constitutional Convention of 1875* 237; See also Seth Sheppard McKay, *Debates in the Texas Constitutional Convention, 1875* (Austin: University of Texas Press, 1930).
39. *Journal of the Constitutional Convention of 1875,* 120; *Galveston Daily News,* September 16, 1875.
40. Brewer, *Negro Legislators of Texas,* pp. 71–72.
41. *Panola Watchman,* December 1, 1875.
42. *Journal of the Constitutional Convention of 1875:* 168.

Chapter 4 THE POST RECONSTRUCTION LEGISLATURES

1. *Galveston Daily News,* January 4, 1876; Rice, *The Negro in Texas,* p. 102: *House Journal of the Fifteenth Legislature,* Regular Session: 148–433.
2. John Cardwell, *The Fifteenth Legislature: Sketches of Legislators and State Officers 1876–1878* (Austin: 1876), p. 104; Sneed's only recorded activity in the House came on the Dog Tax. See *House Journal of Fifteenth Legislature,* Regular Session: 725.
3. Brewer, *Negro Legislators of Texas,* pp. 72–74, 127; W. H. Holland to E. J. Davis, April 30, 1872, Davis Papers; *Austin Daily Journal,* August 2, 1873; Mary S. Barkley, *A History of Central Texas* (Austin, 1970), pp. 168–169; See also Noah Smithwick, *The Evolution of a State* (Austin 1967) p. 320.
4. *Galveston Daily News,* August 14, 1880
5. W. H. Holland to J. S. Hogg, September 1, 1887, James Stephen Hogg Papers (Austin: State Archives).
6. "Notes and Fragments," *Texas Historical Association Quarterly,* Vol. I, pp. 125–126.

7. *House Journal of (25th) Legislature,* first Session: 211.
8. E. N. Swindells, *A Legislative Manual for the State of Texas* (Austin, 2vols., 1876, 1879), p. 246; *Voter Registration List for Harrison County 1867* (Austin: State Archives); *Panola Watchman,* February 19, 1879. Register of Disbursement, Office of Superintendent of Public Instruction 1871–1874. Austin: State Archives 1871.
9. Jacob Freeman came to the Sixteenth Legislature late in the first session because he was involved in a contested election. He probably could have entered the General Assembly earlier, but members of the Committee on Privileges and Election said that it was hard for them to "pull themselves to vote for a black man," *Colorado Citizen,* February 27, 1879. See also Freeman V. Col. I. N. Dennis cited in *Galveston Daily News,* February 20, 1879.
10. Brewer, *Negro Legislators in Texas,* pp. 75, 77, 81, 82; Winkler, *Platforms of Political Parties in Texas,* pp. 232–234; *Galveston Daily News,* April 21, 1875; *Colorado Citizens,* October 2, 1884; Rice, *Negro in Texas,* pp. 107–108; E. L. Blair, *History of Grimes County,* p. 206; *Election Registration List of State and County Officers* (Austin 1879); Swindells, *A Legislative Manual for The State of Texas,*
11. Swindells, *A Legislative Manual for The State of Texas; Galveston Daily News,* May 4, 1882; *House Journal Seventeenth Legislature,* Special Called Session: 43.
12. Texas Legislature, *House Journal of the Sixteenth Legislature,* First Session, (Austin 1879): 208; *Galveston Daily News,* April 1, 1879.
13. J. W. Baker, *History of Robertson County Texas,* pp. 163–164; L. W. St. Clair, *History of Robertson County* (Franklin, 1931), p. 93. In his book, *Members of Texas Legislature 1864–1939* Tommy Yett listed E. C. Mobley as a black representative, but contemporary newspapers confirm that he was a white Independent Democrat.
14. *Ibid.*
15. Swindells, *A Legislative Manual for the State of Texas,* (1879) Brewer, *Negro Legislator for the State of Texas* pp. 75, 128.
16. *Ibid.*; Brewer, *Negro Legislators of Texas;* p. 78; Rice, *Negro in Texas,* pp. 106–107.
17. *Ibid.* Guy's only recorded activity in the legislature was a resolution that he introduced to enable black children to reap the benefits from the Deaf, Dumb and Blind Institute, *House Journal of the Sixteenth Legislature* Regular Session: 565.
18. Will Lambert, *Pocket Dictionary of the Seventeenth Legislature of Texas,* (Austin, 1881); The only bill that Doc Lewis introduced was one to amend article 4875 of the revised civil status, *Austin Statesman,* May 27, 1882.
19. Brewer, *Negro Legislators of Texas,* pp. 84–86; Lambert, *Pocket Dictionary of the Seventeenth Legislature.*
20. *Ibid.*
21. *Ibid.*
22. Lambert, *Pocket Dictionary of the Eighteenth Legislature of Texas* (Austin, 1883); *Colorado Citizen* April 19, 1883; January 18, 1885.
23. *Ibid.*
24. E. H. Loughery, *Personnel of the Texas State Government for 1885* (Austin, 1885); Brewer, *Negro Legislators of Texas,* p. 93; Rice, *The Negro in Texas,* p. 110.
25. *Galveston Daily News,* August 6, 1882, January 15, 20, 26, 1887, March 1, 1892; *Dallas Morning News,* November 5, 1886.

Notes 225

26. Brewer, *Negro Legislators of Texas*, pp. 96–97; L. E. Daniell, *Personnel of Texas State Government*, (Austin, 1887), pp. 249–250.

27. *House Journal of The Twenty-sixth Legislature*, Regular Session: 211–214; Barker, *History of Robertson County, Texas*, p. 164; St. Clair, *History of Robertson County*, pp. 93, 154.

28. Brewer, *Negro Legislators of Texas*, p. vii; See also *Rules of Order of Texas House of Representative 1891* (Austin, 1891).

29. Alice Shannon, (Secretary of San Jacinto Historical Commission) to Merline Pitre, January 15, 1982; Monroe Work, "Some Negro Members of Reconstruction Legislature," *Journal of Negro History*, V, (1920): 111.

30. Brewer, *Negro Legislators of Texas*, pp. 99–100; For contested election see *Texas Legislature, House Journal of the (24th) Legislature*, (1st) (Sess.) 271–277, 285, 290; *Flake's Daily Bulletin*, August 3, 1871.

31. Autobiography of Robert L. Smith, "Robert L. Smith Papers, The Texas Collection" at Baylor University, Waco, Texas; B. L. Bremby, Biography of R. L. Smith (unpublished manuscript in Smith Papers, *Ibid.*; See Louis Harlan, *The Booker T. Washington Papers*, 8 Vols. (Urbana: University of Illinois, 1977). Also see section on Smith pp. 285–299 in the last part of this book.

32. *Texas Legislature, House Journal of the (17th) Legislature*, Sp. Called Sess. (Austin, 1881): 33.

33. *Colorado Citizen*, March 23, 1882: See also *United States V. Dodge*, Federal Case, 14976 (W. D. Texas) 1877. After the passage of the Civil Rights Act 1875, a test case involving a black woman (apparently Mrs. Burton) was brought against the seating policy of the rail companies. The judge upheld the validity of the act, but the decision contained language which was clearly portent of *Plessy v. Ferguson*. He held that a female passenger who had a first class ticket could not be denied access to the ladies car solely because she was of African descent. He further stated, that if the railroad provided two cars "equally fit and appropriate in all respects . . . Then there is no offense under the law in denying a colored female to one and requiring her to ride on the other." There is no evidence that the railroads or black women got the message that the judge had so clearly sent to them. Five years later, the persistent Mrs. Burton was thrown from a slowly moving train when she refused to leave the ladies coach. *Colorado Citizen* March 25, 1882.

34. *Proceedings of the Colored Men's Convention of 1883* p. 5; *Brenham Weekly Banner* October 23, 27, 1883.

35. *Texas Legislature, House Journal of the Twenty-first Legislature*, Regular Session (Austin, 1889): 169.

36. *Galveston Daily News*, February 17, 1889.

37. *Ibid.*, March 26, 27, 1889, January 18, 1891.

38. Robert L. Smith, "A Personal Afterword" in Brewer, *Negro Legislators of Texas*, p. 120.

39. Crouch, "Crisis in Color," 43.

40. *Texas Legislature, House Journal of the Eighteenth Legislature*, Regular Session (Austin, 1883): 362.

41. *Ibid. House Journal of the Twenty-first Legislature*, Regular Session: 169.

42. *Ibid.*, p. 451.

43. *Ibid.*, *House Journal of the Twenty-second Legislature*, Regular Session: (Austin, 1891). 486.
44. *Texas Legislature Senate Journal of the Sixteenth Legislature*, Regular Session: 270.
45. *Galveston Daily News*, January 20, 1881.
46. *Ibid.*, April 1, 1879.
47. *Texas, Legislature, House Journal of the Nineteenth Legislature*, Regular Session: (Austin, 1885): 100.
48. Gammel, *Laws of Texas*, IX, pp. 570–587; *Texas Acts*, (1884), Sec. 79. Chapter 57.
49. *House Journal of the Twenty-fourth Legislature*, First Session: 195; Gammel, *Laws of Texas*, IX, pp. 29–30.
50. *Galveston Daily News*, June 26, 1876.
51. *House Journal of the Fifteenth Legislature*, Regular Session: (Austin, 1876): 126, 639, 666, 703; Willie Tarrant, "A University for Negroes of Texas" (M. A. Thesis, Prarie View College, 1944); George Woolfolk, *Prairie View: A Study in Public Conscience*, (New York, Pageant Press, 1962) p. 30, Gammel, *Laws of Texas*, VIII, p. 135.
52. *Texas, Legislature Senate Journal of the (15th) Legislature*, Regular Session: (Austin, 1876): 247.
53. *Ibid.*, See also Woolfolk, *Prairie View*, p. 30.
54. Alton Hornsby, Jr., "The Colored Branch University Issue in Texas — Prelude to Sweatt *vs* Painter," *Journal of Negro History*, XII (January, 1976): 151. See Frederick Eby, *The Development of Education in Texas*, (New York, 1925), pp 271, 247, and *Texas Acts* (1879), Chapter 159, Secs 1, 2, 3.
55. *Texas Legislature, Senate Journal of the Sixteenth Legislature*, Regular Session (Austin, 1878): 672, 675, *Galveston Daily News*, February 27, 1879; *Austin Daily Statesman*, February 27, 1879.
56. *House Journal of the Seventeenth Legislature*, Special Called Session: 18, 22, 105; *Austin Daily Statesman*, April 22, 1882, See *Galveston Daily News*, February 12, 1881.
57. *House Journal of the Seventeenth Legislature*, Special Called Session: 62, *Austin Daily Statesman*, April 22, 1882.
58. *Austin Daily Statesman*, February 4, 1891; See Woolfolk, *Prairie View*.
59. See *Texas Constitution 1876* Art. 7 Sec 7; See also Merline Pitre "The Evolution of a Black University in Texas," *Journal of Western Black Studies*, III (Fall 1979): 216–223.
60. *Ibid.*
61. W. H. Holland to O. M. Roberts, September 28, 1882, O. M. Roberts Papers, Austin, Texas State Archives.
62. *House Journal of the Nineteenth Legislature*, Regular Session: 43, *Galveston Daily News*, January 23, 1888.
63. *Texas, Legislature, House Journal of the Twenty-third Legislature*, Regular Session (Austin, 1893) 275, 422; February 9, 1893, J. H. Washington headed a black University State Committee which came before the Legislature to make a plea for the said institution, but received nothing in return. Ed Patton had made a sim-

ilar effort two years earlier, but to no avail. See *Galveston Daily News,* March 14, 1891, February 9, 1893.

64. *Texas Legislature, House Journal of the Twenty-fifty Legislature,* First Session: 62, 111, 153, 428. John D. Pitts introduced House Bill #296 on October 16, 1895, "to set apart and grant unto Prairie View Normal School 50,000 acres of land and to set apart the same in alternate sections out of 100,000 [acres] to the permanent free school fund of Texas." A. J. Bell of Karnes County followed this bill up by introducing "an act to provide for the survey of the land set apart as a permanent endowment fund for the branch university for colored people of the state," but this bill died after being tabled. J. T. Curry of Hill County then, introduced House Bill #266, "That the commission of the General Land Office shall designate and set apart public domain for the benefit and use of common schools of the state, state universities and branches to the permanent fund." Later in the session, Smith made a motion to take up this bill and place it on its second reading. Curry's bill was then substituted as House Bill #325, so as to include Prairie View, but was subsequently postponed and dropped from the legislative calendar.

65. *Texas, Legislature, House Journal of the Twenty-sixth Legislature,* Regular Session: 336; *Hogue v Baker* 92, Texas 58 (1898).

66. *Texas, Legislature, Senate Journal of the Seventeenth Legislature,* Regular Session: 129; See *Galveston Daily News,* March 12, 1881.

67. *Colorado Citizen,* July 10, 1879: See also Gammel, *Laws of Texas,* VII, pp. 55–59.

68. *House Journal of the Nineteenth Legislature,* Regular Session: 310.

69. *Ibid., Twenty-fourth Legislature,* Regular Session: 378.

70. *Austin Daily Statesman,* January 20, 1883.

71. *Colorado Citizen,* July 10, 1879.

72. *House Journal of the Seventeenth Legislature,* Special Called Session: 42, *Austin Daily Statesman,* April 13, 1882.

73. *Austin Daily Statesman,* April 13, 1882.

74. *Ibid.,* April 14, 1882, *Galveston Daily News,* March 12, 1882.

75. *Senate Journal of the Sixteenth Legislature,* Regular Session: 197; See also *Galveston Daily News,* July 10, 1876.

76. *Ibid.*

77. *Galveston Daily News,* February 15, 16, 17, 1887.

78. *House Journal of the Twenty-first Legislature,* Regular Session: 524, 613, 870.

79. Ibid., *Fifteenth Legislature,* Regular Session: 188.

80. *Senate Journal Sixteenth Legislature,* Regular Session: 612, *Galveston Daily News,* February 23, 1879.

81. *Senate Journal of Sixteenth Legislature,* Regular Session: 672.

82. Gammel, *Laws of Texas,* IX, p. 732.

83. *House Journal of the Twenty-fourth Legislature,* First Session: 670.

84. *Texas Legislature Senate Journal of the Seventeenth Legislature,* Regular Session 113: *Galveston Daily News,* January 24, 1879; *Austin Daily Statesman,* January 24, 1879.

85. *Galveston Daily News,* January 29, 1879; *Austin Daily Statesman,* January 28, 1879.

86. *House Journal of the Sixteenth Legislature*, Regular Session: 1043.
87. *Ibid.*, *Twenty-first Legislature*, Regular Session: 95.
88. *Senate Journal of the Sixteenth Legislature*, Regular Session: 96, 135.
89. Gammel, *Laws of Texas*, VIII, pp. 914–920.
90. *Austin Daily Statesman*, January 23, 1883.
91. *House Journal of the Twenty-first Legislature*, Regular Session: 375.

The following persons were exempted from jury duty: All persons over 60 years, state and national civil officers, overseers of roads, ministers of the gospel in active ministerial duties, physicians and attorneys in actual practice, publishers of newspapers, schoolmasters, druggists, undertakers, telegraph operators, railroad companies or persons who acted as a jury commissioner during the preceeding twelve months, members of the volunteer guards, i.e. militia and active members of organized fire companies.

92. *House Journal, Fifteenth Legislature*, Regular Session: 465.
93. *Ibid.*, pp. 982–983.
94. *Panola Watchman*, April 2, 1879; *House Journal Twenty-first Legislature*, Regular Session: 588; *Galveston Daily News*, April 3, 1879; see Dick Smith, "Texas and the Poll Tax" *Southwestern Social Sciences Quarterly*, XLIV (September 1964): 167–168.
95. *Panola Watchman*, March 19, 1879.
96. *Ibid.*
97. *Ibid.*
98. *Galveston Daily News*, February 21, 1891.
99. *House Journal of Twenty-fourth Legislature*, First Session: 60.
100. *Ibid.*
101. *Ibid.*: 387.
102. *Ibid.*, *Fifteenth Legislature*, Regular Session: 710, 712.
103. *Galveston Daily News*, February 4, 1879; *Austin Daily Statesman*, February 4, 1879.
104. *Galveston Daily News*, March 3, 1887.
105. *House Journal of the Seventeenth Legislature*, Special Called Session: 59, *Galveston Daily News*, August 23, 1881.
106. *House Journal of the Seventeenth Legislature*, Regular Session: 650.
107. *Galveston Daily News*, February 20, 1881.
108. *House Journal of the Seventeenth Legislature*, Special Called Session: 138.
109. *Ibid.*, p. 43.
110. *Senate Journal of the Fifteenth Legislature*, Regular Session: 290.
111. *House Journal of the Twenty-second Legislature*, Regular Session: 336–337.
112. *Ibid.*, 671.
113. *Ibid.*, *Sixteenth Legislature*, Regular Session: 1089.
114. *Galveston Daily News*, February 18, 1881.
115. *House Journal of the Twenty-third Legislature*, Regular Session: 621.
116. *Ibid.*, *Sixteenth Legislature*, Regular Session: 113.
117. *Galveston Daily News*, February 3, 1881.
118. *House Journal of the Seventeenth Legislature*, Special Called Session: 123; Evans referred to June 19, 1865 as the date of the emancipation of slaves in the United States because that was the day on which General Gordon Granger an-

nounced the news to black Texans of President Lincoln Emancipation Proclamation. Alvin Edward is a state legislator for the 86th Representative District who is responsible for making Juneteenth a State holiday.

Chapter 5   A THORN IN THE SIDE

1. James Baggett, "Birth of the Texas Republican Party," *Southwestern Historical Quarterly*, LXXXVIII (July 1974): 1–20; *Ibid.*, "Origin of Early Texas Republican Party Leadership," *Journal of Southern History*, XL (August, 1974): 441–454; Edward Mydol, "Social Black Leaders in Societies," *A Review of Social History*, IV (1974), 81–110; William C. Nunn, *Texas Under The Carpetbaggers'* (Austin: University of Texas Press, 1962); See also Casdorph, *Republican Party in Texas;* Richard L. Hume, "The Black and Tan Constitutional Conventions of 1867–1889 in Ten Former Confederate States: A Study of Their Membership," (Ph.D. Dissertation, University of Washington, 1969), pp. 637–653; Alwyn Barr, *Black Texans: A History of Negroes in Texas 1528–1970,* (Austin, 1971).

2. Raney Jacob and Anderson Scroggins to J. M. Thorockmorton, May 3, 1867 in *Flake's Daily Bulletin,* May 14, 1867.

3. Winkler, *Platforms of Political Parties in Texas,* pp. 99–102, *Galveston Daily News,* July 5, 6, 1867.

4. *Galveston Daily News,* July 5, 6, 1867.

5. *Flake's Daily Bulletin,* October 24, November 22, 1867.

6. *Ibid.*, December 26, 1867; See also Moneyhon, *Republicanism in Reconstruction Texas,* pp. 75, 76.

7. *Austin Daily Statesman,* June 23, 24, 1868.

8. *Galveston Daily News,* June 23, July 1, 1868.

9. *Proceedings of the Republican State Convention Assembled at Austin August 12, 1868* (Austin: *Daily Republican,* 1868), pp. 3–8; Winkler, *Platforms of Political Parties in Texas,* pp. 112–113; *Austin Daily Republican,* August 12, 22, 1868.

10. Winkler, *Platforms of Political Parties in Texas,* pp. 115–116.

11. *Flake's Daily Bulletin,* August 11, 15, 1868.

12. *Ibid.*, September 9, 10, 24, 1868; See also Woods, "George T. Ruby."

13. *San Antonio Weekly Express,* October 15, 1868 found in Newcomb Papers; *Galveston Daily News,* September 20, 1868; Moneyhon, *Republicanism in Reconstruction Texas,* pp. 91. 96.

14. *Austin Daily Republican,* February 23, 1869; *Galveston Daily News,* February 18, 19, 1869; *Tri Weekly State Gazette,* February 25, 1869.

15. See E. M. Wheelock to E. M. Pease, April 11, 1869, Pease–Graham–Niles Papers, Austin Public Library. Wheelock expressed fear that the party might fall into the hands of such cancille as George Ruby, but still he was opposed to Hamilton's candidacy; See also J. G. Tracy to E. M. Pease, April 8, 1869-Pease–Graham–Nile Papers; *Houston Union* in *Flake's Daily Bulletin,* April 29, 1869; *Galveston Daily News,* April 29, 1869.

16. Winkler, *Platforms of Political Parties in Texas,* pp. 117–119; *Galveston Daily News,* May 6, 9, 1869; *Flake's Daily Bulletin,* May 4, 11, 12, 1869; *Austin Daily Republican,* May 13, 14, 1869; See also M. C. Hamilton to J. P. Newcomb, May 14, 1869; Newcomb Papers.

17. Winkler, *Platforms of Political Parties in Texas,* pp. 119–121; *Flake's Daily Bulletin,* June 10, 1869; *Austin Daily Republican,* June 12, 1869; *Galveston Daily News,* June 11, 1869.

18. G. T. Ruby to J. P. Newcomb, May 6, 1869, Newcomb Papers.

19. The following members of the House of Representative dissented from the action of the Governor in regards to the Grand State Ball: W. G. Robinson, G. Dupree, M. Kendall, H. Moore, S. Mullins, Richard Williams, David Medlock, James F. McKee, W. W. Davis, Richard Allen, J. J. Hamilton, Silas Cotton, John Mitchell, H. R. Allen, D. W. Bailey, and Robert Zapp. They protested because they "believed the whole affair to have been a violation of the rights of certain members as representative of the people and calculated to work political evil-the parties having been excluded on account of the prejudice of color," *House Journal of the Twelfth Legislature,* First Session: 296–297.

20. *Flake's Daily Bulletin,* May 10, 15, 1870; *Galveston Daily News,* May 10, 1870; See also J. H. Williams to G. T. Ruby, July 7, 1870, Newcomb Papers.

21. J. G. Tracy to J. P. Newcomb, June 1, 1871, Newcomb Papers; *San Antonio Express,* May 28, 1871; *Flake's Daily Bulletin,* June 22, 1871.

22. *Galveston Daily News,* May 21, 27, 1871; *Flake's Daily Bulletin,* May 27, June 1, 1871; See also G. T. Ruby to J. P. Newcomb, June 13, 1871, Newcomb Papers; Moneyhon, *Republicanism in Reconstruction Texas,* pp. 157–159.

23. *Flake's Daily Bulletin,* July 14, 1871; G. T. Ruby to Newcomb, June 13, 1871, Newcomb Papers.

24. J. G. Tracy to J. P. Newcomb, June 1, 1871; G. T. Ruby to J. P. Newcomb, July 6, 1871, Newcomb Papers.

25. Address of Matt Gaines to Republicans of the Union League, March 30, 1871; *Galveston Daily News,* April 5, 1871; *Flake's Daily Bulletin,* May 18, 1870, February 24, 1871; *Debates of Twelfth Legislature,* 13, 82, 83.

26. L. W. Stevenson to J. P. Newcomb, February 12, 13, May 26, 1871, Newcomb Papers.

27. *Galveston Daily News,* April 23, 25, May 4, June 21, 1871; See also G. T. Ruby, to J. P. Newcomb, June 29, 1871, Newcomb Papers.

28. *Galveston Daily News,* February 14, 24, 1871.

29. *Flake's Daily Bulletin,* July 16, 1871.

30. *Ibid.,* August 3, 4, 1871.

31. *Ibid.*

32. *Ibid.,* August 4, 5, 23, 26, 1871.

33. *Ibid.*

34. *Ibid.*

35. *Ibid.*

36. *Brenham Banner,* August 15, 17, 1871; *Houston Telegraph,* June 29, 1871.

37. *Flake's Daily Bulletin,* February 25, 1872; *Galveston Daily News,* March 1, 1872; W. T. Clark to J. P. Newcomb, February 19, 1872, Newcomb Papers.

38. *Galveston Daily News,* March 27, April 24, 1872.

39. Winkler, *Platforms of Political Parties in Texas,* pp. 140–143; *Houston Union,* May 15, 16, 1872.

40. J. R. Burns to J. P. Newcomb, September 18, 1872, Newcomb Papers; Moneyhon, *Republicanism in Reconstruction Texas,* p. 178.

41. J. C. Degress to J. P. Newcomb, September 13, 1872; J. R. Burns to J. P. Newcomb September 14, 1872, Newcomb Papers.

42. *Galveston Daily News,* July 5, 6, 1873; *Brenham Banner,* July 4, 5, 1873; Winkler, *Platforms of Political Parties in Texas,* pp. 148–151; *Galveston Daily news,* July 5, 6, 1873.

Chapter 6   MISCALCULATION OR MANIPULATION

1. Alwyn Barr, *From Reconstruction to Reform* (Austin, University of Texas Press, 1971), p. 176.
2. *Norton Union Intelligience,* April 12, May 22, 29, June 12, 1875.
3. Winkler, *Platforms of Political Parties in Texas,* p. 176. See also Casdorph, *The Republican Party in Texas, 1865–1965* pp. 39, 47–48, 66, 251.
4. *Galveston Daily News,* January 12, 13, 1876, May 16, 1882.
5. *Ibid.*; Winkler, *Platforms of Political Parties in Texas,* pp. 176–179; Stanley–Hirshson, *Farewell to the Bloody Shirt,* (Bloomington: Indiana University Press 1962), p. 86.
6. *Galveston Daily News,* October 2, 1878, Virginia Neal Hinze, "Norris Wright Cuney," (M. A. Thesis, Rice University, 1965), p. 61; Barr, *From Reconstruction to Reform,* p. 178.
7. *Galveston Daily News,* October 9, 1878; Casdorph, *Republican Party of Texas,* pp. 38–40; Hinze, "Cuney," p. 61.
8. Winkler, *Platforms of Political Parties in Texas,* pp. 195–197.
9. *Ibid., Galveston Daily News,* March 26, 1880.
10. Barr, *From Reconstruction to Reform,* pp. 195–197; Budd, "The Negro in Politics in Texas," p. 77.
11. *Texas, Secretary of State Report 1881,* (Austin, 1881) pp. 60–64.
12. Winkler, *Platforms of Political Parties,* 212–214; Hinze, "Cuney," p. 64; *Galveston Weekly News,* May 18, 1882; See also E. J. Davis to J. P. Newcomb, October 27, 1881, Newcomb Papers.
13. *Galveston Daily News,* August 25, 1882; Winkler, *Platforms of Political Parties in Texas,* pp. 212–214.
14. *Galveston Daily News,* August 24, 1882; Winkler, *Platforms of Political Parties in Texas,* pp. 212–214; Shack Roberts and Jacob E. Freeman were delegates of this convention, While Hal Geiger was alternate — at-large.
15. *Galveston Daily News,* May 1, 1884; *Dallas Daily Herald,* May 1, 1884; *Official Report of the Republican State Convention Proceedings of 1884 Held at Fort Worth, Texas, April 29, 30, May 1, 1884* (Austin, 1884), pp. 30–31, 42–43; Maude Cuney Hare, *Norris Wright Cuney. A Tribune of the Black People* (Austin: Steck–Vaughn Co., 1969), pp. 55–58.
16. *Dallas Weekly Herald,* April 29, 30, 1884; *Fort Worth Gazette,* May 2, 19, 1884; Winkler, *Platforms of Political Parties in Texas,* pp. 215–216.

Two blacks who played prominent roles in these conventions, but who did not win state offices are Henry and Charles Ferguson. Henry C. Ferguson was born to a slave mother and white father in Jasper County in 1860. He was granted freedom when he reached the age of 30, at which time he migrated to Houston. After the Civil War, he moved to Fort Bend County and served in the state police force. In

1873, he succeeded Walter Burton as sheriff of Fort Bend County. Like Burton, Ferguson had a white deputy to arrest white people. During the 50 years that he resided in Fort Bend, Ferguson accumulated considerable property.

Charles M. Ferguson, brother of Henry was born a slave in Jasper County also, but became free while still a child. At the age of 18, he was sent to Fisk University with assistance by his brother. Three years later, he returned to Fort Bend and was elected district clerk. Unlike his brother, Charles was disliked by many whites. The result of which was that he had to leave his home in 1888 when the Jaybird (Democrats) took over Fort Bend County Government. Returning to Fort Bend several years later, Charles became involved in politics again and joined forces with the whites of the Republican party who were responsible for Cuney's demise. By 1888, Charles Ferguson was economically secured. That is to say, he owned a brick house and fifteen hundred acres of land, Clarence Wharton, *History of Fort Bend County* pp. 181–182.

17. *Galveston Daily News,* August 31, September 3, 4, 1884; Winkler, *Platforms of Political Parties in Texas,* pp. 229–230; Budd, "The Negro in Politics in Texas," p. 87.

18. *Galveston Daily News,* September 14, 24, October 9, 13, 19, 30, 1884; Budd, "The Negro in the Politics in Texas," pp. 86–87.

19. *Dallas Daily News,* August 26, 1886.

20. *Ibid.*, August 27, 28, 1886; Budd, "The Negro in Politics in Texas," p. 91; Winkler, *Platforms of Political Parties in Texas,* pp. 242–244; Hinze, "Cuney," pp. 72–73; Hare, *Cuney,* pp. 13, 26, 27–28.

21. Casdorph, *Republican Party of Texas,* pp. 50–53; Winkler, *Platforms of Political Parties in Texas,* pp. 242–244.

22. Winkler, *Platforms of Political Parties in Texas,* pp. 251–254; *Dallas Morning News,* April 25, 26, 28, 1888; *Galveston Daily News,* April 25, 26, 1888; Budd, "The Negro in Politics in Texas," p. 93.

23. *Galveston Daily News,* September 11, 22, October 10, 22, 1888; Winkler, *Platforms of Political Parties in Texas,* pp. 272–273; *Dallas Daily Herald,* September 22, 1888.

24. *San Antonio Companion News,* September 29, 1888; Hare, *Cuney,* pp. 93, 95–96; Robert Cotner, *James Stephens Hogg: A Biography* (Austin; University of Texas Press, 1951), pp. 278; See Also *White Republican* December 2, 1890; Hinze, "Cuney," pp. 89–90. This white group sent out a circular letter calling for white Republicans to organize without the harmful element of the Negro.

25. *Galveston Daily News,* September 4, 1890; *Austin Daily Statesman,* September 24, 1890; *Houston Daily Post,* September 4, 5, 6, 1890.

26. *Galveston Daily News,* September 22, 1890; Hinze, "Cuney," pp. 94, 97; *San Antonio White Republican,* September 2, 17, 24, 1890; *San Antonio Daily Express,* September 5, 1980.

27. Winkler, *Platforms of Political Parties in Texas,* pp. 290–292; *San Antonio Daily Express,* September 6, 7, 1890; *Austin Daily Statesman,* September 24, 1890.

28. *Fort Worth Gazette,* March 6, 8, 1892; Budd, "The Negro in Politics in Texas," p. 135; *Austin Evening News,* March 8, 9, 10, 12, 1892; *Galveston Daily News,* 10, 1892.

29. *Galveston Daily News,* September 3, 4, 1890.

Notes 233

30. *Galveston Daily News,* March 27, 1892; T. Drinkwood to Ember (sic) Norwood, March 27, 1892 in Embro Norwood Papers, University of Texas at Austin Archives.

31. *Fort Worth Gazette,* March 6, 8, 1892; See also Winkler, *Platforms of Political Parties in Texas,* pp. 301–302; Hinze "Cuney," p. 97.

32. *Proceeding of The Tenth Republican National Convention Held in Minneapolis, Minnesota, June 7, 8, 9, 10, 1892,* (Minneapolis, 1892), 35–36.

33. *San Antonio Daily Express,* November 12, 1894; Barr, *From Reconstruction to Reform,* p. 186; *Galveston Daily News,* October 9, 1894, p. 186; Hinze "Cuney," p. 174.

34. *Dallas Morning News,* August 28, 1894; *Austin Daily Statesman,* August 29, 1894; Winkler, *Platforms of Political Parties in Texas,* pp. 345–349; Budd, "The Negro in Politics in Texas," pp. 150–151.

35. *Galveston Daily News,* August 29, 30, September 4, 1894; Budd, "The Negro in Politics in Texas," pp. 150–153.

36. Barr, *From Reconstruction to Reform,* p. 187; Hare, *Cuney,* pp. 178–181; Hinze, "Cuney," pp. 116–118.

37. *Houston Daily Post,* February 28, 29, 1896, March 5, 1896; *San Antonio Light,* March 8, 1896.

38. Winkler, *Platforms of Political Parties in Texas,* pp. 357–358; *Galveston Daily News,* March 25, 1895; *Austin Evening News,* March 25, 1896.

39. Hinze, "Cuney," 122; *San Antonio Express,* March 27, 28, 1896; *Galveston Daily* News, March 27, 28, 1896.

40. *San Antonio Express,* March 27, 1896; *Galveston Daily News,* March 27, 1896.

41. *Austin Evening News,* March 27, 1896; Winkler, *Platforms of Political Parties in Texas,* pp. 359–360.

42. *Proceedings of the Eleventh National Republican Convention held at St. Louis, Missouri, June 16, 17, 18, 1896* (Minneapolis, Minn. 1896), p. 75; Hare, *Cuney,* p. 195; Richard Baine, *Convention, Decisions and Voting Records,* (Washington, D.C., 1960), pp. 152–159.

43. *Dallas Daily Time Herald* September 7, 1896; *Galveston Daily News* September 7, 10, 1896.

44. Budd, "The Negro in Politics in Texas," pp. 170–171; *Dallas Morning News,* September 18, 1896.

45. Winkler, *Platforms of Political Parties in Texas,* p. 393.

46. Hinze, "Cuney," pp. 126–129; Barr, *From Reconstruction to Reform,* p. 187.

47. H. F. McGregor to J. P. Newcomb, August 29, 1897, Newcomb Papers.

48. *Dallas Morning News,* April 17, 1898.

49. *Ibid.*

50. *Dallas Morning News,* August 16, 1898; Budd, "The Negro in Politics in Texas," p. 178.

51. *Ibid., Dallas Morning News* August 17, 1898.

52. *Ibid.*

53. *Ibid.,* August 18, 1898.

54. *Ibid.,* August 17, 1898.

Chapter 7 FUSION OR FISSION

1. *Marshall Tri-Weekly,* March 16, 1876; *Austin Daily Statesman,* July 26, 1976; Roscoe Martin, "The Greenback Party In Texas," *Southwestern Historical Quarterly,* XXX (January 1927): 167-177; Budd, "The Negro in Politics in Texas," pp. 167-177.
2. *Galveston Daily News,* October 9, 13, November 5, 15, 1878.
3. *Ibid.,* October 31, November 1, 2, 3, 1878.
4. *Ibid.,* August 19, 1878; Barr, *From Reconstruction to Reform,* pp. 177-179; Casdorph, *The Republican Party in Texas,* pp. 38-40.
5. *Brenham Weekly Banner,* October 4, 1878; Budd, "The Negro in Politics in Texas," pp. 73-75.
6. *Galveston Daily News,* August 26, 1880.
7. *Ibid.,* March 23, June 22, 1880; See also Winkler, *Platforms of Political Parties in Texas,* pp. 195-197-201.
8. *Texas, Secretary of State Report,* (Austin: State Archives, 1881), 60-64; Barr, *From Reconstruction to Reform,* p. 60.
9. Barr, *From Reconstruction to Reform,* pp. 64-68.
10. Budd, "The Negro In Politics in Texas," pp. 73-76; *Texas Secretary of State Report 1881,* (Austin, 1881), pp. 60-74.
11. Budd, "Negro in Politics in Texas," pp. 86-87.
12. Duane E. Ginn, "Racial Violence in Texas 1884-1900," (M. A. Thesis, University of Houston 1974), p. 12; *Galveston Daily News,* November 8, 1884.
13. *Dallas Morning News,* February 13, March 9, 10, 1892; *Galveston Daily News,* February 13, 1892.
14. See T. N. Jones to John W. Spivey, November 2, 1892; Leander Travis to Hogg, October 2, 1892, Hogg Papers.
15. S. W. Baker to James S. Hogg, September 21, 1892; W. H. Jackson to Hogg, August 29, 1892; L. Holiday to Hogg, October 21, 1892; Sam Dogley to Hay, May 11, 1892, Hogg Papers.
16. Col. McCuen to J. S. Hogg, October 11, 1892, Hogg Papers.
17. C. Vann Woodward, *The Origin of the New South,* (Baton Rough, Louisiana State University Press, 1951), pp. 188-191.
18. Jack Abramowitz, "The Negro in the Populist Movement," *Journal of Negro History,* XXXVIII (1953); 267-269; Winkler, *Platforms of Political Parties in Texas,* pp. 314-318, 383-384; See also Roscoe C. Martin, *The People's Party in Texas* (Austin, 1933).
19. *Dallas Morning News,* August 18, 1891; Martin, *The People's Party in Texas,* pp. 89-95.
20. Barr, *From Reconstruction to Reform* pp. 151-157; Douglass G. Perry, "Black Populism: The Negro in the People's Party," (M. A. Thesis, Prairie View College, 1954), p. 41; *Galveston Daily News,* August 9, 1896.
21. Jack Abramowitz, "John B. Rayner — A Grass Roots Leader," *Journal of Negro History,* XXXVI (1951): 162-163; See also Jack Abramowitz, "Accommodation and Militancy in Negro Life 1876-1916," (Ph. D. Dissertation, Columbia University 1950).
22. W. Westhoff to J. P. Newcomb, August 22, 1892, J. P. Newcomb Papers

23. *Southern Mercury,* August 1, 15, September 14, 1895; April 9, 16, June 26, 1896; See also Jack Abramowitz, "A Grass Roots Leader."
24. *Houston Daily Post,* August 9, 1896.
25. *Galveston Daily News,* September 3, 1892.
26. Perry, "Black Populism in Texas," pp. 48–52.
27. *Ibid.*; See also Roscoe Martin, "Greenback Party in Texas,"
28. Rice, *Negro in Texas,* pp. 53–67.

Chapter 8   REJECTION, REDUCATION, RETRENCHMENT

1. Allen Trelease, *White Terror: The Ku Klux Klan Conspiracy and Southern Reconstruction* (New York: Harper and Row, 1971), p. 103
2. *Ibid.*, p. xxii
3. Affidavit, George Wilson, September 25, 1871, (Austin: State Archives, Election Return)
4. Affidavit, Monroe Hill, November 19, 1871, *Ibid.*
5. Affidavit, James Taylor, April 8, 1872, *Ibid.*
6. Affidavit, A. M. Mitchell, December 2, 1871, *Ibid.*
7. Affidavit, Matthew Polk, November 19, 1871, *Ibid.*
8. *Galveston Daily News,* July 5, 6, 1867.
9. Matthew Gaines to E. J. Davis, March 6, 1870, E. J. Davis Papers.
10. *Contested Election of the 14th Senatorial District, The Thirteenth Legislature,* p. 68; Gandy, "History of Montgomery County," p. 171.
11. See Map F.
12. *Ordinance Adopted By The Constitutional Convention of the State of Texas, Convened at the City of Austin, September 6, 1875,* cited in Gammel, *Laws of Texas,* VII, pp. 2–9.
13. See Maps A, B, and C.
14. For errors made in taking of the census in Harrison County, which had the second largest black population in the state, see James Turner Marshall to E. J. Davis, January 6, 1871, E. J. Davis Papers. See also *Texas Constitution of 1876,* Article 3, Section 3.
15. *Texas Constitution of 1876,* Article 3, Section 26; As to representation, Section 26 reads as follows: "The members of the House of Representatives shall be apportioned among the several counties, according to the number of population in each as nearly as may be, on a ratio obtained by dividing the population of the State, as ascertained by the most recent United States census, by the number of members of which the House is composed; provided that whenever a single county has sufficient population to be entitled to a Representative, such a county shall be formed into a separate representative district, and when two or more counties are required to make up the ratio of representation, such counties shall be contiguous to each other; and when any one county has more than sufficient population to be entitled to one or more Representatives, such Representative or Representatives shall be apportioned to such county, and for any surplus of population it may be joined in a representative district with any other contiguous county or counties." See Vernon's *Annotated Constitution, 1876: Revised Civil Statues of the State of Texas,* (Kansas City, Mo.: Vernon Law Book Co. 1952), p. 594; See Maps F and G.

16. *Panola Watchman,* December 1, 1875; Rice, *The Negro in Texas,* p. 26.
17. *United State Bureau of Census, Twelfth Census of U.S., 1901,* I (Washington 1901), pp. cxii, cixii; *U.S. Bureau of Census Negro Population,* (Washington 1910), p. 51.
18. *Ibid.;* Austin's decline in population might have had something to do with the Democrats rise to power. The Democrats assumed control in Austin in 1872 when radicals and blacks split and lost control of the county government. For more information, see *Works Projects Administration,* Writer's Project, (Comp.; Houston 1942), 73-74.
19. *U.S. Bureau of Census: Negro Population,* p. 125.
20. *Ibid.,* pp. 70-71.
21. *House Journal of the Seventeenth Legislature,* Special Called Session: 96-97, *Galveston Daily News.* April 18, 1882.
22. *Ibid.*
23. *Galveston Daily News,* February 17, 1895.
24. *Panola Watchman,* October 28, 1874; *Marshall Tri-Weekly Herald,* October 15, 17, 1878; See also White Man's Union Association of Wharton County, Texas, "Constitution, By Laws and Amendments of the White Man's Union Association" (Wharton, Texas: Specator Print, 1900); Rice, *Negro in Texas,* pp. 114-116.
25. Barr, *From Reconstruction to Reform,* p. 195.
26. Gammel, *Laws of Texas,* VIII, pp. 52, 292-294, 1420.
27. *Galveston Daily News,* January 4, 1876.
28. Barr, *From Reconstruction to Reform,* p. 196.
29. Amory R. Starr to My Ward, April 20, 1882, Henry Raguet Papers, University of Texas at Austin Archives.
30. Pauldine Yeldeman, "The Jaybirds Democratic Association of Fort Bend County," (M. A. Thesis, University of Texas, 1938); Rice, *The Negro in Texas,* pp. 115-120; Wharton, *History of Fort Bend County;* See also By Laws of the White Man's Union Association of Grimes County, Texas Jaybird Papers, University of Texas At Austin Archives.
31. Wharton, *History of Fort Bend County,* pp. 186-200.
32. *Houston Daily Post,* September 3, 1888. The message to these blacks read as follows:
Resolve: That in view of the crimes lately committed in our midst, we consider it necessary to the public good that the following persons be notified to leave this county within ten hours from notification, to wit: C. M. Ferguson, H. G. Evans, Peter Warren, J. D. Davis, Tom Taylor, Jack Taylor and C. M. Williams.
33. Rice, *The Negro in Texas,* p. 204.
34. *Ibid.*
35. *Ibid.*
36. *Galveston Daily News,* October 26, 1876; Jaun J. Steighorst, *Bay City and Matagorda County: A History* (Austin: Pemberton Press, 1965), p. 33. Ida Brandon. "The Tax Payers Union in Brazoria County," *Texas History Teachers' Bulletin,* XIV (1926): 86-92.
37. Frank MacD Spindler, "Concerning Hempstead and Waller County,"

Southwestern Historical Quarterly, LIX (April 1956): 458; Rice, *The Negro in Texas,* pp. 200–203, 216–218; *Works Project Administration* Writer's Project 93–94.

38. *Galveston Daily News,* November 6–12, 1884; *Dallas Morning News,* April 15, 1892; *The Report of The Secretary of State 1884,* (Austin, 1884); *Dallas Morning News,* November 8, 1888; See also Robert W. Shook. "The Texas Election Outrages of 1886," *East Texas Historical Journal,* X (Spring 1972): 20–30.

39. *U.S. Senate, Miscellaneous Document, Testimony of Alleged Election Outrages in Washington County Texas, 1886* Fiftieth Congress, Second Session No. 82, (Serial 2618): 126, 130, 137, 202–203, 667–668, 700–701.

40. *U.S. Senate Report Alleged Election Outrages in Washington County, Texas, 1886* Fiftieth Congress, Second Session, No. 2534, (Serial 2618): 19–21, 25–44; *Galveston Daily News,* November 3, 4, 5, 1886; *Dallas Morning News,* November 10, 12, 1886.

41. *Senate Miscellaneous Document: Testimony of Alleged Election Outrages,* 646–649; *Senate Report Alleged Election Outrages,* 89–90. The committee which conducted the hearing recommended the revision of "existing laws regulating election of members of Congress with a proclivity for a more complete protection of the exercise of the elective franchise."

42. *Congressional Record,* Fifty-first Congress, Second Session: 8523–8525.

43. Norman L. McCarver, *Hearne on the Brazos* (San Antonio: Century Press of Texas, 1958), pp. 25–38. According to McCraver, Hearne's first racial killing of Reconstruction occurred when a black state police arrived in the city. This gentleman was requested to come to a certain saloon to quell a fabricated disturbance, whereupon he was shot.

44. Cannon killed the white city Marshall of Hearne for jailing his father-in-law on November 7, 1883. For more on Cannon, See Richard Denny Parkers, *Historical Recollection of Robertson County Texas,* pp. 63, 48–49. See also Roscoe C. Martin, *People's Party in Texas,* pp. 136–137, 179–180, 236.

Chapter 9   MATTHEW GAINES: THE MILITANT

1. *Flake's Daily Bulletin,* August 1, 6, 1871; July 11, 1871; *Brenham Banner,* July 11, 1871.

2. Ann Malone, "Matthew Gaines," pp. 49–54: See *Gaines v States* (607), Affidavit of Matthew Gaines, December 16, 1872 in Case Argued and Decided in the Supreme Court of the State of Texas *XXXIX* (St. Louis, 1875); *Daily State Journal,* July 15, 1870; See also United States *Census* (1850) Schedule 2: Slave Inhabitants, Orleans to West Feliciana, Louisiana.

3. Malone, "Matthew Gaines," p. 54.

4. *Flake's Daily Bulletin,* May 18, 1870.

5. *Debates of the Twelfth Legislature,* p. 13.

6. Ibid.

7. Ibid., p. 82.

8. Ibid., p. 27.

9. *Galveston Daily News,* April 26, 1871; See *Senate Journal, Twelfth Legislature* First Session: 725, 785, 803: See also *Texas Almanac 1873 and Emigrant's Guide to Texas,* (Galveston, 1873).

10. *Galveston Daily News,* April 26, 1871.
11. *Ibid.*
12. *Austin Daily State Journal,* March 30, 1871.
13. *Brenham Banner,* August 15, 1871.
14. *Ibid.*
15. *Debates of the Twelfth Legislature,* p. 13; *Brenham Banner,* February 28, 1871. April 5, 1871.
16. *Brenham Banner,* April 5, 26, 1871.
17. *Ibid.,* August 18, 1871.
18. *Ibid., Galveston Daily News,* September 30, 1870.
19. *Houston Weekly Telegraph,* June 29, 1871.
20. *Austin State Daily Journal,* September 22, 30, 1871; *Austin Daily Statesman,* September 30, 1871; *Senate Journal of Twelfth Legislature,* Second Session: 29.
21. *Ibid.*
22. *Brenham Banner,* September 26, 1871; *Senate Journal of Twelfth Legislature,* Second Session: 29.
23. *Ibid.*
24. *State v Gaines,* Criminal Docket of District Court 1872, Fayette County, Texas; *State v Gaines,* Indictment, November 1872, p. 1, District Court, Fayette County, Texas.
25. *State v Gaines,* Motion to Remove Cause to Federal District Court, p. 5, Fayette County, Texas.
26. *State v Gaines,* Criminal Docket, District Court, Summer Term, 1873, Case No. 1522; See also the *New Era,* (Lagrange), July 18, 1873.
27. *State v Gaines,* Motion for a New Trial in Arrest of Judgement, July 17, 1873, Statement of Facts, Exhibits 1 and 2, July 24, 1873, District Court, Fayette County.
28. *Brenham Banner,* July 17, 1873; *Austin Daily Statesman,* July 19, 1873.
29. *State v Gaines,* (606), Supreme Court M6816 (1873), In an attempt to discredit Gaines, before the Supreme Court handed down its decision, the *Brenham Banner* ran a story which stated that "Matt Gaines belongs in prison. Why is [such a] notorious convict is allowed to run at large?"
30. See "Memorial of Seth Shepard" in *Texas Legislature, Senate Journal Fourteenth Legislature,* First Session: 567–570; See also *Brenham Banner,* quoted in *Galveston Daily News,* March 7, 1874.
31. *Brenham Banner,* April 23, 30, 1875.
32. *Ibid.,* May 27, July 2, August 23, November 8, 1878.
33. *Galveston Daily News,* May 2, 1884.
34. Alice White Wornley to Ann P. Malone, January 29, 1970, interview cited in Malone, "Matt Gaines," pp. 70–72.

Chapter 10 GEORGE T. RUBY: THE PARTY LOYALIST

1. *State Daily Journal,* October 13, 1870.
2. George Ruby, (Bureau Inspector) to Charles Garreston, (Acting Assistant Adjutant General (AAAG) September 14, October 14, 1867, R-86, Box 9, Bureau of Refugees, Freedmen and Abandoned Lands, Record, Group 105, National Ar-

chives, Washington, D.C.); Unless otherwise indicated, all Ruby's correspondence with or from Freedmen's Bureau officials will refer to the Texas Freedmen's Bureau; See also Stephen Shannon, "Galvestonian and Military Reconstruction 1865– 1876," (M. A. Thesis, Rice University, 1975).

3. See Office of the Superintendent of Education, *Record of Teachers*, Vol. XIX, 166–167, Crouch, "Self Determination and Local Black Leaders in Texas," 341.

4. Charles Griffin to Oliver M. Howard, May 24, 1867, AC. LS Vol. V, 55– 56, Texas Freedmen's Bureau; *Weekly State Journal*, July 28, 1870.

5. G. T. Ruby to Joel T. Kirkman, (AAAG), June 23, 1867; AC Letter Received (LR) R-186, Box 4; Ruby to Kirkman, July 26, 1867, Texas Bureau.

6. See Charles Griffin to Oliver Howard May 24, 1867 AC LS Vol. V., pp. 55–56, Texas Bureau; See also Ruby to N. Patton, January 22, 1870, Group 56, Treasury Department, National Archives, For his one year of service, Ruby received $2,000.00.

7. *Senate Journal, Twelfth Legislature*, 70; *Thirteenth Legislature*, 50–51; Winkler, *Platforms of Political Parties in Texas*, pp. 107–108; Woods, "George T. Ruby," 27.

8. G. T. Ruby to J. P. Newcomb, July 27, 1871, *Personal*, J. P. Newcomb Papers.

9. Clipping in E. J. Davis Papers; See also *Texas Almanac*, 1873 and *The Emigrant's Guide to Texas*, (Galveston, 1873); *Debates of 12th Legislature*, p. 90; F. D. Sewalls to George T. Ruby (letter of appointment) June 4, 1867 and Special Order #63, June 18, 1869, Texas Bureau.

10. *Debate of Twelfth Legislature*, p. 90.

11. Ruby to Newcomb, August 4, 1871; See also G. T. Ruby to J. P. Newcomb August 18, 1871, Newcomb Papers.

12. *Flake's Daily Bulletin*, August 17, 1871.

13. *Ibid.*, July 3, 1870; See also G. T. Ruby to J. P. Newcomb, June 13, 1871, Newcomb Papers.

14. G. T. Ruby to J. P. Newcomb, August 18, 1871, *Personal*, Newcomb Papers.

15. *Austin Daily State Journal*, May 4, 1870, May 6, 1871; *Flake's Daily Bulletin*, June 18, 1871.

16. *Galveston Daily News*, June 9, 13, 1871; *Austin Daily State Journal*, June 9, 1871; G. T. Ruby to J. P. Newcomb, August 4, 1871, Newcomb Papers; Moneyhon, "George T. Ruby," 384–385, in Howard N. Rabinowitz (Ed.), *Southern Black Leaders of the Reconstruction Era* (Urbana: University of Illinois Press, 1982).

17. *Galveston Daily News*, July 8, 1873; *Brenham Banner*, July 4, 5, 6, 1873; Winkler, *Platforms of Political Parties in Texas*, pp. 148–151; *Daily State Journal*, July 5, 9, 1873; Eby, *Education in Texas*, pp. 581–582.

18. Woods, "George T. Ruby," 275–276.

19. *Ibid.*, See also *Senate Journal of Thirteenth Legislature*, Regular Session: 297.

20. See C. B. Gardiner to E. J. Davis, September 8, 1870, Davis Papers.

21. *Senate Journal of Thirteenth Legislature*, Regular Session: 171.

22. *Ibid.*, Twelfth Legislature, First Session: 611.

23. *Ibid.*, p. 122.

24. Nunn, *Texas Under The Carpetbaggers*, pp. 153–155.

25. Moneyhon, "George T. Ruby," p. 382.
26. Silas Blonover to E. J. Davis, January 18, 1870, Davis Papers; Wood, "George T. Ruby," 278.
27. *Flake's Daily Bulletin*, May 8, 1870. After Ruby failed to be reelected to the Texas Senate, he returned to New Orleans, where he became clerk to the surveyor for the Port of New Orleans, worked with the Internal Revenue Department and from 1877 to 1882, edited a black newspaper, *The New Orleans Observer*. Ruby died in New Orleans, 1882. *New Orleans City Directory*, 1875, 596, *Ibid*, 1876, 586; *Ibid*, 1877, 558; *Ibid*; 1878, 571; *Ibid*, 1879; 576; *Ibid*, 1880, 662; *Ibid*, 1881, 631; *Ibid*, 1882, 606. For more on Ruby's role in Louisiana politics see William I. Hair *Bourbonism and Agrarian Protest: Louisiana Politics 1877–1900*, (Baton Rouge: Louisiana State University Press 1969).
28. Moneyhon, "George T. Ruby," p. 387–388.

Chapter 11   RICHARD ALLEN: THE OPPORTUNIST

1. *Dallas Herald*, February 8, 15, 1868; *Houston Union*, July 6, 1871; Baggett, "Early Texas Republican Leadership": 14–15; Brewer, *Negro Legislators of Texas*, p. 53; Casdorph; *The Republican Party in Texas*, 39, 47, 48, 66, 251; Rice, *The Negro in Texas*, pp. 38, 57, 201, 202.
2. Casdorph, *Republican Party in Texas*, pp. 249–252; See also Winkler, *Platforms of Political Parties in Texas*, for Allen's activities in party convention.
3. *Houston Telegraph*, July 11, 14, 1869; *Galveston Daily News*, July 3, 4, 1869.
4. *Houston Telegraph*, February 4, 6, 9, 10, 11, 27, March 1, 22, April 20, 21, 26, 28, 1872.
5. *Flake's Daily Bulletin*, August 6, 1871; *Galveston Daily News*, August 3, 1871; See also *Official Proceedings of the Republican Nomination of the Third Congressional District*, cited in *Flake's Daily Bulletin*, August 3, 1871.
6. *Houston Telegraph*, August 12, 14, 17, 24, 1873.
7. *Galveston Daily News*, December 24, 1874.
8. *Ibid*.
9. *Galveston Daily News*, August 19, 1878; Winkler, *Platforms of Political Parties in Texas*, pp. 190–193.
10. *Galveston Daily News*, January 9, 1878.
11. *Panola Watchman*, May 21, 1879.
12. *Official Proceedings of the Colored Convention Held at Houston, Texas, July 4, 1879*, cited in *Galveston Daily News*, July 5, 1879; See also *Houston Telegraph*, July 4, 5, 11, 1879; Leonard Wiliams, Jr., "Texas and the Kansas Fever, 1879–1888" (M. A. Thesis University of Houston 1973); "Proceedings of the Migration Convention and Congressional Action Respecting the Exodus of 1879," *Journal of Negro History*, IV, (1919): 51–52.
13. *Galveston Daily News*, July 5, 1879.
14. *Ibid*.
15. *Ibid*., July 11, 14, 1881.
16. Winkler, *Platforms of Political Parties in Texas*, pp. 359–360; *Austin Evening News*, March 27, 1896.

Chapter 12 ROBERT L. SMITH: THE ACCOMMODATIONIST

1. Autobiography of Robert L. Smith, Smith Papers Baylor University; Robert Carroll, "Robert L. Smith and The Farmer's Improvement Society of Texas," (M. A. Thesis, Baylor University, 1974, Waco, Texas), pp. 1–30; Purvis Carter, "Robert L. Smith, The Farmer's Improvement Society: A Self-Help Movement in Texas," *Negro History Bulletin* XXIX (1966): 175–176; B. L. Bremby, "Biography of Robert L. Smith," (Unpublished Manuscript in Smith Papers), p. 3; See also August Meier, *Negro Thought in America: Radical Ideologies in the Age of Booker T. Washington,* (Ann Arbor, Michigan 1963).

2. Interview with William McDonald, April 16, 1945, cited in Perry "Black Populism," p. 41.

3. Robert L. Smith, "Village Improvement Among the Negroes," *Outlook* I (March 2, 1900): 773; See also Smith, "Elevation of Negro Farm Life," *Independent,* 30 August 1900, pp. 2103–2106. Both the *Outlook* and *Independent* are in Smith Papers.

4. Smith, "Village Improvement Among the Negro," 733–736.

5. *Ibid.*

6. *Ibid.*

7. *Houston Post*, November 14, 1894.

8. Robert L. Smith, "Uplifting Negro Co-operative Society," *The World Work,* XVI (July 1908).

9. R. L. Smith, to Monore Work, March 26, 1918, *Journal of Negro History,* V (1920): 113.

10. R. L. Smith to B. T. Washington, June 9, 1897 in Harlan, *Booker T. Washington Papers,* IV, pp. 295–297; R. L. Smith, "Address of the Seventh Annual Convention," 1902 (Smith Papers, Waco, Texas, no publisher, 1902), pp. 15–16.

11. Autobiography of R. L. Smith, p. 2, Smith Papers.

12. *House Journal of the Twenty-fifth Legislature,* Regular Session: 632; *Ibid,* Twenty-fifth Legislature, First Session: 310.

13. Robert L. Smith to Booker T. Washington, November 1905, in Harlan, *Booker T. Washington, Papers,* VIII pp. 430, cited in August Meier, *Negro Thought in America* (New York: Oxford University Press), p. 253.

14. *House Journal of the Twenty-fifth Legislature,* Regular session: 124.

15. Autobiography of R. L. Smith, p. 2, Smith Papers.

16. Robert L. Smith, "A Personal Afterword," in Brewer, *Negro Legislators of Texas,* pp. 120–121.

17. Autobiography of Smith, p. 6, Smith Papers.

18. B. T. Washington to Theodore Roosevelt, October 7, 1901, in Harlan, *Booker T. Washington Papers,* VI. pp. 232.

19. T. Roosevelt to B. T. Washington, April 4, 1902; *Harlan, Ibid.*, pp. 434–435.

20. B. T. Washington to Theodore Roosevelt, December 14, 1901, Theodore Roosevelt Papers, Library of Congress (Washington, D.C.), cited in Harlan, *Booker T. Washington Papers,* VI, pp. 435–436.

21. Robert Ward to Theodore Roosevelt, October 26, 1901, Roosevelt Papers; *ibid.*, p. 346.

22. Robert Ward to R. L. Smith October 26, 1901, *ibid.*
23. R. L. Smith to B. T. Washington, December 3, 1901, *ibid.*, pp. 363–365.
24. R. L. Smith, "Farmer's Improvement Society Constitution and By Laws 1896," *Preamble,* p. 2, Smith Papers.
25. Emmett Jay Scott to Washington, July 17, 1902, in Harlan, *Booker T. Washington Papers,* VI, pp. 491, 496.
26. Smith to Waller Burns, February 8, 1904, Smith Papers.
27. *The Waco News,* November 9, 1915: During his long and distinguished career Smith also served as President of the American Academy of Social and Political Scientists, Vice President of the American Bible Society and Trustee of the Anna T. Jeanne Foundation.

Chapter 13   NORRIS WRIGHT CUNEY: THE CLIMBER OF SORTS

1. Virginia N. Hinze's interview with Richard Jackson, February 18, 1960, in Hinze, "Cuney," p. 57; Hare, *Cuney,* pp. 12–14.
2. *Ibid*; Hare, *Cuney,* pp. 3–4, 11–13; Paul Casdorph, "Norris W. Cuney and Texas Republican Politics 1883–1896," *Southwestern Historical Quarterly,* LXXVIII (April 1965): 455–464; Carter G. Woodson, "The Cuney Family," *Negro History Bulletin,* XII (1969): 123–125.
3. N. Patton to George S. Boutwell February 3, 1872, February 10, 1872; *ibid.*, September 2, 1872 approved September 9, 1872, Group 56, Treasury Department, National Archives, Washington, D.C.; *Galveston Daily News,* July 26, 1872.
4. N. W. Cuney to E. J. Davis, June 11, 1873, Davis Papers.
5. G. B. Shields to Lot M. Morrill, August 18, 1876, Group 56, Treasury Department.
6. N. W. Cuney to E. J. Davis, April 1, 1876, *ibid.*
7. N. W. Cuney to E. S. Stone, February 26, 1875: See also G. B. Shields to B. H. Bristow, March 16, 1876, *ibid.*
8. D. M. Baker to E. S. Stone, February 22, 1875, *ibid.*
9. G. B. Shields to B. H. Bristow, April 19, May 16, 1876, *ibid.*
10. G. B. Shields to Lot Morrill, August 18, 1876, *ibid.*
11. E. J. Davis to J. P. Newcomb, March 23, 1877, Newcomb Papers.
12. N. W. Cuney to John Sherman, August 30, 1879, Treasury Department, Group 56.
13. C. B. Sabin to John Sherman, July 28, 1879. *ibid.*
14. A. G. Mallory to William Windom, May 31, 1881, approved June 8, 1881; A. G. Mallory to Charles J. Folger, June 17, 1882, approved August 8, 1882, *ibid.*
15. Hinze, "Cuney," p. 22.
16. *Galveston Daily News,* February 12, 13, 16, 18, 19, 29, 1876. Hinze, "Cuney," pp. 36–37.
17. *Ibid.*
18. *Ibid.*
19. *Galveston Daily News,* June 5, 1883; *Minutes of the Galveston City Council,*

March 10, 14, 1883, (City Secretary, Galveston, 1883), Vol. VI, pp. 458–472; 476–490.
20. *Galveston Daily News,* July 31, August 1, 2, 1877.
21. *Galveston Daily News,* March 16, 1883: *Screwman's Benevolent Association Minutes* I: 496, October 11, 1883, in Cuney Collection, Rice University. See also Ruth Allen "Chapter in the History of Organized Labor in Texas" (Austin: University of Texas, 1941); Hare, *Cuney,* 40–42.
22. Hare, *Cuney,* p. 44; *Galveston Daily News,* October 17, 1885.
23. *Galveston Daily News,* November 4, 5, 1885.
24. *Ibid.*
25. *Dallas Herald,* October 22, 1885.
26. *Galveston Daily News,* November 4, 1885; Cuney supervised his men until he became collector of customs in July 1889. He usually worked from early morning until three in the afternoon, but stayed later if ships were scheduled to come in. Hare, *Cuney,* pp. 45–50.
27. In this convention, James A. Garfield received the Republican nomination after a thirty-six ballot fight between James G. Blaine, and Ulysses S. Grant. In this battle, Cuney voted thirty-five times for Blaine before shifting to Garfield on the final ballot. Even though Blaine lost, Cuney's support of him remained unshaken. Thus, when the convention of 1888 rolled around, Cuney was able to commit thirteen out of fourteen votes to Blaine. See *Chicago Daily Tribune,* June 3, 1884; See also *Proceedings of the Eighth Republican National Convention held in Chicago, June 3, 1884* (Chicago 1884), p. 95.
28. *Galveston Daily News,* May 3, 1884.
29. *Galveston Daily News,* July 11, 21, 1889. For some of the people who recommended Cuney for the post, see E. B. Elkins to Benjamin Harrison, May 17, 27, 1889; A. L. Mosley to B. Harrison, January 19, 1889, Treasurer Department, Group 56; James Sherman to B. Harrison, March 5, 1889, Cuney's Letter Press Book III, p. 90.
30. N. W. Cuney to J. S. Clarkson, October 20, 30, 1889, Small Cuney Scrapbook, pp. 105–107, 111–113, Cuney Collection, Rice University.
31. N. W. Cuney for G. M. Patton November 13, 1889, Letter Press Book III, p. 7, Cuney Collection.
32. *Ibid.*
33. Hinze "Cuney," p. 135; Hare, *Cuney,* p. 138.
34. Hare, *Cuney,* pp. 138–139.
35. *Galveston Daily News,* October 18, 1891 found in *Paul Quinn College Monthly,* October 1895, in Cuney Large Scrapbook, pp. 47, 53, 89, 102.
36. Hare, *Cuney,* p. 31; See Also *San Antonio Advance,* August 7, 1899, in Large Cuney Scrapbook, p. 196; Hinze, "Cuney," p. 133.

BIBLIOGRAPHY

Manuscript Sources

Abner Family File. Harrison County Historical Museum, Marshall, Texas.
Cuney, N. W. Collection. Rice University, Houston, Texas.
Davenport, Harry and Crittenden Papers. Archives, University of Texas, Austin, Texas.
Davis, Edmund J. Papers, Archives Division, Texas State Library, Austin, Texas.
Hogg, James Stephens. Archives, University of Texas, Austin, Texas.
Newcomb, James P. Papers, Archives, University of Texas, Austin, Texas.
Pease–Graham–Niles Papers, Austin Public Library, Austin, Texas.
Raguet, Henry P. Archives, University of Texas, Austin, Texas.
Roosevelt, Theodore Papers, Manuscript Division, Library of Congress, Washington, D.C.
Smith, Robert L. Papers, Texas Collection, Baylor University, Waco, Texas.

Unpublished Government Records: National Archives
(All Sources from National Archives, Washington D.C.)

United States Bureau of Refugees, Freedmen and Abandoned Lands, 1865–1869, Records of the Assistant Commissioner for the State of Texas. Record Group 105.
United States Customs Nomination Appointments, Treasury Department. Record Group 56.
Seventh Census of the United States, 1850, Population Schedule 1 (Free Inhabitants, Slave Inhabitants).
Eighth Census of the United States, 1860, Schedule 1 (Free Inhabitants, Slave Inhabitants).
Ninth Census of the United States, 1870, Schedule 1 (Inhabitants).
Tenth Census of the United States, 1880, Schedule 1 (Inhabitants).
Eleventh Census of the United States, 1890, Schedule 1 (Inhabitants).
Twelfth Census of the United States, 1900, Schedule 1 (Inhabitants).

Unpublished Government Records: State
(All Sources from Archives, Texas State Library, Austin, Texas)

Governor's Letters (Governors Hamilton, Pease, Davis, Hubbard and Roberts).
List of Registered Voters by Counties in Texas, 1867.
Records of the Secretary of State. Election Registers, 1870–1898.

———. Election Returns, 1870–1898.
———. Register of Disbursement: Office of the Superintendent of Public Instruction, 1871–1874.
———. State File on Bonds and Oaths of Elected and Appointed Officials, 1870–1989.

Unpublished Government Records: Local

Cemetery Records, Central Texas Genealogical Society, McLennan County Texas (2 vols.; Waco, Texas, 1965).
Deed Records, County Clerks's Office, Bastrop County Courthouse, Bastrop, Texas.
———, County Clerk's Office, Fort Bend County Courthouse, Richmond Texas.
———, County Clerk's Office, Limestone County Courthouse, Mexia, Texas.
———, County Clerk's Office, Harris County Courthouse, Houston, Texas.
———, County Clerk's Office, Harrison County Courthouse, Marshall, Texas.
———, County Clerk's Office, Rapid Parish Courthouse, Alexandria, Louisiana.
Minutes of the Galveston City Council Meeting, 1883, County Clerk's Office, Galveston, Texas.
Minutes of the Houston City Council Meeting, 1868–1870, Houston Public Library.

Published Documents and Source Materials

Austin City Directory, 1870–1890.
Black Citizens in American Democracy: Past, Present and Future (Marshall, Texas: Committee for the Humanities 1976).
Daniell, L. E. (Complier). *Personnel of the Texas State Government.* Austin; City Printing Co., 1887.
———. *Personnel of the Texas State Government.* Austin; Maverick Printing House, 1892.
Gammel, H. N. P. (Complier). *The Laws of Texas, 1822–1889,* 10 Vols. Austin; Gammel Publishing Co., 1898.
Harlan, Louis, *Booker T. Washington Papers.* 8 Vols. Urbana: University of Illinois Press, 1977.
Henderson, N. O. (Complier). *Directory of the Members and Officers of the Fourteenth Legislature of the State of Texas.* Austin: Cardwell and Walker 1874.
Journal of the Texas Constitutional Convention of 1875. Galveston: Daily News Office 1875.
Journal of the Texas Reconstruction Constitutional Convention of 1868–1869. 2 Vols. Austin: Tracy Siemering Company, 1970.
Lambert, Will (Complier). *Pocket Directory of the Seventeenth Legislature of Texas,* Austin; Swindells Book and Job Office 1881.
———. *Pocket Directory of the Eighteenth Legislature of Texas.* Austin: Deffenbaugh and Co., 1883.
Loughery, E. H. (Complier). *Personnel of the Texas State Government for 1885,* Austin: L. E. Daniell, 1885.

New Orleans City Directory 1876–1882.
Proceedings of the Texas State Republican Conventions, 1865–1898.
Proceedings of the National Republican Conventions, 1868–1898.
Proceedings of Colored Men's Convention, 1871.
Proceedings of Colored Men's Convention, 1879.
Proceedings of the Colored Men's Convention, 1883.
State Journal Appendix Containing Official Reports of the Debates and Proceedings of the Twelfth Legislature of the State of Texas. Austin: Tracy Siemering Co., 1870.
Swindells, E. N. *A Legislative Manual for the State of Texas,* Austin; 1879.
Texas State Almanac, 1870, 1872, 1873, 1875, 1875.
Texas State Constitution, 1869, 1876.
Texas, Legislature, House of Representatives. *House Journals, (12th) to (26th) Legislatures 1870–1890.*
——— *Rules of Order of the House of Representatives of the Twenty-First Legislature.* Austin: Smith, Hick and Jones, 1889.
——— *Rules of Order of the House of Representatives of the Twenty-Second Legislature.* Austin: Henry Hutchings, 1891.
——— *Rules of Order of the House of Representatives of the Twenty-Third Legislature.* Austin: Henry Hutchings, 1891.
——— Senate, *Senate Journals of (12th) to (18th) Legislatures, 1870–1883.*
——— Senate, *Rules of Order of the Senate of the Twenty-Second Legislature.* Austin: Henry Hutchings, 1891.
——— *Rules of Order and Standing Committees of the Senate, Fourteenth Legislature* Austin: Cardwell and Walker, 1874.
United States Congress, *Senate Document* (40th) Congress, 2nd Session, no. 53 (Serial 1317).
——— *Senate miscellaneous Documents,* (50th) Congress, 2nd Session, no. 82. (Serial 2618).
——— *Senate Report of Alleged Election Outrages in Washington County, Texas,* (50th) Congress, 2nd Session, no. 2534 (Serial 2618).
Vernon's Annotated Revised Civil Statutes of the State of Texas. Kansas City Mo.: Vernon Law Book Co., 1952.
Winkler, Ernest W. (ed). *Platforms of Political Parties in Texas.* Austin: University of Texas, 1916.
Work Projects Administration, Houston: *A History and Guide,* Houston: Ansar Jones Press, 1942.
Yett, Tommy, et. al. *Membes of the Texas Legislature, 1864–1839,* Austin: 1939.

Theses and Dissertations

Abramowitz, Jack. "Accommodation and Militancy in Negro Life 1876–1916." Ph.D. Dissertation. Columbia University, 1950.
Armstrong, James C. "History of Harrison County, Texas, 1839–1880." M. A. Thesis, University of Colorado 1930.
Baggett, James A. "The Rise and Fall of the Texas Radicals 1867–1898." Ph.D. Dissertation, North Texas State University, 1972.
Budd, Harrell, "The Negro in Politics in Texas 1867–1898." M. A. Thesis, University of Texas, 1925.

Carrier, John P. "A Political History of Texas During Reconstruction, 1865–1874." Ph.D. Dissertation, Vanderbilt University, 1971.
Carroll, Robert, "Robert L. Smith and the Farmer's Improvement Society of Texas." M. A. Thesis, Baylor University, 1974.
Gandy, William H. "A History of Montgomery County." Texas M. A. Thesis, University of Houston, 1950.
Ginn, Duane E. "Racial Violence in Texas 1884–1900." M. A. Thesis, Prairie View College, 1954."
Hinze, Virginia Neal. "Norris Wright Cuney." M. A. Thesis, Rice University, 1965.
Humes, Richard L. "The Blacks and Their Constitutional Conventions 1867–1889 in Ten Former Confederate States: A Study of Their Membership." Ph.D. Dissertation, University of Washington, 1969.
Keener, Charles V. "Racial Turmoil in Texas 1865–1874." M. A. Thesis, North Texas State University, 1971.
Kinsley, Winston, L. "Negro Labor in Texas 1865–1876." M. A. Thesis, Baylor University, 1965.
Lavendes, Mary A. "Social Conditions in Houston and Harris County 1868–1872." M. A. Thesis, Rice Institution, 1950.
Leonard, William Jr. "Texas and the Kansas Fever 1879–1888." M. A. Thesis, University of Houston, 1973.
McKay, Seth S. "Texas Under the Regime of E. J. Davis." M. A. Thesis, University of Texas 1919.
Perry, Douglas G. "Black Populism: The Negro in the People's Party." M. A. Thesis, Prairie View College, 1954.
Sandlin, Betty J. "The Texas Reconstruction Convention 1868–1869." Ph.D. Dissertation, Texas Tech University, 1970.
Shannon, Stephen, "Galvestonians and Military Reconstruction 1865–1869." M. A. Thesis, Rice University, 1975.
Tarrant, Willie A. "University for Negroes of Texas." M. A. Thesis, Prairie View College, 1944.
Thompson, Lloyd K. "Origin and Development of Black Religious Colleges in East Texas." Ph.D. Dissertation, North Texas State University, 1976.
Yeldeman, Pauline. "The Jaybird Democratic Association of Fort Bend County." M. A. Thesis, University of Texas, 1938.

Newspapers

Austin Evening News, 1892–1896.
Austin Daily Republican, 1868–1879.
Austin Daily Statesman, 1868–1891.
Austin Daily State Journal, 1870–1871.
Austin Tri-Weekly State Gazette, 1869.
Austin Weekly Republican, 1868–1869.
Bastrop Advertiser, 1870–1884.
Bishop College Herald, 1975–1978.
Brenham Banner, 1870–1883.

Bibliography 249

Colorado Citizen, 1879–1882.
Dallas Herald, 1867–1896.
Dallas Morning News, 1886–1898.
Dallas Norton's Union Intelligencer, 1875.
Dallas Southern Mercury, 1895.
Flake's Daily Bulletin, 1867–1871.
Fort Worth Gazette, 1892.
Galveston Daily News, 1867–1900.
Grosbeck New Era, 1876.
Houston Daily Post, 1890–1896.
Houston Union, 1868–1871.
Houston Telegraph, 1869–1872.
LaGrange New Era, 1873.
Marshall Tri-Weekly Herald, 1874–1878.
New Orleans Observer, 1877–1882.
Panola Watchman, 1874–1879.
San Antonio Companion News, 1888.
San Antonio Express, 1868–1896.
San Antonio Light, 1896.
San Antonio White Republican, 1890.
Waco Examiner, 1915.
Waco News, 1915.
Washington, D.C. New Era, 1870–1874.

Books

Allen, Ruth. *Chapter in the History of Organized Labor in Texas.* Austin: University of Texas Press, 1941.
Bain, Richard. *Convention Decisions and Voting Records.* Washington, D. C.: Brookings Institution, 1960.
Barker, J. W. *A History of Robertson County.* Franklin: Robertson County Historical Committee, 1970.
Barkley, Mary S. *A History of Central Texas.* Austin: Printing Co., 1970.
Barr, Alwyn. *Black Texans: A History of Negroes in Texas, 1528–1971.* Austin: Jenkins Press, 1973.
———. *From Reconstruction to Reform: Texas Politics 1870–1900.* Austin: University of Texas Press, 1971.
Beadle, J. H. *Western Wilds and the Men Who Redeem Them.* Cincinnati: Jones Brother and Company, 1879.
Blair, E. L. Early History of Grimes County. Trinity, Texas: privately printed, 1939.
Brewer, J. Mason. *Negro Legislators of Texas.* Dallas: Mathis Publishing Co., 1935.
Bryant, Ira. *The Development of Houston Negro Schools.* Houston, privately printed, 1928.
Bundy, William O. *Life of William Madison McDonald.* Fort Worth: Bunker Printing and Book Co., 1925.
Campbell, Randolph. *A Southern Community in Crisis: Harrison County, Texas, 1850–1880.* Austin: Texas State Historical Association, 1983.

Casdorph, Paul D. *The Republican Party in Texas 1865–1965.* Austin: Pemberton Press, 1965.
Cotner, Robert C. *James Stephens Hogg: A Biography.* Austin: University of Texas Press, 1951.
Cotton, Walter F. *A History of the Negroes of Limestone County from 1860–1939.* Mexia, privately printed, 1939.
Du Bois, W. E. B. *Black Reconstruction in America 1860–1880.* New York: Harcourt Brace and Co., 1935.
Franklin, John H. *Reconstruction: After the Civil War.* Chicago: The University of Chicago Press, 1961.
Eby, Frederick. *The Development of Education in Texas.* New York: The Mac Millian Co., 1925.
Hair, William I. *Bourbonism and Agrarian Protest: Louisiana Politics 1877–1900.* Baton Rouge: Louisiana State University Press, 1969.
Hare, Maude Cuney, *Norris Wright Cuney: A Tribune of the Black People.* Austin: Steck Vaughn Co., 1969.
Hicks, John D. *The Populist Revolt: A History of the Farmer's Alliance and the People's Party.* Minneapolis: University of Minnesota Press, 1931.
Hirshsom, Stanley P. *Farewell to the Bloody Shirt: Northern Republicans and Southern Negroes 1877–1893.* Bloomington: Indiana University Press, 1962.
Holt, Thomas. *Black Over White: Negro Political Leadership in South Carolina During Reconstruction.* Urbana: University of Illinois Press, 1977.
Hyman, Harold M. *A More Perfect Union: The Impact of the Civil War and Reconstruction on the Constitution.* New York: Knopf Press, 1973.
Kittrell, Norman G. *Governors Who Have Been and Other Public Men of Texas.* Houston: Dealy-Adey Elgin Co., 1921.
Loyd, Doyal T. *A History of Usphur County, Texas:* Texian Press, 1966.
Martin, Roscoe C. *People's Party in Texas: A Study in Third Party Politics:* Austin, University of Texas, 1933.
McCarver, Norman. *Hearne of the Brazos.* San Antonio: Century Press of Texas, 1958.
McKay, Seth Shephard. *Debates in the Texas Constitutional Convention, 1875.* Austin: University of Texas Press, 1930.
Meier, August. Negro Thought in America 1880–1915: *Racial Ideologies in the Age of Booker T. Washington.* Ann Arbor, University of Michigan Press, 1963.
Moneyhon, Carl H. *Republicanism in Reconstruction Texas.* Austin: University of Texas Press, 1980.
Nunn, William C. *Texas Under the Carpetbaggers.* Austin: University of Texas Press, 1962.
Parker, Richard D. *Historical Recollection of Robertson County, Texas.* Salado, Texas: Ansar Jones Press, 1955.
Rabinowitz, Howard (ed.) *Southern Black Leaders of the Reconstruction Era.* Urbana: University of Illinois Press, 1982.
Ramsdell, Charles. *Reconstruction in Texas.* Austin: University of Texas Press, 1970.
Rice, Lawrence. *The Negro in Texas 1874–1900.* Baton Rouge: Louisiana State University Press, 1971.

Robinson, Edgar E. *The Presidential Vote 1896–1932.* Stanford: Stanford University Press, 1934.

Singletary, Otis. *Negro Militia and Reconstruction.* Austin: University of Texas Press, 1951.

Smallwood, James. *Time of Hope, Time of Despair: Black Texans During Reconstruction.* Port Washington, New York: Kennikat Press, 1981.

Smithwick, Noah. *The Evolution of a State.* Austin: Texas Steck Co., 1967.

St. Clair, R. W. *History of Robertson County.* Franklin, privately printed, 1931.

Stampp, Kenneth M. *The Era of Reconstruction 1865–1877.* New York: Knopf Press, 1965.

Sterling, Dorothy (ed.) *The Trouble They've Seen: Black People Tell The Story of Reconstruction.* New York: Doubleday, 1976.

Trelease, Allen. *White Terror; The Ku Klux Klan Conspiracy and Southern Reconstruction.* New York: Harper and Roe, 1971.

Walter, Ray A. *History of Limestone County.* Austin: Von Boeckmann Jones, 1959.

Webb, Walter Prescott, H. Bailey Carroll and Eldon S. Branda (eds.) *The Handbook of Texas.* 3 vols. Austin: Texas State Historical Association, 1952, 1976.

Wharton, Clarence R. *History of Fort Bend County.* San Antonio: Naylar Co., 1939.

Wharton, Vernon L. *The Negro in Mississippi 1865–1890.* Chapel Hill: University of North Carolina Press, 1947.

Williams, Annie Lee. *A History of Wharton County 1846–1961.* Austin: Von Boeckmann Jones Co., 1964.

Woodward, C. Vann. *Reunion and Reaction: The Compromise of 1877 and the End of Reconstruction.* Boston: Little Brown, 1951.

Woolfolk, George. *Prairie View: A Study in Public Conscience.* New York: Pageant Press, 1962.

Wooten, Dudley G. (ed.) Comprehensive History of Texas 1685–1897. 2 Vols. Dallas: W. G. Scoff, 1898.

Wright, Carroll D. *The History and Growth of the U.S. Census.* Washington, D.C.: Government Printing Office, 1900.

Articles

Abramowitz, Jack. "The Negro in the Populist Movement." *Journal of Negro History,* XXXVIII (July 1953): 257–289.

——— "John Rayner: A Grass Roots Leader." *Journal of Negro History* XXVI (April, 1951): 160–163.

Avillo, Phillip J. "Phantom Radicals: Texas Republicans in Congress 1873–1878." *Southwestern Historical Quarterly* LXXII (1974): 431–444.

Baenziger, Ann Patton. "The Texas State Police During Reconstruction: A Reexamination." *Southwestern Historical Quarterly* LXXII (April, 1969): 470–491.

Baggett, James A. "Birth of the Texas Republican Party Leadership." *Southwestern Historical Quarterly* LXXVIII (July 1974): 1–20.

———. "Origin of Early Texas Republican Party Leadership." *Journal of Southern History* XL (August, 1974): 441–454.

Brandon, Ida. "The Tax Payers Union in Brazoria County." *Texas History Teacher's Bulletin* XIV (1926): 86–92.

Brockman, John M. "Railroads, Radicals and Militia Bill: A New Interpretation of the Quorum Breaking Incident of 1871." *Southwestern Historical Quarterly* LXXIII (October, 1979): 105–122.

Brown, Arthur Z. "The Participation of Negroes in the Reconstruction Legislature of Texas." *Negro History Bulletin* XX (1959): 87–88.

Carter, Purvis. "Robert L. Smith, The Farmer's Improvement Society: A Self-Help Movement in Texas." *Negro History Bulletin* XXIX (Fall 1966: 175–176).

Casdorph, Paul. "Norris Wright Cuney and Texas Republican Politics 1883–1896." *Southwestern Historical Quarterly* LXVIII (April 1965): 455–464.

Crouch, Barry. "Self-Determination and Local Black Leaders of Texas." *Phylon* XXXIX (December, 1978): 344–355.

——— and L. J. Schultz. "Crisis in Color: Racial Separation in Texas During Reconstruction." *Civil War History* XVI (March, 1970): 37–49.

Dann, Martin. "Black Populism: A Study of Colored Farmer's Alliance Through 1981." *Journal of Ethnic Studies* II (1974): 58–71.

Elliott, Claude, "The Freedmen's Bureau in Texas." *Southwestern Historical Quarterly* LVI (July, 1952): 1–24.

Ericson, J. E. "The Delegates to the Convention of 1875: A Reappraisal." *Southwestern Historical Quarterly* LXVIII (July, 1963): 22–29.

Goodwyn, Lawrence C. "Populist Dreams and Negro Rights: East Texas as a Case Study." *American Historical Review* LXXVI (1971) p. 1435–1456.

Hornsby, Alton Jr. "The Freedmen's Bureau Schools in Texas 1865–1870." *Southwestern Historical Quarterly* LXXVI (April, 1973): 397–417.

Lentz, Sallie. "Highlights of Early Harrison County." *Southwestern Historical Quarterly* LXI(October, 1957): 240–256.

Lightfoot, Billy Bob. "The Negro Exodus from Comanche County, Texas." *Southwestern Historical Quarterly* LVI (January 1953): 409–416.

Malone, Ann P. "Matthew Gaines: Reconstruction Politics" in Alwyn Barr and Robert Calvert (ed.) *Black Leaders: Texans for Their Time*. Austin: Texas State Historical Association 1981.

Martin, Roscoe K. "The Granger as a Political Factor in Texas." *Southwestern Social Science Quarterly* VI (March, 1926): 363–383.

———. "The Greenback Party in Texas." *Southwestern Historical Quarterly* XXX (January 1927): 101–177.

Myres, S. D. Jr. "Mysticism, Realism and the Texas Constitution of 1876." *Southwestern Social Science Quarterly* IX (September, 1928): 166–184.

Pitre, Merline. "The Evolution of a Black University in Texas." *Western Journal of Black Studies* III (Fall, 1979): 210–223.

Reese, James V. "The Early History of Labor Organization in Texas, 1838–1876." *Southwestern Historical Quarterly* LXXIII (July, 1968): 9–22.

Richter, William. "The Army and the Negro During Reconstruction 1865–1875." *East Texas Historical Journal* X (Spring 1972): 7–13.

Russ, William A. Jr. "Radical Disfranchisement in Texas 1867–1870." *Southwestern Historical Quarterly* XXXVIII (July, 1954): 40–52.

Shook, Robert W. "The Texas Election Outrage of 1886." *East Texas Historical Journal* X (Spring, 1972): 20–50.

Smith, David. "The Poll Tax: The Case of Texas." *America Political Science Review* XXXVIII (August, 1944): 693–709.

Smith, Ralph A. "The Farmer's Alliance in Texas 1875–1900." *Southwestern Historical Quarterly* XLVIII (January, 1945): 346–369.

Smith, Robert L. "Village Improvement Among the Negroes." *Outlook* I (March 2, 1900): 773–774.

———. "Elevation of Negro Farm Life." *Independent* I (August 30, 1900): 2103–2106.

———. "Uplifting Negro Cooperational Society." *The World Work* XVI (July, 1908): 1–3.

Somers, Dale A. "James P. Newcomb: The Making of a Radical." *Southwestern Historical Quarterly* LXXXII (1969): 449–469.

Spindler, Frank Mac D. "Concerning Hempstead and Waller County." *Southwestern Historical Quarterly* LIX (April, 1956): 455–472.

Strong, Donald S. "The Poll Tax: The Case of Texas." *American Political Science Review* XXXVIII (August, 1944): 643–709.

Woods, Randall, "George T. Ruby: A Black Militant in the White Business Community." *Red River Valley Historically Review* I (Autumn, 1974): 269–280.

Woodson, Carter G. "The Cuney Family." *Negro History Bulletin* XII (1968): 123–125.

Work, Monroe. "Some Members of the Reconstruction Legislature." *Journal of Negro History* V (1920): 111–112.

INDEX

A

Abington, C. W., 55
Abner, 51
   David, 41, 42, 47, 48, 49, 200
   David Jr., 121
Adams, Henry, 176
   P. P., 15
Allen's Houston Manufacturing and Furniture Co., 33
Allen, 95, 176
   R., 97
   Richard, 22, 23, 28, 29, 31, 32, 33, 34, 35, 39, 41, 95, 98, 99, 100, 101, 102, 104, 112, 117, 118, 119, 174, 175, 177, 197, 200
Allison, William, 110
   William B., 110
Anderson, Edward, 39, 41
Armstrong, Robert, 105
Arthur, Chester, 194
Asberry, 74
   Alex, 108
   Alexander, 61, 64, 106, 107, 150
Austin, Samuel, 105

B

Baggett, James, 202
Bailey, A., 117
Baker, M. A., 106
Ball, George, 192
Ballinger, W., 171
Barr, Alwyn, 99
Bashon, George B., 188
Bassett, H. A. P., 61, 73, 78, 120, 145
Beck, 144
   Thomas, 41, 42, 43, 57, 59, 69, 74, 75

Bell, James, 86, 87, 88, 89
   James H., 84
Bishop, Marshall E., 117
Blaine, James G., 194
Bledsoe, A. A., 17
Blount, W. H., 104, 105, 106, 120
Bolton, D. C., 148
Booker, George E., 16
Brewer, J. Mason, 24
   J. M., 50
Brinkley, C. C., 102
Broiles, H. M., 109
Brown, Edward, 41, 42, 48
   Miles, 16
Bryant, 12, 13, 14, 15, 18
   Charles, 16, 88
   Charles W., 8, 17
Bumstead, Horace, 180
Burns, J. R., 97
Burton, 44, 49, 73, 74, 122
   Mrs. Walter, 64
   Senator, 57
   Thomas Burke, 43
   Walter, 36, 55, 66, 67, 71, 72, 79, 101, 105, 117, 118, 119, 121, 146, 200
   Walter M., 43
   Walter Moses, 43
Butler, James P., 18

C

Cain, J. J., 22
Caine, B. F., 111
   John, 110
Caldwell, Colbert, 18
Campbell, Israel S., 94
Canby, Edward R., 19
Cannon, O. D., 58, 61, 150
Carson, W. R., 102

Carter, G. W., 15
  J. R., 104
  W. Frank, 19
Cass, John, 98
Child, J. D., 56
Choce, C. F., 108
Clark, 95, 96, 122
  Congressman, 97
  George, 108, 109, 121, 196
  William, 161
  William T., 93, 94, 169, 171
Clope, L. A., 98
Cochran, A. M., 101
Coke, Richard, 47, 117
Colwell, A. H., 109, 112
Cotton, Silas, 24, 28, 34
  Silas (Jiles), 23
Culberson, Charles A., 48
  David B., 125
Cuney, 113, 127, 178, 190, 194, 196, 197
  95, 110, 111, 122, 192
  Joseph, 195
  N. W., 98, 99, 102, 103, 104, 105, 106, 107, 111, 170, 172, 191
  Norris, 110
  Norris W., 35, 98, 100, 101, 103, 105, 118, 120, 169, 184, 193, 202
  Norris Wright, 93, 94, 188
  Phillip, 188
Curtis, 18
  Stephen, 9, 15, 19, 85, 132

D

Davenport, W. H. C., 130
Davis, 25, 27
  Bird, 49
  E. J., 97, 102
  Edmund, 12, 15, 19, 88, 100
  Edmund J., 24, 47, 91, 99, 101, 103, 117, 121
  Governor, 31, 36, 44, 45, 98, 170, 176, 189, 191
  J. D., 146
  W. W., 104
  Willie, 104
Debruhl, John, 91, 98, 103, 104, 170
Degress, Jacob, 98, 106, 168
  Jacob C., 195
Dennis, Patrick, 145
Despallier, Martin G., 22
  Matt C., 164
Dillard, J. E., 44, 160
Dodge, Samuel, 172
Dohoney, E. L., 159
Douglass, Frederick, 183
Du Bois, W. E. B., 33
Dupree, Goldstein, 23, 24, 28, 36, 41, 132

E

Easton, W., 112
Elliott, J. P., 111
Evans, 144
  73, 74, 78, 79
  Andrew J., 11
  J. R., 77
  R. J., 57, 59, 63, 68, 72, 80, 103, 104, 117, 119, 144

F

Ferguson, C. M., 104, 105, 106, 109, 126, 146
  Charles, 110, 147
  Charles M., 107, 108, 114, 184, 185
  H. C., 104, 106, 111
  Henry, 110
  Henry C., 112, 147
Ferris, J. R., 104
Fields, Scott, 74
Flake, Ferdinand, 13, 89, 90, 158, 173
Flanagan, James, 110
  James W., 24, 91
  Webster, 111, 160
Fountaine, Albert J., 31
Francis, Patrick, 55
Freeman, Jacob, 41, 42, 57, 98, 117, 122, 146
Frost, 147
  Henry, 146
Fulton, Robert L., 191

Index

G

Gaines, 159, 160, 161, 164
  27, 28, 30, 37, 94, 96, 165
  Matt, 25, 26, 32, 36, 41, 45, 46, 93, 97, 132, 150, 158, 160
  Matthew, 22, 43, 44, 92, 95, 98, 157
  Senator, 163
Gardiner, C. B., 172
Geiger, 58
  Hal, 66, 73, 77, 95, 117, 118, 150
  Harriel G., 57
Gieger, 144
Goddin, M. H., 49
Granger, Gordon, 155
Grant, Dr. John, 111, 112
  John, 109, 110, 114, 178
Green, 113
  E. H. R., 113
Greens, Duff, 15
Griffin, Charles, 167
  William, 93
Griffith, D. W., 186
Gross, F. W., 111
Guy, A. B., 117
  B. A., 57, 58, 59

H

Haller, 78
  N. H., 98
  Nathan, 36, 62, 70, 74, 79, 95, 96, 144, 147
Hamilton, A. J., 87, 90
  Andrew, 17, 18
  Andrew J., 89
  J. J., 98, 100
  Jeremiah, 200
  Jeremiah J., 23, 28, 117
  Morgan, 12, 19, 24, 86, 88, 90, 167
Hanna, Marc, 110
Harrison, 109
  Benjamin, 106, 108
  J. T., 112
Hawley, H. B., 185
  R. B., 111, 113, 114
Hayes, John L., 90
  R. H., 126

Hill, Polk, 149
  W. A., 105
Hoffman, Joseph, 149
Hogg, Governor, 121
  James S., 108, 120
  James Stephen, 65, 196
Holland, 56
  Boyd, 55
  J. K., 55, 56
  W. H., 70, 76, 100, 101, 102, 146
  William H., 55, 67, 119
Hollard, William H., 55
Holt, Thomas, 200
Houston, Joshua, 106
Howard, Oliver O., 167

I

Ireland, John, 64

J

Jenkins, Coote, 98
Jennings, Henry J., 126
  R. L., 145
Johnson, 12, 18
  A. J., 106
  Burriell, 104
  Wiley, 9, 10, 14, 17, 19
  William, 80
Jones, George W., 101, 102, 103, 119
  T. B., 58
Jordan, Barbara, 62

K

Kearby, Jerome C., 125
Kendall's town of Marshall, 33
Kendall, 18
  Mitchell, 9, 10, 19, 22, 28
Kerr, 144
  78
  Major A., 59
  R. A., 104, 118, 119
  Robert, 79
  Robert A., 59, 73, 118, 119
Keyes, C. D., 111
Kirk, Lafayette, 148, 149
Knoxson, H. H., 148

L

Lawson, M. W., 112
Lea, Pryor, 15
Lewis, Doc, 59, 146
Logans, O. T., 105
Long, 12, 13, 18
  Ralph, 9, 10, 15, 17, 19
Lucas, H. G., 146
Lumpkin, Fred, 95

M

Makemson, W. K., 111
Mallory, 104
  A. G., 103, 178
  A. J., 195
Malone, Ann, 158
Marshall, Eugene, 111
Martin, Marion, 106
Maxes, Lewis, 148
Mayes, Elias, 57, 58, 61, 64, 76, 117
McCabe, 51
  Henry L., 200
  L. H., 49
  Lloyd H., 36
  Lloyd Henry, 49, 50
  Mac, 50
McCauley, A. J., 114
McComb, John, 68
McCormick, A. P., 73
McCoy, Samuel, 104, 195
McDonald, 113
  Bill, 112
  W. M., 111
  William, 113, 114, 180
  William M., 110
McGregor, H. F., 113
McKee, Scipio, 17, 85
McKinley, 111
  William, 110, 112, 125
McMahan, T. H., 172
  Victor, 35, 171, 172
McWashington, 14, 15, 18
  James, 8, 19
Medlock, David, 24, 28
Miller, S. H., 31
Mills, Robert, 51
Mitchell's town of Lexington in Burleson, 33
Mitchell, E. M., 132

John, 23, 24, 28, 32, 41, 42, 49
Moneyhon, Carl, 173
Moore, Henry, 23, 28, 31, 39, 41, 46
  J. B., 109
  R. J., 36, 60, 61, 65, 66, 70, 71, 73, 74, 75, 98, 119, 120, 148
Morris, J. R., 23
Mosley, A. G., 114
Mullins's Waco Light and Gas Company, 33
Mullins, Shepard, 9
  Sheppard, 22, 28, 32, 36, 85
Mutual Aid Society of Houston, 33

N

Nelson Richard, 93, 94, 101, 170
Newcomb, 93
  J. P., 91, 92, 169, 191, 194
  James, 88, 113
  James P., 89, 92, 97, 168, 195

O

Ochiltree, Thomas, 170
Ogden, Judge, 114

P

Paddock, B. P., 78
Parson, W., 169
Patton, Ed, 65, 69
  Edward, 62, 77, 79
  Edward A., 61
  G. M., 195
  Nathan, 195
Pearson, P. E., 146
Pease, Elisha, 11, 86
  Governor, 87, 88, 89
Perry, R. H., 86
Pete, W. A., 106
Peterson, Davis M., 159
Phelps, Henry, 39, 40, 45, 146
Pier, P. F., 58
Pitts, John D., 70
Polk, Matthew, 132
Price, W. A., 98, 100
Pridgen, J. B., 163

Index

R

Raney, Jacob, 85
Rayner, J. B., 124, 125
Rector, J. B., 105
Redpath, James, 8
Reed, John, 98
    Johnson, 92, 168
    Thomas B., 111
Reynolds, 51
    Joseph J., 15, 24, 90
    William, 49, 50, 200
Rice, Lawrence, 67, 127
Richardson, H. T., 105
Richer, W. C., 98
Ripetoe, Senator, 78
    Walter, 55, 56, 74, 75, 79, 98, 145
Roberts, O. B., 39
    Oran, 68
    Oran M., 57, 65, 70, 102
    Shack, 39, 45, 48, 49, 55, 71, 72, 76, 78, 117, 119, 145
    Shack R., 41, 42
Rogers, M. M., 106
Roosevelt, President, 185
    Theodore, 184
Rosenthal, A. J., 105, 111
Ross, Lawrence S., 147
Ruby's Galveston Mutual and Life, 33
Ruby, 12, 15, 18, 19, 26, 37, 45, 89
    G. T., 16, 17, 88, 97, 98, 160
    George, 41, 170
    George T., 8, 13, 22, 25, 35, 85, 86, 87, 91, 92, 93, 94, 95, 161, 166, 169, 172, 173, 189, 194, 200
    George T., 88
    Senator, 30, 47

S

Sabin, C. B., 172, 191
    Chaucey B., 173
Sawyer, J. N., 193
Scroggins, Anderson, 85
Shamblin, 147
    J. M., 146
Sheppard, Seth, 164
Sherman, John, 191
Shields, G. B., 190
    General, 191
Sinclair, William, 35, 171
Slaughter, George, 92
Sledge, Andrew, 57, 58, 75, 77, 80, 117
Slvonker, A. B., 89
Smith, 49, 78
    R. K., 16
    R. L., 70, 112
    Robert, 74, 89, 197
    Robert L., 64, 67, 71, 77, 112, 185, 186, 200
    Robert Lloyd, 62, 179, 181, 183, 184
    Tillman, 48
    W. F., 111
Sneed, Henry, 55, 76, 78
Sprague, H. G., 35
Starr, Amory, 145
Stevenson, 95, 96
    Lewis, 93, 95
    Louis, 92, 94, 169
Stewart, James H., 60
Stuart, Adelina, 188
Summer, Fred, 15
Sutton, Fanny, 164
Swisher, J. M., 76

T

Talbot, Joseph W., 31
Taylor, Jack, 146
    James, 131
    Tom, 146
Terrell, E. Henry, 111
    E. H., 111
Thomas, Harry, 16
    W., 15
Thornmenheimer, J. M., 36
Throckmorton, James, 85
Tracy, 93
    J. G., 100
    James, 92
    James G., 90, 162, 175
Trelease, Allen, 131
Tyle, William R., 19

U

Urwitz, Max, 107

W

Wade, Melvin, 105, 126
Ward, Robert, 185
Warren, Peter, 146
Washington, 40, 186
  Booker T., 179, 183, 184, 185
  J. H., 96, 97, 98, 100, 192
  James, 41, 119
  James H., 39, 96, 98
Watrous, 12, 13, 18
  Benjamin, 88
  Benjamin O., 9, 19, 158
Webb, Frank, 100
  J. J., 98
Wheelock, Edwin M., 90
White, A., 105
Whitemore, George, 92
Whitmore, George W., 93
Wilder, Allen, 39, 40, 46, 55

Allen W., 148
Williams, 12, 13, 18
  B. F., 13, 17, 19, 29, 31, 32, 33, 34, 55, 57, 60, 72, 88, 97, 98, 99, 118, 146, 147, 200
  Benjamin, 66
  Benjamin F., 22, 27
  Benjamin Franklin, 9
  C. M., 146
  C. P., 109, 110
  Richard, 24, 28, 31, 41, 45, 46, 47, 95, 96
  Richard, 39
Work, Monroe, 62
Worthman, Louis J., 114
Wright, Arvin, 17
  Sam J., 107
Wyatt, George, 119, 146
  George W., 60, 148